Portrait Stories

Portrait Stories

MICHAL PELED GINSBURG

FORDHAM UNIVERSITY PRESS
New York 2015

Copyright © 2015 Fordham University Press

All rights reserved. No part of this publication may be reproduced, stored in a retrieval system, or transmitted in any form or by any means—electronic, mechanical, photocopy, recording, or any other—except for brief quotations in printed reviews, without the prior permission of the publisher.

Fordham University Press has no responsibility for the persistence or accuracy of URLs for external or third-party Internet websites referred to in this publication and does not guarantee that any content on such websites is, or will remain, accurate or appropriate.

Fordham University Press also publishes its books in a variety of electronic formats. Some content that appears in print may not be available in electronic books.

Library of Congress Cataloging-in-Publication Data is available from the publisher.

Printed in the United States of America

17 16 15   5 4 3 2 1

First edition

In memory of Helen Tartar, an extraordinary editor, a true friend

CONTENTS

	Acknowledgments	ix
	Introduction	1
1.	Poe's "Oval Portrait"	13
2.	The Portrait's Two Faces: James's "The Special Type" and "The Tone of Time"	27
3.	The Portrait Painter and His Doubles: Hoffmann's "Die Doppeltgänger," Gautier's "La Cafetière," and Nerval's "Portrait du diable"	43
4.	On Portraits, Painters, and Women: Balzac's *La Maison du chat-qui-pelote* and James's "Glasses"	59
5.	Portraits of the Male Body: Kleist's "Der Findling," Hardy's "Barbara of the House of Grebe," and Wilde's *The Picture of Dorian Gray*	81
6.	Portraits, Parents, and Children: Storm's "Aquis submersus" and Sand's "Le Château de Pictordu"	110
7.	Gogol, "The Portrait"	141
	Afterword: Reading Portrait Stories	158
	Notes	167
	Works Cited	199
	Index	209

ACKNOWLEDGMENTS

This book would have never been written if it were not for Moshe Ron, who first introduced me to portrait stories and shared with me his ideas about them. Lorri Nandrea read many drafts of the entire book over the years; her comments, insights, and friendship have greatly contributed to making it a better one. I thank also friends and colleagues who have taken the time to read parts of the book and discuss them with me and whose critical observations were invaluable: Françoise Gaillard, Dorothy Kelly, Jörg Kreienbrock, Claudia Brodsky Lacour, Jules Law, Nasrin Qader, Liran Razinsky, and Domietta Torlasco. I am grateful to the three readers for Fordham University Press—Marshall Brown, Ross Chambers, and Susan Winnett—for their comments, suggestions, and, above all, support. For help with art historical matters I thank Marco Ruffini and Claudia Swan; special thanks to Sarah Betzer, especially for the cover image. Thanks are also due to Nina Gourianova and Leona Toker for their assistance with questions concerning the Russian text of Gogol's story; and to Denis Depo and Steven Tester for their research assistance.

My gratitude to Helen Tartar, for her friendship and unfailing support over so many years, is as deep as my sorrow that she is not here to receive it.

An earlier version of chapter 2 appeared in *The Henry James Review* 33.1 (2012): 165–76; an earlier version of chapter 4 appeared in *Comparative Literature* 62.2 (2010): 122–43. I would like to thank Johns Hopkins University Press and Duke University Press for permission to reprint.

In the parenthetical references to the French and German texts, the first page citation is to the original, the second to the English translation. Translations from French and German were silently modified when necessary; all emphasis within quotes is in the original, unless otherwise noted.

INTRODUCTION

"Portrait is a curious bastard of art, sprung on the one side from a desire which is not artistic, nay, if anything, opposed to the whole nature and function of art: the desire for the mere likeness of an individual," wrote in 1885 the art critic Vernon Lee in an essay entitled, somewhat self-contradictorily, "The Portrait Art" (212).[1] While in ancient times the desire "for the mere likeness of an individual" could have been judged useful since the individuals depicted were "great men," whose example could inspire posterity,[2] in the modern period this is no longer the case: everyone can have his or her portrait painted—that is, everyone who can pay. And though throughout history painters of all sorts have been paid for their work, and some of them even grew very rich, the portrait painter's situation was perceived as different: the reversal of cash flow whereby the painter is paid by the sitter (rather than paying the model) compromises the painter's freedom and authority. A comment to a portrait sitter attributed to Jean Auguste Dominique Ingres—"I would like to be able to give you 5 francs, Madame, for then you would be forced to hold the pose like the poor girls we pay expressly so to do"—captures this reversal of power relations whose ultimate outcome is the painter's "servitude" to the whims of his subject.[3]

But what has prompted "aesthetic purists" to consider portraiture an inferior form of art (or no art at all)—its interest in particular individuals and its entanglement with worldly interests and monetary transactions[4]—is precisely what makes it a compelling subject of narrative and gives stories about portraits their unique characteristics. For one, since portraiture itself is far from a purely aesthetic practice, stories that center around portraits do not deal with purely aesthetic issues; indeed, they often undermine the very idea of a purely aesthetic realm (of production or consumption). This does not mean that portrait stories do not sometimes represent a painter's ambivalence toward the "portrait art" or the desire (of the painter, the sitter, the person who commissions the portrait) to transcend the individual—the particular, contingent, real—that is, the desire to "idealize." Such stories, however, often show the dangers or impossibility of this attempt.

Centered around the portrait as a particular form of visual representation, portrait stories deal with transactions and exchanges among painters, sitters, and viewers—all interested parties, whose interests, moreover, are often conflicting and whose interactions are shaped by power differentials (especially those determined by gender). The conflicts these interactions produce are particularly charged precisely because the portrait is a representation of a particular individual: what is at stake is this individual's identity or subjectivity as well as that of the painter and/or viewer(s) whose interests are inscribed in the portrait.

That portrait stories are primarily about the relation between subjectivity and representation may seem obvious, as may the idea that representation is a social practice inflected by particular interests and power relations. And yet both have been obscured by two interpretative tendencies among critics. The first is the tendency to discuss stories about portraits as stories about "art," thus ignoring and erasing the specificity of the portrait as a particular form of representation. The second tendency is that of linking portraits to the supernatural or the fantastic, which often inhibits further interpretation: since the portrait's power is said to be supernatural, since the events surrounding it are said to be fantastic, there seems to be no reason to ask about the nature of the portrait's power or the reasons for these events.

In this book, by contrast, I will show how, in the stories I analyze, the portrait's role is inseparable from its specificity as a visual representation of a particular individual. I will argue that portrait stories deserve our attention because they provide us with varied and differentiated accounts of the ways in which subjectivities are formed in relation to a particular kind of image, whose own production is complicated by intersubjective relations, themselves inflected by social determinants. In telling about the portrait's production these stories show the interestedness of the painters and the power that can accrue to them from the act of representation (often at the expense of the portrait's subject) while also exposing the vulnerability of the portrait painter's sense of self. In telling about the viewer's relation to the portrait (and the viewer can double up as subject and/or painter) they show how the portrait functions as a site for the formation of subjectivity, problematizing the very act of seeing with its attendant acts of identification, misrecognition, projection, and imitation.

That portrait stories are, in a general way, about the relation between subjectivity and representation does not, of course, mean that all portrait stories deal with the same problems or tell the same story. In narratives about portraits, I will argue, the portrait functions as a topos, that is, a set of variables that can be combined in different ways and with different emphasis in order to articulate a variety of issues. These variables do not have a predetermined meaning that remains always the same but rather receive different meanings as well as different valuations in different contexts. So while a certain family resemblance can be found among portrait stories—a resemblance that gives them their specificity as a subgenre—there is not one overarching issue, theme, or problem that they can all be said to exemplify.

In what follows I analyze nineteenth-century portrait stories—short stories and novellas—from a variety of literary traditions (American, British, French, German, Russian). Though portrait stories are as old as portraits themselves (and those, in turn, go back to the very beginning of the art of painting),[5] if we limit ourselves to Western literature of the modern period we can see that the nineteenth century functions as an important watershed in the history of this subgenre. In narratives from the seventeenth and eighteenth centuries the portrait appears as an object already existing in the world and about whose producer and process of production not much (most often nothing) needs to be said. In such texts the portrait appears as an incontrovertible token of the identity of its subject. In Madame de Lafayette's *Zaïde* (1670–71), for example, the portrait that captivated Zaïde's attention and that Consalve was thought to merely resemble is proven to be in fact his own portrait. Thus the prophecy that Zaïde will marry the subject of the portrait, though grounded in error and deceit, proves ultimately to be "a true prediction" (235). As a result, Zaïde and Consalve can marry and Zaïde's father is finally convinced to convert to Christianity, an act upon which he has decided before Zaïde's birth but neglected to accomplish. In Horace Walpole's *Castle of Otranto* (1764), to take another example, there is no doubt that the portrait that at the beginning of the narrative "quit[s] its panel and descend[s] on the floor with a grave and melancholy air" (22) is that of Manfred's grandfather, whose criminal acts are the cause of all the disasters related in the narrative. There is also no doubt that the other portrait featured in the narrative is that of Alfonso, the rightful ruler who was poisoned by Manfred's ancestor. The resemblance of Theodore to the portrait, first observed by Matilda, establishes Theodore as the rightful heir so that as the crimes of Manfred's grandfather are revealed they are also redressed (even if belatedly). In *The Portrait*, "a novel in two volumes by Miss Elliott, Novelist" (1783), there is no doubt that the portrait the heroine, Maria, sees at the picture gallery in her grandfather's castle is that of her dead father, who was cast away by his own father for marrying against his wishes. Maria's reaction to the portrait—"She faintly exclaimed, while her eyes, filled with tears, were fixed on it, oh! My father, my revered, my beloved father, and instantly sunk to the floor in a swoon" (2: 193)—shows that her love for her father is stronger than any selfish wishes she may have had to ingratiate herself with her grandfather; the grandfather, convinced by her filial duty and reconciled with his granddaughter, removes his opposition to her marrying her cousin, who is also his heir.[6]

In all these examples (drawn from the traditions of romance, gothic, and sentimental narrative, respectively) the portrait is perceived as referring unambiguously to a real, existing, specific person. It also embodies unresolved residues of past conflicts and helps bring about their resolution (or dissolution). For this double purpose the figure of the artist who painted the portrait and the process of its production are irrelevant; indeed, including these elements would bring to the fore the status of the portrait as the product of someone's act of representation, and this might cast ever so small a doubt on its purely referential status.

This view and use of the portrait does not die out at the end of the eighteenth century; far from it. Indeed, many nineteenth-century portrait stories that feature a "haunted" or "magic" portrait conform to this model and do not include a painter.[7] Nevertheless, it is still the case that, unlike the preceding centuries, the nineteenth century also produced a considerable body of narratives about portraits, primarily short stories and novellas, that pay as much attention to the painter as to the portrait itself and deal with the circumstances and process of production in addition to the subsequent effects of the portrait. This shift testifies to the emergence, toward the end of the eighteenth century, of the painter as a likely hero for fiction, an emergence that owes much to the Romantic myth of the artist and that, in prose works, we usually associate with the appearance of the Künstlerroman.[8] Stories about portraits, however, should be distinguished from "portrait of the artist novels," which rarely feature portraits. This point is often missed because critics tend to conflate painted portraits with verbal portraits (that is, character description). Thus neither James Joyce's *The Portrait of the Artist as a Young Man* nor Henry James's *The Portrait of a Lady* are portrait stories (although the former is a Künstlerroman).[9] One important difference between the two subgenres is that, unlike Künstlerromans, portrait stories are rarely about the formation, or aesthetic education, of the painter (one exception is George Sand's story "Le Château de Pictordu," which I discuss in chapter 6).[10]

With the introduction of the painter, the status of the portrait changes: it can no longer be seen as an unmediated document of the past presence of its subject since it also bears the imprint of its producer, whose way of seeing and view of the subject are inscribed in the portrait. The inclusion of the painter calls attention to the fact that no portrait is simply a portrayal of its subject (is never purely "denotative," to use Richard Brilliant's terminology); it is also, to a certain degree, a portrait of the painter. The represented subject, in addition, is to some extent the construct of the painter. For these two reasons, the act of viewing, or seeing, can no longer be (as it was in portrait stories of previous centuries) a simple identification of the "real subject."[11] Indeed, the subject can no longer be seen as prior to and independent of its representation, as having an "identity" of which the portrait is merely the token; rather, subjectivity (of sitter, painter, and viewer) is seen as produced by and in relation to representations.

Though portraits represent both their subjects and their painters, they do not do so in quite the same way. Charles Sanders Peirce's typology of signs can be helpful in articulating this difference since it defines signs (or more precisely sign-functions) according to the kind of relation they entertain with their object.[12] Using Peirce's terminology, we can say that in the modern European tradition, the relation between a portrait and its subject is primarily iconic, that is, grounded in resemblance: the portrait is a "likeness." However, since resemblance is relative rather than absolute, the degree of resemblance necessary for a representation to count as a likeness is determined in a general way by cultural conventions (conventions of portrait painting prevalent at the moment of production or of viewing, which, in turn, may depend on specific understanding of what constitutes subjecthood). Therefore, to use Peirce's terminology again, the relation of portrait to its subject is also symbolic (that is, grounded in convention).[13] The impossibility of absolute resemblance to the original is, of course, not unique to portraits; but the interests and desires that motivate the production of a portrait render disagreement over resemblance anything but a theoretical issue.

Disagreement over resemblance is not limited to the rendering of physical traits since a great portrait is supposed to show the sitter's true self (variously defined as social status, character, soul, etc.). Such features are never unequivocally coded, so the mere demand for their pictorial representation leaves open the possibility of disagreement and conflict. Moreover, whereas we normally assume that a portrait merely re-presents the sitter's physical aspect, when it comes to portraying moral or psychological traits, such an assumption cannot be automatically made. The painter may be bringing out a hidden truth about the sitter or merely imagining he is; he may be imposing his own view, unconsciously or deliberately. Thus the iconic dimension of the portrait—its status as a likeness—is fraught with ambiguity and is subject to differing, even conflicting interpretations.

While the relation of the portrait to its subject is iconic-symbolic, the relation of the painter to the portrait is primarily, in Peirce's terms, indexical (grounded in causality).[14] As the portrait's producer, the painter leaves his or her trace in the work. Whereas art history sees the imprint of the painter in the portrait as having to do with the "telltale signature of his personal style" (Brilliant 142), portrait stories show that the painter's presence in the portrait has to do with motives, intentions, and interests that are not exclusively artistic. Such motives and interests can very well be in conflict with those of the portrait's subject. This is most obvious in portraits that do not simply strive to represent the physical aspects of the subject, his or her appearance at a specific moment in time, but rather to bring out the subject's spiritual, psychological, or moral qualities, sum up a life, or present the subject as a general type. Not only is it equally possible that the painter reveals what the subject would like to hide or that the soul or character so revealed are only the painter's own vision, inspired by various motives; the very attempt to transcend the merely physical, ephemeral aspect of the subject (by summing up a whole life or bringing out the subject's essence), appears, from this point of view, as a manifestation of the painter's will to power over his particular, contingent subject, if not at the expense of this subject.

Both the subject's iconic presence and the painter's indexical presence in the portrait may or may not be recognized by the portrait viewer or viewers. What the viewer sees or does not see has now to do with the viewer's relation to either the subject or the painter (or to both). To put it in the Peircean terms I have been using: the viewer can be inscribed in the portrait iconically if he or she sees himself/herself in the portrait's subject (that is, if he or she "identifies" with the subject's image); if what the viewer sees in the portrait is his or her traces (that is, his or her influence on either the subject or the painter), then the viewer is present in it indexically.

The clear distinction between the way the subject and the painter are inscribed in the portrait gets complicated, however, since the portrait is an index or a trace not only of the painter but also of the subject's past presence.[15] The subject, then, is represented in the portrait both iconically and indexically. Indeed, in the history of art, the idea of portraits as iconic signs of their subjects, as likenesses, emerged relatively late; until the late Middle Ages the identity of the portrait's subject was indicated primarily by emblems.[16] Some scholars hypothesized that resemblance emerged as the defining relation between the portrait and its subject when the belief that the portrait retains something of its subject—that is, a certain understanding of the indexical relation of the image to its subject, associated with magic and ritual use of images—declined.[17] The belief in "the identity of picture and depicted" is often attributed to primitive belief in the power of images.[18] And yet common practices in our own day, such as the ubiquitous display, under certain regimes, of the image of the ruler, the desecration or destruction of images or statues of hated or deposed rules, as well as that of images of rejected or unfaithful lovers, all testify that this view of the portrait's "power," produced by its indexical (rather than iconic) relation to its subject, has not been entirely left behind or overcome. At the same time, as we shall see, the idea that subjectivities are produced by and in relation to representations endows the portrait with a different kind of power.

The status of the portrait as both icon and index of its subject is expressed with great clarity in the story about the origins of the portrait (and of all plastic arts), told by Pliny the Elder in his *Historia naturalis*.[19] This is the story of the daughter of the potter Butades, who, on the eve of her lover's departure for war, traced his profile on the wall while he was asleep, following the outlines of his shadow;[20] her father later made a clay model out of this tracing. As a tracing of a person's shadow, the portrait is an icon—a perfect replica of the body's contours.[21] But the story also emphasizes the existential (or indexical) relation between person, shadow, tracing, and clay model: like the shadow, the portrait is not only a likeness but also a trace of the person's presence. That the portrait is drawn as the lover is about to leave for war suggests that the portrait's function is to keep the person present (alive) even in his absence (death). But drawing the portrait while the lover is asleep suggests that the painter is "stealing" her lover's likeness; and the indexical relation between body, shadow, and portrait strengthens the impression that painting the portrait constitutes an appropriation of some part of the subject's being and hence may constitute a threat to his integrity as subject: "It is as if Butades' daughter has appropriated an actual part of her lover by furtively tracing the shadow of the sleeping young man, acquiring some essential part of his being that she would be able to possess even in his absence" (Bettini 43).

The story of Butades's daughter brings to the fore the uncanny aspect of the portrait's indexical and iconic dimensions. It is therefore important to remind ourselves that the portrait's indexical relation to its subject makes it a prime example of referential representation (as Peirce puts it, as an index of its subject the portrait signifies the subject's existence). In addition, a portrait that is a likeness—that is, has an iconic relation to its subject rather than referring to its subject by emblems, for example—is a clear example of mimetic representation (which in the story about Butades's daughter appears as a perfect copy, unmediated by convention).[22] It is thus within (a certain understanding of) referential and mimetic representation that the magic or uncanniness of the portrait resides—a point that the common association of portrait stories with the supernatural or the fantastic tends to obscure.[23] But the portrait painted by Butades's daughter is neither supernatural nor fantastic; if it is uncanny, it is because tracing the shadow, as an extreme instance of the portrait's indexicality and iconicity, risks erasing the difference and upsetting the hierarchical relation between sign and object that is at the foundation of representation. It shows us the uncanniness that lurks within referential and mimetic representation.

The story of Butades's daughter also shows the intimate relation between portraiture and death: the portrait is painted against death, against time, decay, and oblivion; its function is to re-present the subject, keep it present in its absence, extend its presence beyond physical life. But portrait stories that in one way or another convey a resistance to the "overcoming" of the individual—contingent, particular, subject to death—bring to the fore a different understanding of the relation between the portrait and death: death not as the opposite of life but as immanent in life, the portrait as registering death rather than overcoming it.

The very few previous studies of the portrait story as a distinct category took the form of historical surveys. Both Theodore Ziolkowski and Sergio

Perosa see the portrait as a "motif" that undergoes changes over time.[24] Ziolkowski discusses what he calls "the haunted portrait" under three categories—genius loci, figura, and anima—and argues that they go through four stages of "disenchantment": "from conventional acceptance of magic through rationalization and psychological internalization to inversions of various sorts" (145). Perosa, for his part, studies the "ghostly, telltale, uncanny, and finally killing portraits" as projecting and expressing a growing uneasiness with assertions about the superiority of art over life: "The killing portrait becomes a figurative and figural image of the anxiety, the dread, the unexpected torment which irrepressibly arise when Art claims to substitute Life" (93). Maurizio Bettini's study, though also a survey, is somewhat different: his corpus consists primarily of texts from classical antiquity, and he considers the portrait not as a motif but as a scenario—what he calls "the fundamental story"—consisting of two lovers and a portrait. Bettini argues that "there are very many ways in which these elements can be combined, a large number of stories that can be told about these characters" (4), and his book follows these mutations and combinations.

My approach is different from that of Ziolkowski and Perosa primarily in that I do not see the portrait as a "motif" that has a life, or a history, of its own. In my opinion, studying the portrait as a motif—that is, a detachable textual element that can be traced historically from text to text—results in separating it from other aspects of the text, thematic and formal, and therefore flattens its meaning.[25] Rather than attributing the differences among the portrait stories I analyze to the evolution of a detachable motif, mirroring a broader historical process, I see them as resulting from the particular concerns (thematic and formal) of each text and the choices each author makes in manipulating the topos of the portrait in order to explore these concerns. I therefore do not detach the portrait from the rest of the text but rather analyze its role in relation to the text's plot, narrative structure, and thematic concerns.

Like Bettini, I see the portrait story as a set of variables that can be combined in different ways. My scope, however, is broader than his "fundamental story" since the corpus of portrait stories in the nineteenth century cannot be reduced to stories about two lovers and a portrait (just as it cannot be limited to Ziolkowski's "haunted" or Perosa's "killing" portraits). Moreover, my focus on the role the portrait plays in each particular text also means that, unlike Ziolkowski, Perosa, or Bettini, I am not interested in a survey where, necessarily, the relation of one text to others in a tradition is more important than each text's particular choices. It is worth noting that though Ziolkowski and Perosa write historical surveys, neither one remarks on the literary-historical change in portrait stories that occurs in the nineteenth century with the introduction of the painter.[26] My approach, by contrast, is attentive to the specificity of each text; I offer close readings where comparison among texts is in the service of illuminating their differences, as well as similarities.

Besides studying the portrait as a motif or a scenario, critics also have discussed portrait stories in the context of the relation between the "sister arts" of painting and literature, the principle of "ut pictura poesis," and the capacity of language to describe art objects and the use of such descriptions in literary works (ekphrasis).[27] Such studies tend to consider the portrait as an object of description, and therefore see the representation of a portrait in a literary text as marking the place where language attempts to rival painting in the art of making objects visible, or as the place where writing reflects upon itself. There is no doubt that the presence of an image in a literary text raises, at least implicitly, the question of the relation between image and text, and I will be discussing this question in texts where it seems particularly important. But studies of portrait stories as sites for literature or language self-reflection tend to subsume the portrait within broader categories. Thus Françoise Meltzer, in her introduction to *Salome and the Dance of Writing*, a book that investigates how literature imagines representation by looking at literary texts featuring a portrait, says: "The choice of the portrait is essentially arbitrary on my part; I could as well have considered music, landscapes, tactile expressions and so on" (1). Though she concedes that there is something "curiously alluring" about the way "eidetic images" function in literature, she firmly asserts that "The portrait qua portrait is not at issue" in her book (2).[28] By contrast, what interests me is precisely the way the portrait, as a very particular kind of visual representation, a material object, and a complex sign, functions in a literary text. I see the portrait's function as residing not in foregrounding the literary text's ability to describe and produce an object for the reader's viewing (the reader views nothing except black marks on white surface) but rather in its serving as the site where intersubjective relations of desire, identification, rivalry, projection, aggression, guilt, idealization, misrecognition, get organized.

I have been arguing that the study of portrait stories has been impoverished by considering only those texts that fitted within certain preconceived ideas about this subgenre and that this limitation has obscured what is both distinct and important about these stories. In constituting the corpus for this study I tried to remedy this situation by deliberately choosing texts that do not conform to these preconceived ideas (such as Honoré de Balzac's *La Maison du chat-qui-pelote* or Theodor Storm's "Aquis submersus") as well as texts that have received very little critical attention of any sort (such as Henry James's "The Special Type" and "The Tone of Time," Thomas Hardy's "Barbara of the House of Grebe," or George Sand's "Le Château de Pictordu") while also including some obvious and much-analyzed examples of this subgenre (such as Oscar Wilde's *The Picture of Dorian Gray*).

The book's first three chapters center around the portrait's defining feature—its status as a representation of an individual—and the attending impulse to go beyond this particularity, which manifests itself as the tension between the real and the ideal or that between the portrait's subject and the painter's "vision." The first chapter, "Poe's 'Oval Portrait,'" deals with the challenge that a representation of a particular individual poses for interpretation. I argue that critics' tendency to conflate the puzzling story of the portrait's viewer (the frame narrator) with the more conventional, allegorical story of its painter in a way that subordinates the former to the latter arises from the desire to go beyond the particular individual—in other words, from the very desire that has led to the death of the woman in the painter's story. Chapter 2, "The Portrait's Two Faces: James's 'The Special Type' and 'The Tone of Time,'" deals with the tension between two views of the portrait: the first considers it as a re-presentation of a real person that preserves the likeness of that person in his or her absence, whereas according to the second the portrait's subject is the product rather than the ground of representation; hence, according to the latter view, the portrait is not a re-presentation but rather a simulacrum, a double, or a ghost. The comparison between the stories shows that the first view is linked to the portrait's entanglement with worldly interests and desires while the second (the portrait as a ghost) is linked to the withdrawal of portrait and painter from these entanglements. Whereas Poe's "Oval Portrait" dramatizes the danger the portrait entails for its subject, and James's stories show the power that can accrue to the painter from the act of portraiture, chapter 3, "The Portrait Painter and His Doubles: Hoffmann's 'Die Doppeltgänger,' Gautier's 'La Cafetière,' and Nerval's 'Portrait du diable,'" analyzes the different ways in which the portrait painter's own subjectivity is problematized by the act of portraiture, whether it is understood as reproducing the real or as an attempt to merge an ideal with the real.

Chapters 4 and 5 address more directly the question of gender difference (which is already discussed in chapters 1 and 2). Chapter 4, "On

Portraits, Painters, and Women: Balzac's *La Maison du chat-qui-pelote* and James's 'Glasses,'" presents us with the common scenario in which a male painter paints a woman's portrait (or portraits); it thus invites us to explore the way the power to represent another person (and thus construct or produce subjects) relates to gender. I argue that as stories that demonstrate the social function and power of the portrait qua representation and show the painter's artistic production to be inseparable from his interests and desires, they also show how, and under what conditions, the power to represent is gained, kept, or lost. Chapter 5, "Portraits of the Male Body: Kleist's 'Der Findling,' Hardy's 'Barbara of the House of Grebe,' and Wilde's *The Picture of Dorian Gray*," presents us with the less common scenario in which a man is the object, rather than subject, of vision and desire. In all three texts, we find a full-body representation of an idealized male that is kept hidden (as opposed to the texts discussed in chapter 4 where we have portraits of women's faces that are exhibited in public). These full-body representations are the sites of conflicting desires and identifications for multiple viewers, male and female. I argue that though we can understand some of these viewers' relation to the image in terms of narcissistic identification and mimetic desire, this paradigm cannot fully account for what takes place in these stories.

The issue of gender is crucial also for chapter 6, "Portraits, Parents, and Children: Storm's 'Aquis submersus' and Sand's 'Le Château de Pictordu,'" in which I discuss the way portraits function as means of transmission—of traits but also of authority, knowledge, and the past. I argue that both Storm's story, centered around the relation between father and son, and Sand's fairy tale, dealing with the relation between mother and daughter, question prevalent ideas about the relation between gender and transmission. Storm's story puts into question genealogical transmission and the power of the father while Sand's story de-idealizes the father and represents a successful transmission from mother to daughter.

Nikolai Gogol's "The Portrait," discussed in the final chapter, deals with the relation between portraits and money. I argue that the story has two conflicting strands: in one strand, where representation is understood as a relation between original and copy, money is seen as what destroys art; in the other strand, where representation is understood as a relation of adequation, art is seen as analogous to money.

Finally, in the afterword, I reflect on the relation between "portrait" and "story," between the characters' experience of seeing the portrait and the reader's experience of reading about it.

CHAPTER I

Poe's "Oval Portrait"

As we have seen in the introduction, portrait stories expanded their scope in the nineteenth century to include, besides the viewer and the portrait, the painter and his subject. This means not only that the story of the portrait's production is now added to that of its after-effects but also that the portrait can no longer be considered as purely referential. The attenuation of the portrait's referential status, in turn, means that viewing it cannot be reduced to an identification of its subject. Edgar Allan Poe's short story "The Oval Portrait" (1845; originally published as "Life in Death" in 1842) is a good example of this expansion and complication of the portrait story: it features, besides the oval portrait, the full array of character-positions—a painter, a subject, and a viewer—and in three short pages tells the story of both the portrait's production and its subsequent effect on a viewer. Moreover, the experience of the viewer in Poe's story is dramatically different from the one typical to portrait stories in pre-nineteenth-century texts, whether in the gothic, sentimental, or romance tradition. Indeed, though the story opens with an explicit allusion to the gothic novel, this allusion, I will argue, serves to mark the *difference* of the viewer's experience in the story from the one we find in the gothic novel.[1]

The complexity of the story is reduced considerably, however, when critics see the frame narrator (the viewer) as replicating the predicament of the painter in the main narrative, as they often do (going as far as to claim that they are one and the same person).[2] The result of such a reading is to simplify the frame narrative (dealing with the viewer's experience), depriving it of its most puzzling aspects.

In what follows I will focus on these two points—the differences between "The Oval Portrait" and gothic fiction and the differences between the two parts of the text (the story of the painter and that of the viewer), in order to come to terms with the story's unsettling effect. I will conclude by considering the reasons for critics' tendency to conflate the stories told in the two parts as well as what I see as at stake in resisting this tendency.

Rewriting the Gothic Portrait Story

"The Oval Portrait" starts with an explicit reference to the gothic novel: the chateau in which the wounded narrator of the frame narrative takes refuge is described as "one of those piles of commingled gloom and grandeur which have so long frowned among the Apennines, not less in fact than in the fancy of Mrs. Radcliffe" (*Poetry and Tales* 481). As I have argued in the introduction, in the gothic novel (as in other seventeenth- and eighteenth-century texts featuring a portrait) the portrait is the sign of unresolved past conflicts; often the character who discovers the portrait (or any other mysterious object that refers to past misdeeds) gets involved, as a result of this viewing, in adventures that eventually lead to the uncovering of past wrongs and to their righting. In Poe's story, the frame narrator finds in the castle a portrait that fascinates and appalls him; the story of the portrait's production he reads in a book he finds by his bedside tells of the death of one person (a woman) as a result of the actions of another person (the painter); the narrator himself, as I have mentioned, is severely wounded. However, neither one of these "crimes" gets clarified, punished, or avenged by the viewer; the frame narrator's actions remain limited to gazing at the portrait and reading the story of its production. Whatever wrong occurred in the past is not rectified.

The main narrative, dealing with the painter, describes a double process by which, on the one hand, an empty canvas gradually fills up and becomes a painting and, on the other hand, a living human being is drained of life and becomes a corpse; the tale's conceit is that the former is the cause of the latter.³ In other words, the painter's story is not that of a metamorphosis, where a woman becomes a work of art.⁴ The narrator's story, therefore, cannot be a symmetrical reversal of such a metamorphosis—that is, of a work of art, a portrait, coming to life. The narrator is explicit on this point when he insists that, drowsy as he was, he had not "mistaken the head [in the portrait] for that of a living person" and, further on, that "the peculiarities of the design, of the *vignetting*, and of the frame must have instantly dispelled such an idea [that the portrait is not a picture but the head of a living person]" (482). The coming to life of a portrait is one of the scenarios we find in gothic fiction, where it leads to the avenging of a crime or the rectifying of a wrong of which the portrait is the sign. That the frame narrative does not—indeed, cannot—stage a coming to life of a portrait marks one of the differences between Poe's story and the gothic novel (and at the same time suggests that the frame is different from the main narrative, rather than being its repetition-through-inversion).

The gothic in Poe's story is primarily a space—a chateau in the Apennines, and even more precisely, a turret room in the chateau. We should note that there is no plausible motivation for the wounded narrator choosing "a remote turret" (481) for his place of rest inside the deserted chateau. Similarly, it is not obvious why, in the main narrative, the painter, who is presented to us only as an artist and a husband, should be painting in a castle, and specifically in a "dark high turret-chamber" (483). Without realistic motivation, "turret" appears as the purely conventional site of the literary tradition of the gothic. But whereas characters in gothic fiction end up leaving the chateau with its scary turrets at the end of their travails, this is not the case with the characters of "The Oval Portrait." The painter, the woman who is the subject of the portrait, the narrator who views it, and the portrait itself all occupy the space of the turret and none of them leaves it: the woman dies in the turret room where the portrait was painted; we are not told what happened to the painter after he finished painting the portrait or to the narrator after he finished reading the story of the portrait so that they, too, in some sense, remain forever in a turret room.

By leaving the painter and the narrator in the turret room, with the portrait (as well as the corpse of the dead woman, in the case of the painter, and the book, in the case of the narrator), Poe does not allow them the possibility of stepping outside the site of their horrific experience. The absence of an outside is also conveyed through the lack of realistic motivation for the transmission of the story. Since the narrator of the frame narrative is "desperately wounded" (481), it is not at all clear whether or why he could or would write it. The main narrative ends when the painter completes the portrait and realizes that his wife is dead; a few lines before we were told that "as the labor [of painting] drew near to its conclusion, there were admitted none into the turret" (483). It is, therefore, not clear who could have witnessed the completion of the portrait and the death of the woman and hence who could have told the painter's story. The origin of the story cannot be the painter himself not only because the story is in the third person but also, indeed primarily, because the story relates what the painter did not—indeed would not—notice. Thus both the main narrative and the frame narrative dispense with providing a realistic motivation for the act of transmission (a feature we find also in other Poe stories, such as "The Pit and the Pendulum" or "Manuscript Found in a Bottle").

The lack of realistic explanation for the story's transmission casts a doubt on the narratives' status as records or re-presentations of past experience; they appear, rather, as coextensive with the experience itself. Lived experience is repeated in the narratives but without the distance or difference (of re-presentation) that would allow one to overcome or "redeem" this experience (to use Leo Bersani's term).[5] If the gothic is alluded to in order to suggest a horrifying, "appalling" experience, in Poe's story, contrary to what happens in gothic fiction, this experience has no "outside" and cannot, therefore, be either left behind or mastered and overcome.

As readers we, of course, can leave the space of the turret/tale, go "outside" it and gain a distance that would allow us to comment on it (rather than relive it) or, alternatively, simply leave it behind and read or do something else. But though this is true empirically, it is also the case that the structure of the story is such as to make our own exit impossible: the frame narrative precedes the main narrative, which is chronologically prior to it and is its necessary precondition; the frame does not "close," and at the end of the main narrative we do not return to the narrator to find out what happened to him after he finished reading the story of the painter. Given these two features, when we finish reading the story of the painter and his wife, we should, logically, continue by going back to the frame narrative that tells of the subsequent history of the portrait; we would then read again the story of the painter and his wife, and so on, ad infinitum: we, too, would never leave the turret/tale.

Rewriting the gothic portrait story in "The Oval Portrait" thus amounts to exposing a crime or an act of violence that cannot be avenged, a wrong that cannot be rectified, creating a horrifying experience that cannot be overcome or neutralized in any way.

Painter and Viewer

We have seen that the three characters of the tale share the same predicament, which the reader is also invited to assume. This, however, does not mean that they are interchangeable: While the narrator both sees the portrait and reads the book, the reader only reads the book and the painter only sees the portrait. Since, as we shall see, the portrait and the book where the painter's story is written seem to be mutually exclusive, the frame narrator's position seems to be the most complicated one.

As critics have long noticed, the frame narrative is considerably longer than the main narrative; it is also more complex. The story of the painter, his wife, and the portrait, with all its uncanniness, is relatively easy to understand because it is structured around a series of symmetrical oppositions such as art/life, life/death, seeing/not seeing, looking/withholding of the gaze, man/woman, and so on. Indeed, several critics have commented upon the clichéd nature of the painter's story.[6] The story of the narrator, on the other hand, though it resembles that of the painter in some respects, involves less clear-cut oppositions: instead of gazing/withholding the gaze, gazing/reading; instead of portrait/woman, portrait/story. In addition, rather than generating its meaning through stark oppositions, the frame narrative emphasizes middles. We have already seen that the narrator occupies a mediating position between painter and reader (since he both sees the portrait and reads the story). Wounded, the narrator also occupies a middle ground between life and death. When he reaches the turret room he creates, through a series of instructions to his valet, a space of light, where gazing and reading will take place, and that lies, again, in a middle ground between the darkness of the outside world (night outdoors, the danger of death) and the darkness of the inside—the bed with its heavy curtains (sleep, danger of delirium): "I bade Pedro to close the heavy shutters of the room—since it was already night—and to throw open far and wide the fringed curtains of black velvet which enveloped the bed itself" (481). In collapsing the narrator's story into that of the painter we risk, therefore, subsuming what is strange and even incomprehensible in what is known and familiar.

Though the painter is described as a complex figure (for example, he is both "passionate" and "austere" [483]), he is a fairly conventional representative of the Romantic artist. Art is his first love; he takes "a fervid and burning pleasure" (483) at the task of painting his wife so that implicitly at least artistic pleasure replaces for him erotic pleasure and artistic creation takes the place of sexual procreation. In producing a portrait that he considers to be "*Life* itself" (484), he shows himself to be a Promethean figure who dares to compete with God. Though he "ha[s] high renown" (483), we don't hear of his exhibiting or selling his art, and though he is "studious" (483), there is no indication that he has learned his art from a master; he is a genius, a born artist who lives solely for his art. In using his art—his first bride and his wife's "rival" (483)—to paint a portrait of the latter he, like other Romantic artists depicted in fiction (one thinks of stories by E. T. A. Hoffmann, such as "Die Jesuiterkirche in G.," or "Der Artushof," for example), tries to resolve the conflict (overcome the opposition) between the real and the ideal. In stating that the portrait is "*Life* itself" (484), the painter claims that he succeeded in transcending the particular, concrete, contingent (and in so doing has gone beyond painting a portrait of an individual), though he also realizes belatedly that this was achieved at the price of the life of the depicted woman.

If the painter is an easily recognizable figure, the narrator remains mysterious since we know practically nothing about him except that he is wounded and has a valet named Pedro. And while the painter's story lends itself easily to interpretation, the narrator's story remains puzzling. We can see the difference between the two narratives through the way in which light and the gaze are used in both. In the main narrative, gaze and light are the equivalent of love or attention (just as blood/paint is the equivalent of life). As the painter paints he gradually looks more at the painted face than at the real one until he "turned his eyes from the canvas rarely, even to regard the countenance of his wife" (483). Deprived of his "regard"— his gaze and attention—the woman gradually loses life. In order to live, the woman also needs light. The description of the turret room as "dark" (483) is linked to her experience (since presumably the turret room has enough light, indeed, the right light, for the painter to paint): "she . . . sat meekly for many weeks in the dark turret-chamber where the light dripped upon the pale canvas only from overhead" (483). Following the logic whereby the creation of the portrait is the destruction of the woman, either the light that enables the painter to paint is withheld from her, as is her husband's gaze, so that she dies from the paucity of light, its relative absence (the light drips on the canvas, not on her); or, alternatively, the light can be read as a symbolic equivalent of the painter's transcendentally oriented idealism, in which case it actively kills her. In either case, light and the gaze cannot serve both the interests of life (of the woman) and of artistic creation (by the painter).

In the frame narrative, on the other hand, the competition for light/gaze between the woman and the portrait becomes a competition (or disjunctive alternative) between the book and the portrait—an alternative whose meaning is less readily available. The narrator alternates between gazing at pictures and reading the book he finds by his bed: "Long—long I read—and devoutly, devotedly I gazed" (481). The analogy between the gaze and light, and the competition for them between book and portrait, become explicit when the narrator shifts the light in order to see the book better and, in so doing, makes the oval portrait visible for the first time, thus diverting his gaze and attention from the book to the portrait. When he moves the candelabrum back, the portrait is shut off from view and then he seeks the book "eagerly" (482). The whole sequence of actions, carefully noted, is not entirely logical: if the narrator moved the candelabrum in order better to read, why, after discovering the portrait, would he need to move the light back in order to read? And for that matter, why, to begin with, does he move the candelabrum rather than the book? The insistence on shifting and reshifting the light (which attracts our attention precisely because it does not make practical sense) may suggest an incompatibility between book and portrait, other than the empirical impossibility of reading and gazing at the same time. The disjunction between portrait and book appears as a difference that cannot be overcome: there cannot be a synthesis between book and portrait that would allow the narrator (or us) to grasp them together.[7]

The painter's reaction to the completed portrait is described as a logical progression: Having put the last brush strokes onto the face in the picture, the painter first stood "entranced before the work which he had wrought." In the next moment, while still gazing at the painting, "he grew tremulous and very pallid, and aghast," and cried "This is indeed *Life* itself." In a third moment, he "turned suddenly to regard his beloved" and found that "—*She was dead!*" (484).

Whereas the painter's reaction is characterized by a logical progression, the reaction of the narrator to the portrait is more complex and not entirely comprehensible. As a shifting of the light/gaze brings the portrait into view, the narrator's first reaction is: "I glanced at the painting hurriedly, and then closed my eyes" (482). He does not understand, at first, why he shut his eyes; with his eyes still closed he tries to figure out the reason for his action and concludes that "It was an impulsive movement to gain time for thought" (482). There is a certain panic at being exposed to viewing without thinking, maybe because such viewing might be a projection of one's imagination, desire, obsession; thought intervenes "to calm and subdue my fancy for a more sober and more certain gaze" (482). After the interval of thought he "look[s] fixedly" at the portrait, gives a detailed description of its style and its frame, and tries to account for his first reaction to it—that it "had so suddenly and so vehemently moved [him]"—by rejecting three possible causes for the impression it made on him: "the execution of the work," "the immortal beauty of the countenance," and that "fancy . . . had mistaken the head for that of a living person" (482). He then remains "for an hour perhaps" both "thinking earnestly upon these points" and gazing "riveted upon the portrait" (482). The result of this "thoughtful vision" is that he finds the solution to the "true secret of [the portrait's] effect" in its "absolute *life-likeliness* of expression" (though as noted above this "expression" apparently comes neither from the painter's skill nor from the subject's beauty). At the same time he elaborates on the effect this "absolute *life-likeliness* of expression" had on him: "at first startling, [it] finally confounded, subdued, and appalled [him]." Satisfied with his solution to the origin of the "spell," he moves the light away from the portrait "with deep and reverent awe," and, with the "cause of [his] deep agitation being thus shut from view," he starts reading (482–83).

This is a very detailed and complicated account of a reaction to a portrait. It seems to have two contradictory threads to it. On the one hand, there is an attempt to master and bind affect. This is done, first, impulsively, by shutting off the source of affect. This impulsive act then becomes in itself a source of anxiety, itself in need of mastering and binding. Thinking or rationalizing is then used first to explain the impulsive act and then to master its source—the portrait. Describing the portrait as an artifact with a specific style, as well as its frame, is one way of mastering the portrait. Finally comes the explanation that satisfies him and brings the viewing to a close. On the other hand, there is the sense that all this control and rationalization ultimately do not result in neutralizing the portrait. The narrator's thinking and fixed gazing do not eliminate affect, only allow him to spell out more clearly of what this affect consists. Even though he is satisfied with his solution, the portrait still remains a "cause of deep agitation" and needs again to be "shut from view" (482) as it was at the beginning. In trying to control an impulsive first reaction the narrator does not deny the power of the portrait to confound, subdue, appall and agitate him as a portrait.[8] Since we do not get the narrator's reaction to what he has read in the book, the story of the painter cannot be seen as solving the riddle of the portrait for the narrator, explaining it or dissolving the horror and agitation it causes.[9]

The Life-likeliness Effect

> I prefer commencing with the consideration of an *effect*.
> —EDGAR ALLAN POE, *"Philosophy of Composition"*

The narrator's final judgment that the effect of the portrait comes from its "absolute *life-likeliness* of expression" is much less clear than the painter's final exclamation: "This is indeed *Life* itself." The very fact that Poe created a neologism of sorts—"life-likeliness"—in order to describe the portrait's expression indicates that he was trying to describe something for which he did not have ready-made terms.

Whatever idea the word "life-likeliness" was designed to communicate, it does not seem to have been grasped, since most critics substitute, more or less systematically, the clear and relatively common "life-likeness" for the alliterative, synthetic "life-likeliness."[10] The reason for that is fairly obvious: the word Poe creates introduces into the relatively simple notions of resemblance (likeness, another word for a portrait) and resemblance to life (lifelike) the heterogeneous term of likelihood or probability. It is the intruding "li" of "likelihood" that seems incongruous in this context (and therefore is eliminated by critics) since we normally do not speak of a portrait as "likely," though we do refer to stories as "likely" (either ironically or not). If "life-likeliness" suggests the coming together of portrait and story, it does so by keeping their heterogeneity and incompatibility intact.

The portrait's "life-likeliness" is said to be absolute, which causes a further problem of interpretation since the modifier "absolute" seems to negate the meaning of both "likeness" and "likelihood": absolute likeness is identity and not resemblance; absolute likelihood is certainty and not probability. This "absolute life-resemblance-likelihood" is an "expression" that, as we have seen, cannot be anchored in either the skill of the painter or the beauty of the model and is not the result of taking the portrait to be an actual living person.

What sense can we make of Poe's "absolute *life-likeliness* of expression"? "Life-likeliness" appears only one other time in Poe's work, in the story "The Premature Burial."[11] The story lists cases of premature burial, arguing that such occurrences take place frequently. The particular incident to which the expression refers has to do with the application of a galvanic battery to a person who, supposed to be dead, was buried and then disinterred, in order to be dissected. The application of the galvanic battery, we are told, produced "the customary effects" on the body, "except, upon one or two occasions [when it produced] a more than ordinary degree of life-likeliness in the convulsive action" (671)—that is, likeliness of being alive. It is worth noting that in the earlier version of "The Oval Portrait," entitled "Life in Death," the narrator is startled "into waking life" by the view of the portrait "as if with the shock of a galvanic battery."[12]

We have seen that unlike the painter who is horrified by having created "*Life* itself," the narrator is horrified by what he insists is only a picture, by its "expressing" something that is both life-like and likely (or, if we take into account the modifier "absolute," the same as life and certain). The narrator sees something that appears life-like, looks alive—"a young girl *just ripening* into womanhood" (251; my emphasis) who, the comparison with "The Premature Burial" suggests, is buried alive in the portrait, imprisoned within a frame.[13] The comparison to "The Premature Burial" (together with the story's earlier version) also suggests that the narrator himself may be in the same predicament of a living corpse, buried prematurely. This may explain his strong reaction to the portrait without imputing to him knowledge or recognition of the portrait's subject. The painter's double reaction when he views his completed work—the painting is "*Life* itself" and his wife is dead—is replaced by the narrator's reaction—the portrait's spell comes from its "absolute *life-likeliness*," suggesting that both he and the woman in the portrait are buried alive, that is, are both dead and alive. Again, a symmetrical opposition (and the desire to overcome it) is replaced with a middle ground partaking of both terms of the opposition, which, hence, cannot be overcome.

The theme of premature burial is common enough in Poe's work so that suggesting that this is what the portrait in some sense "expresses" comes as no great surprise. Previous critics have explained the presence of this theme in Poe's work either in terms of a psycho-pathological obsession, or, more recently, as an expression of a more general preoccupation, produced by certain social and cultural concerns.[14] In the context of an analysis of "The Oval Portrait," "buried alive" can be read as a sign of an impossibility or a refusal to transcend the particular, to generalize, to allegorize.[15]

As critics pointed out, the painter's story invites being read as an allegory of (a certain kind of) art:[16] art that aspires to transcend the particular. In painting the portrait of his beautiful wife the artist does not engage in mimesis in the sense of copying, slavishly or mechanically imitating, the contingent, particularized real (indeed, as he progressed in his work, the painter "turned his eyes from the canvas rarely, even to regard the countenance of his wife" [483]). Rather, he attempts to capture an essence—

Life itself rather than this or that life, this or that moment in life. In attempting to represent an essence through the painting of his beloved's portrait, the painter marks his effort as a deliberate attempt to overcome art's dependence on the real and contingent (while using a genre defined by its commitment to the particular, real, and contingent).

The frame narrator's reaction to the portrait sidesteps these issues. Unlike the visitors to the turret, who see the portrait's "mighty marvel" in its resemblance to the original (483), the narrator is not struck by the portrait's mimetic accuracy; there is no textual evidence to suggest that he recognizes the portrait's subject. Nor does the narrator express admiration for the portrait as capturing the essence of life, being "*Life* itself," as the painter put it. The narrator's strong reaction to the portrait, then, is not the result either of the portrait's realism or of its ability to transcend the real but rather of its "life-likeliness." As we have seen, the source of the narrator's reaction is not exactly *in* the portrait (the painter's skill, the subject's beauty): in declaring the source of the portrait's spell to be in its "absolute *life-likeliness*," the narrator describes its effect on him, what the portrait "expresses" to this particular viewer.[17]

Unlike the story of the painter, the story of the narrator's reaction to the portrait cannot be generalized, or allegorized: it remains the story of one individual's affective response or reaction to a particular portrait. That we know practically nothing about the narrator except that he is a wounded man paradoxically contributes to this particularization (since attributes indicate the belonging of an individual to a category). His being a wounded man is, of course, of the greatest importance since it indicates his similarity to the woman in the portrait, his being, like her, a living dead, buried alive. We can read this as a general statement (there is no life that is not already partaking of death, we are all living dead), but the response of the narrator to the portrait would still remain irreducibly particular since it involves affect rather than knowledge (and affect is anchored in the body, hence in the particular). The overcoming of the particular that the painter seeks (creating "Life itself") and that his story performs (it invites being read as an allegory) thus remains disjunctive in relation to the narrator's unsublatable affective experience of viewing the portrait.

In telling the story of a painter devoted to his art who, in painting a portrait of his wife, shifts his gaze and attention (his "regard") away from her and onto the image he is painting and thus brings about her death, the main narrative explicitly claims what in many other portrait stories involving a painter remains implicit: that the painting of a portrait causes in some way the annihilation of its subject. In Poe's story this is not attributed to a quasi-magic power of the portrait. Rather, the story suggests that when a portrait is considered superior to its subject, for instance by being "Life itself" rather than but one instance of life, the real subject, rejected as not deserving of attention ("regard"), is symbolically annihilated.

As I have argued in the introduction, the portrait has been often seen as inferior to other art forms because of the particular, singular nature of its subject. A portrait, it was claimed, would not be of much interest to a viewer unless it transcends the particular, is more than a portrait.[18] The narrator's story suggests, however, that the portrait can engage a viewer not because it reveals a general truth or an essence but because it has the power to affect: it can create an effect. The creation of effect has been one of Poe's main goals as a writer (as he himself argued, for example, in his "Philosophy of Composition" or in his review of Nathaniel Hawthorne's *Twice-Told Tales*), and it may be one of the reasons why he is often regarded as not a very serious artist (an artist not to be taken very seriously). Critics' tendency to conflate the narrator's story with that of the painter in a way that subordinates the former to the latter suggests that they prefer the "serious"—that is, generalizable—part of the story (its meaning, its "message") to its affective one. In so doing, critics not only attempt to master and overcome affect (which, as we have seen, the frame narrator also does but without denying the power of affect or obliterating it). They also perform a reading where the production of knowledge or understanding (general) is carried out at the expense of—through the sacrifice of—experience (the particular)—something that the story, in its lack of "outside," lack of distance between experience and narrative, is designed to preclude.[19]

Though, as I have argued above, the structure of the story is such that we, readers, remain imprisoned in the turret and, like the characters, cannot step outside the site of a horrifying experience and gain a cognitive distance from it, it is also true, as Hélène Cixous has noted, that the tale's structure entails that we, as readers, would repeatedly forget the narrator as we become absorbed in the painter's story. This forgetting duplicates the painter's own "forgetting" of his wife in favor of her painted image (Cixous 28). Both acts of forgetting have to do with the preference for the general, essential (Life itself, the painter's allegorical tale) over the particular, singular (the woman, the narrator's reaction to the portrait). Thus Poe's story both prefigures and resists the critical response it generates. Put otherwise, it shows us, the readers, the inevitability, but also the price, of "forgetting" the particular text we are reading as (or when) we draw from it a general meaning, and suggests that not discarding our affective reaction to it in favor of its "message" is a way of countering the urge to generalize. Another way of countering this urge is, of course, committing oneself to a close reading of the text, being attentive and having "regard" for its particularities—to what is different in each text and within each text—rather than sacrificing this difference for some general truth that is, more often than not, already known and familiar.

Poe's story introduces us to some of the issues I will be discussing in the rest of the book. To begin with, the tension between the portrait as a representation of a "mere individual" (hence, debased art form) and the portrait as transcending the particular will be a recurrent issue. As in Poe's story so in many of the others, it will often be mapped onto gender difference. Portrait stories thus provide us with the opportunity of using the undervalued half of the binary opposition particular/universal as means for a critical reflection on how and for what purposes this opposition has been used.

Poe's story also introduces the issue of the painter's power over the sitter or subject—the power to represent. The painter's tale presents this power as absolute: it is the power to create and annihilate life. The lack of any recognizable social setting in the story strips this power of any determinants other than gender difference. Most importantly, the painter who wields this absolute power is presented as a disinterested, "pure," artist-creator who has no worldly concerns, who aspires to transcend the real, and who paints only for the love of art, his first bride. Thus, Poe's story presents the view of art as a separate sphere, outside the world, and hence, presumably, outside power relations, as dependent upon or grounded in a gender differential that gives the male painter complete power over the woman. It can be read as showing how this notion of art founds, justifies, and perpetuates assumptions about male power.[20] The frame narrative, on the other hand, presents the narrator-viewer as wounded and his attempt to master the affective charge of the portrait as only partially successful. It suggests that the male gaze is not always and everywhere conscripted to objectify the woman and (or as) her image. The narrator-viewer's possible identification with the image of the woman suggests an alternative view of the male subject and his association with vision, contesting the notion that "the gendered dynamics of looking are reducible to the relations of empowered male subjects and disempowered female ones."[21] I will return to this question in my discussion of Henry James's story "Glasses" in chapter 4.

Poe's story also addresses the main tension legible in the title of my book: that between portrait and story. By insisting on the disjunction between book and portrait, Poe's story asks us to remember that a story is not a portrait even when it is a portrait story. This issue will be raised in different ways in some of the stories I will be analyzing, and I will discuss it more fully in the afterword.

CHAPTER 2

The Portrait's Two Faces: James's "The Special Type" and "The Tone of Time"

Henry James had a strong and enduring interest in the portrait as a particular kind of representation, and we find in his fiction a large number of texts dealing with portraits and portrait painters. If this fact has not received, on the whole, the attention it deserves, it is, at least in part, because portraits and portrait artists feature prominently primarily in his short fiction, which is still less studied than his novels.[1] But another reason is critics' tendency, when discussing portrait stories, to subsume the portrait within a larger category—such as painting, picture, visual representation, art—rather than to explore the specificity of the portrait as a form of representation.[2] To some extent James himself is responsible for this approach since the analogy between painting and writing, picture and novel, is frequent in his writings. It is worth noting, however, that though in his critical reflections on the novel, most famously in his essay "The Art of Fiction" (1884), James often uses general terms such as "painting," "picture," and "painter" as terms of comparison for literary production, when it comes to his *fiction* he is, by necessity, more specific and the painters he represents are, more often than not, portrait painters.[3] This specificity is by no means marginal or accidental since none of events told in stories such as "The Liar," "The Story of a Masterpiece," "Glasses," "The Sweetheart of M. Briseux," or any of the other portrait stories could have taken place had the stories been about landscape painters or about history paintings. Notwithstanding the general analogy between fiction and painting, then, portraits seem to have, in James's fiction, a specificity all their own. A passage from *The Tragic Muse* provides a good starting point for discussing the portrait's "great peculiarity":

> Nick shared his box at the theatre with Gabriel Nash, who talked during the entr'actes not in the least about the performance or the performer, but about the possible greatness of the art of the portraitist. . . . He insisted above all on the interest, the richness arising from this great peculiarity of it: that unlike most other forms, it was a revelation of two realities, the man whom it was the artist's conscious effort to reveal and the man (the interpreter) expressed in the very quality and temper of that effort. It offered a double vision, the strongest dose of life that art could give, the strongest dose of art that life could give. (992)

According to Nash (in Nick's account), the portrait's "peculiarity"—indeed, its superiority—lies in the perfect symmetry and balance it achieves between art and life: "the strongest dose of life that art could give, the strongest dose of art that life could give." The portrait represents a real person in the real world, but it also reveals, and to the same extent, the painter's art. The artist's imprint—"the very quality and temper of [his] effort"—his "style" or "manner"—is as visible as the portrait's subject and the experience of viewing a portrait consists in our recognizing in it both the sitter and the painter.

In this passage Gabriel Nash gives a particularly serene account of the relation between these two aspects of the portrait (what I discussed in the introduction as its status as both an icon—a likeness—of its subject and an index or trace of its producer). However, toward the end of the novel, when at Nick's request he agrees to sit for his own portrait, Nash seems ill at ease. Nick speculates that "what made his friend uncomfortable was simply the reversal . . . of his usual terms of intercourse. He was so accustomed to living upon irony and the interpretation of things that it was strange to him to be himself interpreted, and (as a gentleman who sits for his portrait is always liable to be) interpreted ironically" (1234–35). The emphasis in this passage is no longer on a "double vision" but rather on a competition between sitter and painter over the power to interpret and exercise irony. Nash's reluctance to sit indicates that under the eye of the painter he feels diminished and powerless. Thus in this passage, as in some of James's other texts ("The Liar" being the most obvious example), the portrait's "double vision" does not produce a peaceful coexistence: the portrait is rather a field of tension, if not of outright conflict, between sitter and artist. Texts such as "The Liar" also show that the presence of the painter in the portrait cannot be reduced to artistic manner or style; the interpreter's "effort to reveal" and the "quality and temper" of this effort expressed or revealed in the portrait may involve motives and intentions not necessarily pertaining to the domain of art. Thus in "The Liar," for example, Everina's first words upon seeing Lyon's portrait of her husband are, "It's cruel—oh, it's too cruel!" (*Complete Tales* 6: 429): the portrait reveals (or Everina sees in it) not only the sitter, Capadose, as a liar but also—even primarily—the painter Lyon as cruel, resentful, vindictive (and possibly also as a liar). Thus the neat distinction and balance between the "dose of life" and the "dose of art" is compromised.

In *The Tragic Muse* we get yet another turn of the screw. After three sittings, Gabriel has stopped showing up and disappeared "'without a trace,' like a personage in a fairy-tale or a melodrama," leaving Nick with an unfinished portrait. While waiting for Nash to turn up, Nick begins

> imagining that the picture he had begun had a singular air of gradually fading from the canvas. He couldn't catch it in the act, but he could have a suspicion, when he glanced at it, that the hand of time was rubbing it away little by little (for all the world as in some delicate Hawthorne tale), making the surface indistinct and bare—bare of all resemblance to the model. Of course the moral of the Hawthorne tale would be that this personage would come back on the day when the last adumbration should have vanished. (1236)

Whereas one of the functions of the portrait is to preserve and transport the likeness of a particular person beyond his or her actual presence and even natural life, the mention in this passage of the effect on the portrait of "the hand of time" suggests that temporality, and death, have not been overcome: the disappearance of the subject is (or is imagined to be) duplicated by the fading of the portrait. The portrait "imitates" its original but not in the way we expect a representation to do. Moreover, the idea that the sitter would reappear "when the last adumbration should have vanished" suggests that the portrait was the cause of the sitter's absence rather than the means of making up for it; the portrait is seen as competing with the subject for the same place, so that Nick's musings come close to the view that the portrait may be a threat to the person portrayed, usurping the person's place, annihilating him rather than preserving him or his image. In this passage the portrait has become uncanny if not outright magic; it belongs to the world of fairy tales, melodrama, or allegorical tales à la Hawthorne.[4]

The three passages I have quoted from *The Tragic Muse* provide us with a concise account of different aspects or potentials of the portrait. In the first passage, the portrait is presented as a superior form of art because it makes visible both an object in the world and a particular way of seeing it (and making it visible to others). We can see how the portrait's "double vision" would fit with James's notion that the novel should represent reality as it is refracted through the vision of some privileged consciousness and his concern that these two aspects of representation remain balanced. In the second passage, the relation between art and real life, between painter and sitter, is presented as potentially conflictual: the painter's "vision" may not accord with the way the sitter sees himself/herself or would like to be seen by others. Moreover, the painter's ironic interpretation, his effort to "reveal" some hidden truth about the sitter, may have more to do with his vision than with the real object (not to mention that this ironic view, the hidden truth he intends to reveal, may not be seen by others, may be seen by some but not by others). In the third passage, the focus moves from an intersubjective relation between sitter and painter, a power struggle where what is at stake is the subjecthood of both, to the relation between the real and its representation where what is at stake is their ontological status. Here the difference between sitter and portrait, reality and representation—the gap that constitutes the portrait *as* representation and establishes the portrait's secondary status, its dependence on the real object—is tampered with if not downright abolished. The portrait then is no longer, strictly speaking, a representation but rather has the status of a double (interchangeable with the real), of a simulacrum (a copy without an original), or of a phantom (an apparition with no objective reality).

The collapse of the difference between reality and representation, the "real" sitter and his/her portrait, occurs also in other texts by James involving a portrait (besides *The Tragic Muse*), when the portrait in one way or another takes the place of its subject rather than re-presenting it. This happens, for example, when the subject is seen as already a portrait (as is the case in "The Beldonald Holbein" or in "Glasses") or when the status of the portrait's subject as "real" is put into question.

From the point of view of the problematic of the "double vision" we have been pursuing, the portrait is, for James, a metaphor for a certain formal ideal that he strove to achieve in his fiction. The permutations I have discussed represent various deviations from this formal ideal (and indicate, at the same time, situations that can be found in stories about portraits). From this point of view, when the status of the portrait's subject as "real" is put into question, the balance between "life" and "art" becomes skewed, with the "dose" of life drastically wanting. But this situation raises another issue besides the formal one of balance or lack thereof. Putting into question the status of the portrait's subject as "real" undermines the portrait's status as a re-presentation that makes the absent or dead present again, makes up for absence and death. Rather, as a simulacrum or phantom the portrait registers absence and death. This registering, in the portrait, of what the last passage from *The Tragic Muse* called "the hand of time"—that is, of the negativity that the portrait is supposed to overcome—calls into question the very possibility of the economy of the "double vision."

To follow this set of issues I will analyze and compare two stories by James that have received very little critical attention: "The Special Type" and "The Tone of Time," both published in 1900.[5] Though the "germs" for the two stories are totally different, reading these two stories alongside each other, and reading them as stories about portraits, reveals striking similarities between them.[6] Indeed, since "The Tone of Time" was first published in November 1900, a few months after "The Special Type" (first published in June 1900), and since it immediately follows "The Special Type" in collections of James's stories, it can be read as a rewriting of the earlier story. In that "revision," it is not only the dose of "life" and of "art" that has changed but also the portrait's relation to absence, loss, and death.

Like some other portrait stories by James, "The Special Type" and "The Tone of Time" involve a love triangle. But whereas in portrait stories such as "The Liar," "The Story of a Masterpiece," or "Glasses," the object of desire is a woman, these two stories tell of the rivalry between two women over a man. In "The Special Type," both Mrs. Cavenham, whom Frank Brivet intends to marry after he gets his divorce from his wife, and Alice Dundee, the woman of the "special type" with whom he pretends to have an affair in order to get the divorce, are in love with Frank. In "The Tone of Time," the painter Mary Tredick is commissioned by the painter-narrator to provide Mrs. Bridgenorth with the portrait of the husband she probably has never had; Mary ends up painting the likeness of the man she herself loved and who jilted her and who is no other than the man who might have married Mrs. Bridgenorth had he not died. In both stories, the man is presented as superlatively attractive and totally unscrupulous. The rivalry between the two women establishes and exhausts the relationship between them: in "The Special Type," Mrs. Cavenham and Alice meet only once, briefly; in "The Tone of Time," Mary and Mrs. Bridgenorth never meet. In both stories, the women's rivalry over the man becomes a rivalry over his portrait. The nameless male painter-narrator plays a crucial role in both stories, mediating and negotiating the relations among the other characters, thus adding a fourth corner to the love triangle.

In both stories, the description of the man is given primarily through that of his portrait (already suggesting a certain primacy of the portrait over its living subject), and in both cases it is the narrator who gives it. In "The Tone of Time," he concludes his long description of the nameless man in the portrait painted by Mary by saying: "Nothing has ever happened to humiliate or disappoint him, and if my fancy doesn't run away with me the whole presentation of him is a guarantee that he will die without having suffered. He is so handsome, in short, that you can scarcely say what he means, and so happy that you can scarcely guess what he feels" (*Complete Tales* 11: 202). In "The Special Type," it is the narrator who paints Brivet's portrait, which, according to him, will "give the pitch of [his] aspect" by showing him as if saying, "See how clever and pleasant and practicable, how jolly and lucky and rich I've been!" (188). Thus in both tales the portrayed man (the man as/in the portrait) is, for the narrator-painter, an idealized (indeed fantasmatic) male figure who is either beyond need and desire ("so happy that you can scarcely guess what he feels") or has the means fully to satisfy all his needs and desires without any diminution of his self-regard: "His cheer was that of his being able to say to himself that he got all he wanted precisely *as* he wanted: without having harmed a fly" (188).

Both men are seen as singular, irreplaceable, as opposed to the women, who are always many: Mrs. Cavenham's insulting reference to Alice as "they" implies that she is but one of the many women who might desire Brivet, and Alice's "plurality" is echoed by the multiplicity of pictures in the studio depicting her (whereas the painter refuses to make a second portrait of Brivet). Likewise, Mary claims that Mrs. Bridgenorth is one of the many women who tried to steal the man who jilted her and get him to marry them. But whereas what makes Brivet unrivalled is his being "disgustingly" rich (175), the nameless man in "The Tone of Time" is represented as hyperbolically beautiful—"the most beautiful man in the world" (200). This difference between money and beauty as the markers of the uniqueness of the object of the women's desire (and of the narrator-painter's admiration cum envy) accounts for the apparent difference between the two stories in the "dose" of life and of art (to use the formulation of *The Tragic Muse*) each receives. "The Special Type" appears as a realistic representation of vulgar (indeed, sordid) social and monetary transactions in which both portrait and painter are entangled. "The Tone of Time," on the other hand, appears as the somewhat unlikely tale (a story that "stretches the long arm of coincidence about as far as it has been made to reach")[7] where a work of art, "a breathing masterpiece" (209), though painted in hatred and in order to expose the subject's infamy, reveals only his superb beauty (the narrator tells Mary: "The beauty, heaven knows, I see. But I don't see what you call the infamy" [203]); at the end, it is "saved" from the entanglements of the social world and from the money nexus and removed into a private space and the sanctuary of art.

What is at the root of the difference between the two stories, however, is the ontological status of the man in question and, hence, the status of the portrait as representation. In "The Special Type," the man, Frank Brivet, is present as an actual character, a living person who interacts with the other characters in the present time of the story. His portrait is seen primarily as a guarantee of his presence: as the narrator explains, painting his portrait will require Brivet to come back from his travels and the possession of the portrait itself "would constitute for [Mrs. Cavenham] the strongest possible appearance of holding [Brivet's] supreme pledge" (183)—his binding promise to marry her. Though the need to bring Brivet back and the anxiety that gives rise to the wish for a pledge already suggest the danger of loss and absence, this danger is minimized. Mrs. Cavenham's reaction to the finished portrait is described by the narrator thus: "it was the dear man in his intimate essence for those who knew him; and for any one who should ever be deprived of him it would be the next best thing to the sound of his voice. We of course by no means lingered, however, on the contingency of privation, which was promptly swept away" (189). The irony, of course, is that it is Alice, the person who was "deprived" of Brivet (according to Mrs. Cavenham, she never saw him alone), who is given the portrait, of which she says: "It will be *him* for me. . . . I shall *live* with it" (191). The danger of loss that motivated the commission of the portrait is minimized while at the same time the portrait is seen as the means of compensating for absence and loss—it is a re-presentation.

In "The Tone of Time," on the other hand, the portrait's function is to stand for the husband Mrs. Bridgenorth never had; it is to be the picture of a man who is absolutely rather than contingently absent (a "never-existent person," as James put it [*Notebooks* 283]), and it is this radical absence that motivates its commission. The portrait is to be painted with no sitter; as the narrator puts it to Mary, it is a portrait "quite in the air," "of nobody" (193, 194). Though Mary ends up painting somebody, the man she paints is not only absent as a character in the story but has also been dead for years; the portrait remains without a sitter. That Mary does not base the portrait on drawings made during the man's lifetime (she has destroyed them all) means that the existential (or indexical) link between sitter and portrait—the way in which a portrait, besides being a likeness, is also a trace of the sitter's past presence—is severed. Moreover, with the exception of the two women, no one who sees the portrait recognizes the man, and he remains anonymous to the end. "No one," says the narrator at the close of the story, "has ever recognized the model, but everyone asks his name" (215). The general lack of recognition with which the portrait is received casts doubt over the man's past presence; he seems to exist only as a portrait. The fact that only the two women "see" the man in the portrait makes him (and/or the portrait) akin to a ghostly apparition. Mary tells the narrator that her suspicion that Mrs. Bridgenorth was the woman who caused the man to fail her grew through the night: "I *saw* them there—in your studio—face to face" (214), as if the man or the ghost of the man were there in the studio—but the man/ghost is the portrait.

In both stories, portraits are linked to the production of social appearances in which the painter is actively involved. This is most explicit in the case of "The Tone of Time," where Mary is asked, and agrees, to help Mrs. Bridgenorth rewrite her past by providing her with a picture of a man she can pass as her dead husband. "The tone of time," which the narrator insists is the portrait's most important feature, refers to the faking (rather than preserving) of a past, here in the service of producing the appearances of social respectability. The narrator explains to Mrs. Bridgenorth that she would want the picture to look old (197) and that this is what Mary is good at; what is wanted and what Mary can produce is a "mere clever humbug" (197). In "The Special Type," it is Brivet who stages the fake love affair with Alice, the woman of "the special type," so that he can provide his wife with grounds for divorce without tarnishing the reputation of Mrs. Cavenham, whom he intends to marry. But the painter-narrator is not simply a passive observer of this charade. Mrs. Cavenham's untarnished reputation is the result of Brivet's having been "so d—d particular" (176) in keeping their intimacy secret, and it is produced in part by Brivet's money (he pays for her to go to America while his fake affair with Alice is going on); but it is also produced and fixed by the portrait the narrator paints of her. When Brivet impresses upon the narrator the need to keep Mrs. Cavenham away from "splash" or "spattering," he revealingly links her untarnished reputation to her representation: Mrs. Cavenham, he says, "stands on a pinnacle; she stands as she stands in your charming portrait—lovely, lonely, untouched. And so she must remain" (176). The use of the portrait to create social appearances indicates the role played by representations in establishing status and reputation; the painter involved in creating such representations can therefore achieve a certain amount of power (as does the narrator-painter in "The Special Type"), whereas withdrawing the portrait from the arena of social relations (as Mary will do at the end of "The Tone of Time") would mean abdicating such power.

The portrait that is central to the plot of "The Special Type" is that of Brivet himself. In painting Brivet's portrait, the narrator intends to reveal Brivet's complacent confidence in the unlimited power of his money, a confidence and a power the narrator both admires and resents. But in a marked difference from a story such as "The Liar," this project of exposure has no consequences: both Mrs. Cavenham and Alice cherish the portrait as they do the man himself and the narrator does nothing to suggest that they might be mistaken. The idea that the portrait might reveal the man as other than what he seems or that it might reveal the painter's view of or relation to him, is briefly suggested but not followed up; it would diminish the status of the portrait as substitute ("the next best thing") for the model. In "The Tone of Time," by contrast, the portrait is not, strictly speaking, a substitute for its subject. It is commissioned by Mrs. Bridgenorth to *appear* as a substitute, is a "substitute" for a nonexistent person, an empty sign whose function is to produce (rather than represent) its supposed referent; it is painted by Mary not in order to make up for the absence of the man she loved but as a sign of her loss of him, of his betrayal of her (it will show his infamy). When the portrait is completed and its sitter recognized by Mrs. Bridgenorth, the portrait does not become "the next best thing" to the man but rather the man himself. Whereas Alice says of Brivet's portrait, "It will be him for me" (191), marking the difference between the man (him) and the portrait (it) and the relation of substitution, Mary says that in giving the portrait to Mrs. Bridgenorth, she had "so blindly and strangely given him back" to her (214), and later that Mrs. Bridgenorth "by a prodigy . . . unwittingly gives him back" to her (215).

As we have seen, in "The Special Type," both Brivet and his portrait are marked by presence: Brivet is present in the story and his portrait represents him. While Brivet has the power to satisfy (or not) the women's desire for him, the painter has "the next best thing"—the power to represent

Brivet and, as we see at the end of the story, the power to dispose of his portrait. Though the narrator is not Brivet's rival for the love of either one of the two women (he does not care much for Mrs. Cavenham and readily admits to Brivet that he likes Alice "ten times more than she likes me; so *that* needn't trouble you" [180]), through Brivet's portrait he acquires the power to satisfy or frustrate the desire of either.

Brivet controls the story's plot through his money: he finances his wife's divorce as well as the show of his supposed affair with Alice, and pays for Mrs. Cavenham to go away while the faked affair goes on; he also pays for the two portraits the painter is doing. At the end of the faked affair, Brivet offers Alice "whatever in the world [she] most desire[s]" (190), thus affirming his own belief in the power of his money to settle all accounts. But the narrator forestalls Brivet: In giving Alice Brivet's portrait, commissioned by Mrs. Cavenham, the narrator usurps Brivet's power to remunerate Alice—thus beating him at his own game. Since the portrait is his "high-water mark" (188), he gives her also something that represents his own power as a painter. By giving the portrait to Alice he frustrates Mrs. Cavenham's desires, and Mrs. Cavenham is in some sense a screen for Brivet himself: she manifests the same selfish complacency as Brivet except that, as the narrator admits, what he cannot bear in her he tolerates in him (188). Getting the better of Mrs. Cavenham is thus another way of getting the better of Brivet without doing so directly. At the end of the story the narrator still has the portrait in his keeping—he is holding onto it until he hears of Brivet's marriage. Since the portrait is seen as a pledge of faith (for Mrs. Cavenham) and as a substitute for an intimate experience that may or may not have taken place (for Alice), having it in his keep gives the narrator considerable potential power over the other characters.

The power of the painter-narrator over the three other characters is expressed already by the fact that all three of them repeatedly seek him at his studio—and not only in order to be painted; he himself never has reason to leave his studio. It is in his studio that the most important transactions and exchanges take place, and when the action takes place in other spaces (as is the case with the faked affair between Brivet and Alice or Mrs. Brivet's decision to divorce Frank), others bring the news to him at his studio. The painter's studio is the site where the characters meet and where exchanges of all sorts take place since the painter himself is not a mere observer but rather an active mediator without whom none of the events could have taken place. And, as in other portrait stories by James (notably in "Glasses," to be discussed in chapter 4), his role as a go-between cannot be separated from his role as painter, the producer of representations. Though Brivet's portrait is described (by the narrator-painter) as a great artistic accomplishment, both painter and portrait are implicated in transactions where money and sex (the real in all its vulgarity, for James) play a determining role.

Though the painter-narrator of "The Tone of Time" also plays the role of mediator and participates (at least vicariously) in the production of social appearances, he does not have the same power as the narrator of "The Special Type." Rather than holding court in his studio, he busily moves back and forth throughout the story between his own studio, Mary's studio, and Mrs. Bridgenorth's house, engaged in a shuttle diplomacy that ultimately fails. At the end of the story he is an old man who has inherited the portrait after the death of both women. Mary herself is a Jamesian artist who has given up everything except her painting, but (unlike the narrator-painter in "Glasses," for example) she does not (or cannot) exercise any power through her art. Unlike the painter in "The Special Type," she is a woman; she is not a successful portrait painter but primarily copies other works, imitates other imitations, and is thus at the bottom of the Platonic ladder. She does not even get to copy what she likes so that rather than shaping the desires of others she is merely the instrument of satisfying others' desires; and even this is not quite true since she seems to have hard time making a living (which is why the narrator is keen on getting her a lucrative commission). When given the opportunity to literally create for another person her past and the grounds for her social standing, Mary chooses instead to project the object of her own failed desire and then reappropriate it. Unlike the painter-narrator of "The Special Type," whose hold on Brivet's portrait makes him the arbiter of the two women's fate, Mary's reappropriation of the portrait means the relinquishing of all power and profit she could have gained from her work, the severing of all relations with Mrs. Bridgenorth, and a retreat into her own, solitary world. If holding onto the portrait gives her the consolation of art, it also leaves her in the same situation as at the beginning of the story, that of the one who "had given up everything but her work" (193). The inability or refusal to exercise power seems to be a correlative of the particular view of the portrait as a sign of absent presence rather than as that which makes present again what was present in the past (or is still present but in another place).

Centered around a present character, and emphasizing what we can call the positive "face" of the portrait, "The Special Type" operates according the conventions of realism. The rivalry between Alice and Mrs. Cavenham is entirely within the realm of the *vraisemblable*; in fact, it is predictable—and more or less predicted by the narrator—that Alice will fall in love with Brivet. In "The Tone of Time," the rivalry between the two women for the love of the unnamed man whom neither one wins is not the subject of the story. The story, rather, deals with the "astounding coincidence" (205), the "prodigy" (215) that brings them together through the mediation of the portrait. But what multiplies infinitely the coincidence—and lack of verisimilitude—and renders the tale truly uncanny is that only the two women recognize the man in the portrait. Different as they are in "reality" (that is, socially), the two women become, in relation to the portrait, almost indistinguishable, mirroring and echoing each other repeatedly. Both are sure from the start that no one will recognize the man in the portrait (Mrs. Bridgenorth claims that "no one else would see" the resemblance to a known individual [206]; Mary says that "nobody will ever know" who he is [200]). Mrs. Bridgenorth anticipates that Mary will be jealous of her (208), and Mary guesses that Mrs. Bridgenorth has told the narrator that she would be jealous (214). Knowing "what happened when he made *me* jealous" (208), Mrs. Bridgenorth can anticipate what Mary might do in her jealousy. Moreover, if at first it seems to Mary that in painting the portrait she has "so blindly and strangely given [the man] back" to Mrs. Bridgenorth (214), who had taken him from her, at the end she says that it was Mrs. Bridgenorth herself who "by a prodigy . . . unwittingly gives him back" to her (215). "Seeing" the same thing constitutes the two women not only as rivals but also as mirror image or echo of each other—thus "de-realizing" both. If the man in the portrait is a ghost, an apparition that only the two women see, the specular relation between the women compromises the status of "seeing" itself as part of the real. Whereas in James's official view, the artist's vision gives us access to reality in all its fullness and nuance, here seeing de-realizes both seers and what is seen.

A portrait is commonly understood as in some sense immortalizing the living, protecting them against the ravages of time, against decay, death, and oblivion by keeping an image of them as living. But in "The Tone of Time," preserving the past is (also) faking the past. Rather than painting a portrait of a living person so that after he dies the portrait will keep his image, Mary not only paints the portrait after the man has died ("He was dead—he had been dead for years" [203]) but also paints him in the style of the past, creating the *illusion* that the portrait was painted years before, when the man was alive. Since a portrait is supposed to resemble its model as much as possible, the highest praise for a portrait is to say that the painted figure appears alive. But in the portrait produced by Mary, appearing alive has two contradictory meanings: an image appears as if it were a living man, and a man who is dead is represented as if he were alive. Because the portrait is that of a dead man, painted after he died, while at the same time it creates the false impression of having been painted in the past, the fiction of painting and the fiction of the man's being alive become the same. The "high artistic impertinence with which [the portrait] offered itself as painted about 1850" (202) has its parallel in the "unconscious insolence" of the man who appears full of "the joy and pride of life" (202), appearing alive though he is dead and/or appearing unconscious, not knowing that he is dead. Moreover, the presence of the "tone of time," for which the narrator praises the portrait, is not restricted to the style of painting; it characterizes also the subject of the portrait who is "dressed, the observer gathers, in a fashion now almost antique and which was far from contemporaneous with the date of the work" (201).[8] It is as if the sitter himself, and not only the manner of painting him, is predated, sounding the tone of time. Thus "the tone of time" is here not the preservation of the past, of life, through representation; rather it is associated with fiction as deception and illusion: that of the painting having been painted in 1850, of the portrait being that of a live sitter.[9]

According to the narrator, Mary would be able to produce the "tone of time" since she has experience copying masterpieces of the past. In successful copies of masterpieces, the copier's identity is hidden behind that of the original painter. But in producing the portrait Mary does not copy another painter; she does not copy herself (since she destroyed all drawings of the man made during his life), nor does she, strictly speaking, copy "the real," paint a sitter. She paints what her memory has retained of what she saw and drew in the past. Without direct reference to the real or to other paintings (hers or others'), this painting should be one that reveals to the highest degree the artist's "effort" and "temper," the artist's vision. But this is not the case. Not only is the "infamy" of the man—her view of what he really was—invisible to its closest viewer, the narrator-painter, but, more generally, the imitation of the style of the 1850s disguises Mary's identity (without, however, her assuming that of another painter, as in her copies). In this portrait without a sitter, the painter, too, is absent; if the name of the sitter does not appear (the portrait does not reveal his identity; there is no caption), neither does that of the painter (there cannot be a signature). Neither painter nor sitter can be recognized in the portrait. This explains why the production of the ghost-portrait turns its producer into a ghost-portrait, too. After Mary makes her decision to keep the portrait, she appears to the narrator "quite on the other side of the gulf of time" (214). Later he adds: "For a moment we stood there, and I had again the sense, melancholy and final, of her being, as it were, remotely glazed and fixed into what she had done" (215).[10] If this suggests the narrator's appreciation of the portrait as a masterpiece—a work of art through which a painter has achieved immortality—immortality here is linked to both the loss of name and the loss of life (hence "the sense, melancholy and sad").

What the portrait in James promises, I have suggested, is a balanced economy of "life" and "art"—sitter and painter, or, in more general terms, brute reality and the vision, the interpretation of the artist (or his surrogate). The symmetry of the exchange suggests that a balance between "art" and "life" is what one should strive for. But the very notion of a balance also suggests that loss or lack on one side of the equation may result in a gain or excess on the other. Thus the gain or increase in vision (of the artist, of the vessel of consciousness) may result in the loss of grounding in reality (the most extreme example of which is James's *The Sacred Fount*). Conversely, too much investment in the real might reduce the scope of the artist's vision; "The Special Type" can be read as an example of this permutation.

"The Tone of Time," however, does not abide by any version of this economy: the portrait is marked both by a double gain (no loss) and by losses that produce no gain (only further losses). To begin with, the portrait Mary painted is, as the narrator puts it, "much more than has been covenanted" (209), and this excess has two contradictory meanings. On the one hand, Mrs. Bridgenorth, who wanted a fake portrait to pass as that of the husband she never had, got the portrait of the man she loved and wanted as her husband. For the narrator, on the other hand, what was supposed to be "a decorative trifle" ended up being a "breathing masterpiece" (209). What was supposed to be a "portrait in the air" ended up being a likeness after all; but it also ended up "too fine" for the part it had to play in the charade of social respectability (201). Instead of being a fiction, it is "too sincere" (201). Even the "tone of time," which for the narrator was what the picture should be all about, is in excess (202). This excess in both referentiality and genuine artistic accomplishment is ultimately translated, by the narrator, into more money, and it is the excess of payment that reveals that what is to be exchanged is not exactly what was bargained for and hence the transaction falls apart.

And yet with all this excess—of referentiality, of art, of beauty, of the past, of money—the portrait is also a sign and a site of a loss that cannot be turned into a gain. On the level of plot, in the battle over the ownership of the portrait, Mrs. Bridgenorth, who wanted a portrait to make up for an absence, loses, and Mary, who represented in the portrait her loss (the man's infamy), gains. Loss has the upper hand; it is loss that gains, and what is gained is loss. That both women recognize the man in the portrait does not increase his reality but rather de-realizes both the man and the two women. The loss of the indexical relation between the subject and the portrait, which means that the portrait is indeed "in the air" rather than grounded in the real, is not made up by a gain in vision (no one sees the infamy; one cannot recognize the painter).

As an index of its subject, a portrait indicates that this subject "was there" while it also tells us, by its very existence, that one day the subject will no longer be there: the portrait will make up for this loss. But the portrait of someone who is already dead (the representation of loss) disrupts this economy. The portrait then can neither tell us that the subject "was there" (unless it lies, but then what it does is create a fiction or a simulacrum of life rather than preserve and represent) nor that the subject is going to die.[11] Rather than overcoming loss (absence, death, oblivion), the portrait registers it: the person was not there, was not present, he failed to be there (for Mary), he died, he is dead. The tone of time that, for the narrator was the fiction of the past, becomes in Mary's portrait the truth of loss and death—hers as well as of the man. When the narrator asks Mary if she is "getting" the tone of time (that is, managing what for him is a "clever trick"), she answers: "Getting it, my dear man? Didn't I get it long ago? Don't I *show* it—the tone of time? . . . I can't give it to him more than—for all these years—he was to have given it to *me*" (201). The darkness that "lurks" in the portrait, as the narrator puts it at the end of story (215), is that of the tone of time as loss and death that cannot be recuperated.

"The Tone of Time" is one of the very few portrait stories featuring a woman painter (others include Balzac's "La Vendetta" and Sand's "Le Châteaux de Pictordu"). I will briefly discuss the representation of the woman artist in the next chapter (in the section on Hoffmann) and will analyze it more fully in the second part of chapter 6, dealing with Sand's story. For the moment, I would like to suggest that James's choice to attribute to a woman painter the portrait of the unknown man—a portrait that, in my reading, registers loss and death rather than overcoming them—can be read in at least two different ways. It can be seen as a sign that the male painter-narrator subscribes to a view of woman as a site and sign of lack and loss.[12] What the portrait as an index of its producer would register, then, is not Mary's vision of the man's villainy but rather her own weakness—loss and lack—as a woman. This would accord with the narrator's characterization of the portrait: calling it "extraordinary" (201), he, nevertheless, "hasten[s] to add" that it is "an appreciably feminine rendering, light, delicate, vague, imperfectly synthetic—insistent and evasive, above all, in the wrong places" (203). "Feminine" here means lacking force, gravitas, determination, the ability to grasp the totality—all more or less stereotypical attributes of woman. But the strong affective reaction of the narrator to the portrait suggests that he responds to the darkness that lurks in it—to the way it registers death. The focus or point of the story, then, would be not loss as lack, signified by woman, but rather the impossibility of overcoming loss in and through representation, and more specifically through portraiture. We have encountered this issue already in the frame narrative of Poe's story, in the idea that the woman in the portrait, as well as the frame narrator, is a living dead, "buried alive" (rather than "Life itself," as the painter claimed)—that is a to say, the idea that death is immanent in life and therefore cannot be overcome. I will come back to this issue in the next chapter, in the discussion of Nerval's "Portrait du diable."

As we have seen in "The Tone of Time," portraying a dead man as if he were still alive disrupts the temporality within which the portrait is usually understood to function (the subject was there in the past and is not here in the present except as a re-presentation). Portraying the dead thus tests the limits of the portrait, which, as the emblematic inscription in some Renaissance portraits—V.V.—proclaims, is of and for the living (it stands for *vivens vivo*, or "[painted] during a lifetime for the living [beholder]").[13] This important difference between portraying the living and portraying the dead, between attempting to immortalize and registering death, has been often ignored by critics. I will explore this question in more detail in my discussion of Theodor Storm in chapter 6.

CHAPTER 3

The Portrait Painter and His Doubles: Hoffmann's "Die Doppeltgänger," Gautier's "La Cafetière," and Nerval's "Portrait du diable"

As we have seen, the nefarious effect the portrait has on the real woman in the main narrative of Poe's "Oval Portrait" is related to the painter's desire to transcend the real, that is, the contingent, ephemeral, imperfect individual. It is through this transcendence that a representation would become "art." In this respect, Poe's story resembles portrait stories by E. T. A. Hoffmann, such as "Der Artushof" (1816), "Die Jesuiterkirche in G." (1816), and "Die Doppeltgänger" (1822). All feature a portrait painter who tries to merge the real woman with the ideal one—the painter's two "brides" in Poe's story—going beyond their opposition. "Die Jesuiterkirche in G." in particular demonstrates the danger of this project but suggests that it affects not only the woman subject but also the painter himself. While the painter Berthold, directly or indirectly, causes the death of his wife—the ideal woman of his painterly vision turned flesh and blood—he himself does not survive this disaster: after the disappearance/death of his wife and son, for which he feels responsible, Berthold sticks to architectural paintings as a penance but eventually completes successfully a painting he could not paint while they were alive and near him, and then commits suicide. The embodiment of the ideal in the real proves to have catastrophic effects on both subject and painter. No wonder then that the painters in the other two Hoffmann stories decide to resist the urge to merge the ideal and the real.

Hoffmann's stories thus raise the question of the relation between the act of portraiture and the portrait painter's own subjectivity (a question also raised, as we have seen, in James's "The Tone of Time"). In this chapter I will discuss three stories that deal with this question and that have received little critical attention: Hoffmann's "Die Doppeltgänger" (1822), Théophile Gautier's "La Cafetière" (1831), and Gérard de Nerval's "Portrait du diable" (1839). All three focus on the portrait painter, and in all three the author uses some strategy (parody in the case of the first two, framing in the case of the third) to distance himself from the figure of the painter, as if trying to protect himself from the dangers the portrait painter faces. All three dwell on the way the painter's own subjectivity is at stake in the act of portraiture. While all three stories tell of a portrait painter's love for an ideal woman, they also include, in one way or another, a diabolic figure, whose power (in the first two stories) derives from producing a perfect replica of the real or creating the illusion, the fiction of reality. They therefore also pose the question of the relation between the reproduction of the real and its transcendence.

Hoffmann's "Die Doppeltgänger"

Hoffmann's "Die Doppeltgänger" tells the common story of a painter who falls in love with the beautiful woman he paints. Through the young painter Georg Haberland talking to his friend, the engraver Berthold, Hoffmann underscores the clichéd nature of this scenario:

> You have long been able to guess that I am in love. The story of this love—it is so simple, so ordinary, that you can read about it in any insipid novel. I am a painter, and so it is in the ordinary course of events that I should fall deeply in love with a lovely young girl I was drawing. That really did happen to me during my stay in Strasbourg. . . . I acquired the reputation of being an excellent portraitist who could steal likenesses for miniatures right out of mirrors; and so it happened that [I was begged] to paint a young lady. . . . I saw, I painted Natalie. O ye eternal powers! My fate was sealed! Now truly . . . there is nothing special in all that, is there? But . . . let me tell you that since my earliest childhood the picture of a divine woman, towards whom all desire and love were directed, has

hovered in my dreams and presentiments. The crude attempts of the artistic boy reveal this picture, as do the more finished paintings of the maturing artist. It was Natalie! (430; 287–88)

In asserting that one "can read about [his predicament] in any insipid novel," Haberland raises, in an offhanded, half-serious way (designed perhaps to encourage us not to take it too seriously), the issue of the relation between representation and the real. On the one hand, if his experience repeats stories in novels, then the relation between reality and representation is reversed; on the other hand, in a sleight of hand common to realist fiction, the very mention of the way things happen in novels serves to create the impression that what we are reading is not a novel but "real." In presenting his story as a repetition of what one can read "in any insipid novel," Haberland both casts himself as a product of fiction and comments on the power of representation to create effects in "the real world." The reversibility between the real and its representation, where each can be the source of the other or "pass" for the other, undermines the hierarchical relation between reality and representation.

What is clichéd about Haberland's story—what happens "in the ordinary course of events"—is his falling in love with the girl he paints, which means that he falls in love with, or through, his own creation. In claiming that what he paints is "the picture of a divine woman, towards whom all desire and love were directed"—that is, in claiming that Natalie is a figure of the "ideal"— Haberland tries to counter the banality of this scenario, of the fact that, as he himself puts it, "there is nothing special in all that." Thus, he tells us, the model for his painting is not the real Natalie but an image in his mind of which she herself is but an embodiment. In painting her, he does not copy a real person, Natalie (with whom he then falls in love), but gives form to an ideal that precedes and exceeds her (and which is the true object of both his love and his art). In making this assertion, Haberland diminishes both the importance of the real woman and the status of his portrait as a representation of a real person. He casts himself as a painter with his own personal "vision" (and hence not at all like a character in an insipid novel) and, by the same token, claims to himself the status of a creative painter, rather than a mere copier of the real. Casting himself as an artist inspired by an ideal serves then to bolster his "originality," that is, serves to deny or disavow both his being a copier of the real and himself a copy. What the painter in search of the ideal needs to exorcise is the power of representation to create "doubles"—a power he himself wields (in his portraits "stolen" out of mirrors) but that also threatens his sense of selfhood.

We now understand why the tale of Natalie's portrait and of the painter's love for her (or for the ideal she embodies) appears in a story whose main subject is ostensibly quite different—the antagonistic relation between doubles. Georg Haberland and Deodatus Schwendy are each the mirror image of the other. As we find out later on in the story, they are actually young Graf von Törny and young Fürst Remigius, respectively; they were both separated from their parents in their childhood and their true identity was hidden from them. The resemblance between them is absolute, and they can eventually be told apart only because of "a little mark on the left breast" of the young Fürst, made by a doctor when he was a baby. Through the machinations of others (of which they remain unaware), the two finally confront each other as rivals for the love of Natalie. This rivalry serves to articulate the fundamental antagonism between them: each threatens the sense of selfhood of the other:

> "Ha!" cried the raging young Törny [i.e., Haberland], "Ha, Fürst! Are you a doppelgänger come from Hell who has stolen my ego [mein Ich], who is plotting to steal my Natalie and to snatch my life from my lacerated breast? Vain, mad thought! She is mine, mine!"
>
> The young Fürst [i.e., Schwendy] replied, "Why are you thrusting into my ego [mein Ich]? What do I have to do with you that you ape my features [Antlitz], ape my figure [Gestalt]! Away with you! Natalie is mine!" (462; 313)

The young Graf accuses the Fürst of being the devil and stealing his ego, and the young Fürst returns the compliment by accusing his double of imitating his features and figure. In other words, each accuses the other of being the kind of portrait painter who imitates his subject so well that it is as if he stole likenesses out of mirrors, a kind of imitation that is also attributed to the devil. Each attributes this power to the other while at the same time both feel threatened in the very root of their being by this painterly/diabolic power.

Hoffmann never gives a full, explicit explanation for the absolute resemblance between the two young men who are not related by blood (even their handwriting and voice are identical [415, 419; 275, 279]). We are told that the resemblance of the baby Fürst to the old Graf von Törny has led the old Fürst (incited by his envious brother) to suspect his wife of adultery. We are assured, however, that this was not the case. True, the Fürstin loved von Törny passionately, but "only the spirit had sinned" (458; 310). Thus, while the resemblance of the painter Georg Haberland to the Graf von Törny can be explained by heredity, that of the young Fürst Deodatus Schwendy to the Graf cannot. Rather, it can be explained by a theory that prevailed from classical antiquity to the Renaissance and that posited "the power of images over the mother's imagination and the power of the mother's imagination over the fetus."[1] If the young Fürst resembles the Graf, then, it is because it was the Graf's image that was before the Fürstin's eyes during the sexual act and/or during pregnancy. Thus though both young men "clearly had Graf von Törny's features [Züge]" (457; 309), the source-cause of this likeness—of their own status as "portraits" of the Graf—is different: the painter Haberland's resemblance to the Graf is that of a son to his biological father, the result of a "natural" reproduction, whereas Schwendy's resemblance to the Graf results from the ability of the mother's imagination to reproduce a copy of the real. As Marie-Hélène Huet has argued, theories of generation are also theories of art; the tradition that attributed to the mother's imagination the power to imprint an image on the fetus saw the mother as an artist: "For Paracelsus, 'By virtue of her imagination, the woman is an artist and the child the canvas on which to raise the work.'"[2] Conversely, when the theory about the power of the mother's imagination was superseded at the end of the eighteenth century, it was replaced not only by new theories of reproduction but also by a new theory of art: Romantic aesthetic theory, where imagination is defined as the power to create images rather than reproducing them, the male power to transcend rather than re-produce the real. Hoffmann's story can then be read as staging an encounter between two ways of thinking about the imagination, one of which has already been discredited by his time of writing but which he uses to challenge the dominant view.[3]

The perfect resemblance of Haberland and Schwendy to the Graf means that neither son resembles his mother. This accords with theories of reproduction according to which the mother functions only as the carrier for the sperm so that the son never bears her likeness. (I will get back to this question in the discussion of George Sand and maternal transmission in chapter 6.) In the case of the young Graf, the effacement of the mother, her invisibility, reaffirms the power of the father and the legitimacy of patrilineal descent.[4] In the case of the young Fürst, by contrast, the resemblance of the son to the Graf indicates both the mother's transgressive desire (which threatens patriarchal authority) and the power of her imagination to override the laws of nature from within natural reproduction. Rather than being bound by the authority of the father and by the laws of nature, the mother's imagination follows and expresses her desire. The perfect resemblance of her son to the Graf—the status of the son as a perfect likeness—is not the result of servile, mechanical copying but rather the product of an imagination fed by transgressive desire. We can understand why the Fürstin is rumored to be a witch.[5]

As we have seen, Haberland himself also produces "doubles." The portraits he paints appear uncanny since they seem to be produced by magic—by "stealing likenesses"—that is, there is no labor involved in their production. They seem to be perfect reproductions of the real, not mediated in any way by the painter's agency or by convention: they are transposed from the objective reflection of the mirror, and the painter's vision—his imagination, his desire, his effort—do not leave their mark on them. Thus it is a *male* painter who faithfully reproduces the real and is totally invisible in his creation, while the mother, who was supposed to remain invisible (both in the process of procreation and in the role of a mere copier of the real often attributed to her), is a "witch" who produces a portrait as "real" as its model while also representing (indexically, as a trace) her transgressive desire and power over nature.

The likenesses Haberland steals out of mirrors also do not seem to have anything to do with the ideal of the divine woman that he "recognizes" in his portrait of Natalie. Nor does Haberland recognize himself in his double, who appears not as a narcissistic confirmation of his selfhood but rather as a rival, a menace. It is this double, whose very being and status as a double derives from the mother's power of imagination, who ultimately brings about Haberland's loss of Natalie. Though we see him first as the lover of the beautiful who tries (and indeed seems to have succeeded) to merge the ideal with the real, and though in the portrait he paints the image of the real Natalie coexists peacefully with his vision of a "divine woman," Haberland ends up losing the real Natalie: after she realizes that she cannot tell the difference between the doubles, Natalie wisely decides to withdraw to a nunnery. Haberland's friend Berthold tries to diminish the sense of loss by telling Haberland that since his true love is art, he has not lost anything. Haberland agrees with his friend that what is important for an artist is the "pure ideal of [his] art, which inspires [him], which breathes from [his] work" and which has nothing to do with the "real" since it is "enthroned above the stars" (464; 315). The devotion of the painter to the pursuit of the ideal thus appears not as an overcoming of the real but rather as the result of (or as a response to) the loss of the real woman as well as a response to the danger the double posed to the painter's sense of selfhood: at the end of the story, Haberland leaves behind him not only Natalie but also his double.

Gautier's "La Cafetière"

Gautier's "La Cafetière" (1831) can be read as a parody of the gothic convention of the portrait coming back to life to reveal a past crime.[6] The narrator is a guest at the house of a nameless friend and spends the night in a room full of portraits of his host's ancestors. These portraits come to life, become real: "I saw clearly that what I had assumed were merely paintings [de vaines peintures] were in fact reality; the eyes of these framed individuals [ces êtres encadrés] shifted and shone in a remarkable way; their lips opened and closed like the lips of people talking" (*Récits fantastiques* 14–15; *Spirite and the Coffee Pot* 20). The narrator is appropriately scared: "an overwhelming terror gripped me" (15; 20), but the parody makes itself apparent already in the description of the figures that come to life ("Chubby little priests, dry sallow dowagers, serious-looking magistrates shrouded in great black robes, dandies in silk stockings" [16; 21]) and especially in the comic description of the way they stumble out of their frames. Ultimately we discover that, in the best gothic tradition, a tragic death had occurred; however, the young and beautiful Angéla was not murdered but rather died "after catching pneumonia at a ball [d'une fluxion de poitrine à la suite d'un bal]" (22; 26).

The parody of the fantastic convention, however, does not account for the entire tale and does not explain its peculiarities. These have to do with the narrator himself—an aspiring painter—and with Angéla, the beautiful young woman whom he never met in life and whose loss he mourns at the end of the story. During the night the narrator spends in the room, the figures in a tapestry representing an Italian concert come to life and play music; the figures in the portraits come out of the their frames and speak, dance, drink coffee. But though the narrator dances and talks with Angéla, she, unlike the other figures, does not come out of a painting, for the very simple reason that her portrait does not feature among those hanging on the wall of the room, and, indeed, it will be painted only *après coup* and by the narrator himself.

The narrator also sees inanimate objects, such as armchairs, becoming animated. The coffee pot is one such object: "a coffee pot threw itself down from a table on which it had been standing and hobbled over to the hearth, where it settled itself amongst the embers" (15; 21). The narrator sees the coffee pot becoming animated but he does not see its metamorphosis into a woman—and neither do we. Therefore, the appearance of Angéla, the dream woman ("Never, even in my dreams, have my eyes been presented with anything so perfect" [18; 23]) remains unaccounted for:

"I saw something which had escaped my notice: a woman who had not been dancing. She was sitting in an easy-chair in a corner by the fireplace and seemed not in the least concerned with what was going on around her" (17; 23). It is only at the end of the dance, as Angéla leaves the narrator and collapses on the floor and he rushes to lift her up, that her provenance is hinted at: "All I found was the coffee pot shattered into a thousand pieces" (20; 25). In the morning his friends find him "stretched right out on the floor . . . clutching a piece of broken porcelain in [his] arms as though it were some young and pretty girl" (20–21; 25).

When the narrator finds himself holding a broken coffee pot instead of the dead Angéla he is persuaded that he was the victim of "some diabolical illusion" (20; 25); the diabolic illusion proves to be, however, none other than that of his own artistic production. After recovering from his swoon, the narrator "began to draw." And we read: "Without my thinking [sans que j'y eusse songé le moins du monde], the almost imperceptible outlines traced by my pencil happened to represent [se trouvèrent représenter], with the most amazing accuracy, the coffee pot which had played such an important role in the scenes of the night" (21; 26). The narrator's host, however, takes the drawing of the coffee pot for a portrait of a woman, which, he states, resembles his dead sister Angéla. The narrator then observes: "In fact, what had seemed to me a moment earlier to be a coffee pot, was really and truly Angéla's sweet and melancholic profile" (21; 26), thus echoing and supplementing his experience of the night before when he "saw clearly that what [he] had assumed were merely paintings [de vaines peintures] were in fact reality" (14; 20). The transformation of Angéla occurs here, at the moment when crayon lines drawn on "a square of vellum" and representing "with the most amazing accuracy" a coffee pot (21; 26), are revealed to be—are "really and truly [bien réellement]"—the profile of a woman. The missing portrait out of which Angéla should have come out (and whose placeholder is the coffee pot), is the portrait he himself draws when he draws the coffee pot. The "real" Angéla, a "mysterious and fantastic creature" (20; 24), the object of an eternally frustrated love, can thus be said to come out of the narrator's drawing.

If the resemblance of the idealized woman to a coffee pot ironizes the narrator's romantic nostalgia ("I realized that there was no happiness left for me on earth" [22; 26]), the fact that he cannot see Angéla's metamorphosis during the night scene and is not aware of it when he draws the coffee pot (it is his host who points it out) suggests that this metamorphosis includes him in an act of phantasmatic desire. The ideal woman lost forever is the product of his painting, which he mistakes for reality. The story tells of the coming back to life of a dead, lost woman (who can thus be mourned and idealized) but then shows that woman to be the creation of the painter who mourns her. In mourning the death of the ideal woman who momentarily appeared as real so that she can be lost again, the painter posits the reality of the ideal whereas it is only his art that both produces the ideal and makes it appear real.

The other, complementary peculiarity of the story is that the narrator never sees his own metamorphosis. When he gets to his room he undresses quickly and gets into bed (14; 20), and when he sees the beautiful woman by the fireplace he jumps out of bed: "I leapt out of bed, where I had been rooted until now" (18; 23). And yet when his two friends find him in the morning lying unconscious on the floor holding the broken coffee pot he is dressed up in an old wedding suit. One of his two friends suggests that he "must have found it all tucked away in a corner and put it on for the fun of it" (21; 25), but the narrator does not know anything about this part of his nightly activities. In addition, the friend, Borgnioli, recognizes the costume as that of his own grandfather, but it is far from clear why a costume of his grandfather would be in that room since Borgnioli, like the narrator, is just visiting the castle. If, on the other hand, the costume is that of the *host*'s grandfather, it is not clear how or why Borgnioli recognizes it: "And here are the paste buttons with their tracery decoration which he told us [who are these "us"?] so much about" (21; 25). As in the case of the drawing of the coffee pot, here, too, recognition is delegated to another character: it is not the narrator who recognizes the clothes he is wearing, he is not aware of his own metamorphosis just as he neither sees Angéla's metamorphosis nor recognizes her on his own in his drawing of the coffee pot. But in the case of the narrator's clothes, the double who recognizes for and instead of the narrator is himself doubled, divided between the friend and the host. The presence in the room of the costume the narrator casts away as a "ridiculous outfit" (21; 26) is never explained, and its putting on is the one action the narrator never sees—either when it happens or *après coup*, through his drawing. His own participation in the animated picture, in the trompe l'oeil where a representation becomes real, is not something he can see, precisely because he is the one who produces it. It can be recognized only through a double—the friend (who, like the narrator, is an aspiring painter), doubled by the host (the owner of the castle whose ancestors are depicted in the portraits). In assigning recognition to a double, the story allows the narrator to remain unconscious of his role in the creation of what he himself defines as a diabolic illusion. The diabolic consists of creating the illusion of life through representation but also the illusion of the ideal becoming real; the power to create doubles is both that of creating a fiction of the real and that of making the ideal appear real. It is thus the work of the devil, who both creates perfect resemblances and makes the ideal appear real, both producing and frustrating the subject's desire.

The presence of the devil as the figure for and double of the painter is only alluded to in "La Cafetière"; we can find it in a more developed form in Gautier's "Onuphrius" (1832; translated as "The Painter"), a story of a poet-painter who goes mad, having been dispossessed by a diabolic double. This double, who comes out of a mirror without silvering, both frustrates and expresses Onuphrius's desires. On the one hand, the diabolic double prevents Onuphrius from completing the portrait of his beloved Jacintha just at the moment when it is about to come to life: "The blood began to flow beneath the flesh tones [sous les chairs], the outlines grew sharp, the forms filled out, the light values were established against the dark [la lumière se débrouillait de l'ombre], and half the canvas was already alive. The eyes were particularly successful. . . . The gaze was firmly fixed [la prunelle regardait bien]" (*Récits fantastiques* 27; *My Fantoms* 55). As the portrait is about to become alive, as the painter is about to complete a creation of a living being, the devil, his double, interferes. On the other hand, the diabolic double causes Onuphrius to transform the portrait so that "It was no longer Jacintha, but much more like one of her friends, with whom she had quarreled because Onuphrius thought she was pretty" (35; 64), thus suggesting that he—the diabolic double—is the agent expressing Onuphrius's unconscious, hidden desires. The double also transforms Jacintha's portrait by providing it with "masculine insignia"—"a pair of moustaches that would have done honor to a drum major" (26; 54)—which can be read either as frustrating or revealing Onuphrius's desires.

The intervention of the diabolic double, who ultimately usurps Onuphrius's place as a poet, painter, and lover, can be interpreted in various ways, but what is clear is that it relates to the common idea that the production of the illusion of reality, of life, through mimetic representation is a deception and falsity (hence its association with the devil); the more deceiving the image, the more it bears the sign of the devil—hence the trompe l'oeil. The devil's deception is also that of making one think that the ideal is (or can be merged with the) real. Thus in Gautier as in Hoffmann, the story about the search for the ideal is also a story about mimetic representation. For Gautier it is the artist (the devil) who transforms what he copies (the coffee pot) into the ideal (the perfect woman) whose imaginary referent (Angéla) he then mourns.

Nerval's "Portrait du diable"

In Nerval's "Portrait du diable," the relation to the devil is much more enigmatic since nowhere in the tale can we find either a portrait of the devil or the devil himself. The distancing that in "La Cafetière," "Onuphrius," and "Die Doppeltgänger" was produced through parody is here produced by the creation of a frame. The first-person narrator differentiates himself from his friend Eugène, "a skilled painter" (165), whose sad story of persecution and madness he hears and then relates to us. Eugène's painterly career is derailed when he meets Thomas Wilkinson, a rich Englishman, and falls in love with his daughter, Laura. Wilkinson leads him to believe that he admires his art, but his regard is only illusory: he rebuffs and rejects Eugène when he asks for Laura's hand, and she later cruelly pretends not to recognize him.

As in "La Cafetière," the idealized and desired beautiful woman both precedes her portrait and comes out of it. As we shall also see in chapter 4, in the discussion of Balzac, the beautiful woman is always already a painted image, an incarnation of painterly beauty. Thus, in Nerval's story, Laura Wilkinson is loved by Eugène since she resembles "the most beautiful feminine types ever produced in Greece" (170). The loss of the beautiful woman is the loss of an object of desire, which is, at the same time, the source of the male painter's artistic creation. It thus preludes the painter's dispossession as both a lover and a painter. In "Onuphrius," the agent of this double dispossession is the devil, the powerful double who steals Onuphrius's ideas, signs his paintings, and becomes Jacintha's lover. In Hoffmann's "Die Doppeltgänger," dispossession is averted (or the sense of loss is minimized) when the painter is convinced by his friend that the real woman (object of desire) is different from the ideal one (source of artistic creation) and that losing the former does not rob him of his art (though it makes it impossible for him to be a portrait painter). In Nerval's story, the painter Eugène cannot separate his love for the real woman from his artistic ideal; like Onuphrius he goes mad, though the devil appears nowhere except in the story's—and a painting's—title.

After being rebuffed by Laura's father, Eugène follows father and daughter to Paris but fails to find them. He decides to paint Laura's picture from memory and exhibit his painting in a gallery visited by tourists with the hope that the painting will become the means of resuming his relation with her and maybe even gaining her love. The idea that one could win the love of a woman by painting her is predicated on the assumption that, seeing herself in the image the painter has created, the woman will recognize herself, and especially the beauty that defines her, as *his* creation and therefore will love him. We will see such a scenario at work in Balzac's *Maison du chat-qui-pelote*, where the painter Sommervieux wins Augustine's love by painting her portrait and displaying it at the Salon.

But in Eugène's case, the plan fails. On the face of it, this failure can be attributed to Laura's falseness—her regard for him, just like her father's, is illusory; rather than being Petrarch's Laura she is, as we shall see, the infernal woman, Lilith, the devil's bride.[7] But it might be that the reason for the failure lies also in the picture itself. Rather than trying to win Laura's love by painting her portrait, Eugène decides to paint from memory his last interview with her, that is, he paints his own love story. But his hope to achieve through the painting what he failed to do on his own, fails. Laura does visit the gallery, but she pretends not to recognize him—either as the man who declared his love to her or as the painter of the displayed picture. This annihilation, however, is already prefigured in the painting by the ambiguity concerning the place Eugène himself occupies in it. Though, logically, the painting should include his own likeness, since it is a painting of his last meeting with Laura, Eugène does not expect Laura to recognize him by his resemblance to the figure of the lover in the picture. Nor does he expect her to recognize him as the picture's painter (by his manner of painting, his style, or the trace of his love he leaves in the picture). His only hope is that the picture "will attract the attention of Laura and that she will be able to find out the name of the artist who has painted it" (173). It is as if Eugène is absent from the painting both as a subject, a lover, and as a painter, though (or because) the painting tells/anticipates the story of his dispossession and annihilation. Surprisingly, this absence suggests that he himself is, in some sense, the devil, since the latter is also defined by his absence (from both the story and the painting that bear his name).

After Laura ignores him in the gallery, Eugène finds himself in the street, held by policemen, with his painting torn to thousand pieces, apparently by himself (though he has no recollection of the act). Following this unconscious murder cum suicide, Eugène leaves for Venice. "A bizarre fantasy" (175), he says, caused him to go there to see a certain picture. This repeats his previous decision to go to Paris, "To what end? I would not be able to say" (172), so that the search for the picture can be seen as the repetition of the senseless search for Laura. The two-hundred-year old picture that obsesses him is "a picture whose subject was furnished by the most horrifying story" (174). What this subject is remains ambiguous; all we hear is that "the painter did not complete his painting; but when he examined attentively his bizarre work, which represented the Devil's Betrothed [la Fiancée de Satan], he lost his mind and ended up killing himself" (174). The "horrifying story [effroyable histoire]" seems to be that of the painter's madness and death *following* the act of painting rather than what provided the subject for the picture. The painting represents "la Fiancée de Satan" so that it does not seem to represent either the painter, whose "horrifying story" is the only one mentioned, nor the devil whose portrait the title of the story promises us; both are absent-present in the picture. What is called the subject *of* the painting is the story of what happens *as a result of* the painting. The painting's subject is its own history, and this history seems to be subject to endless repetitions: it is both adumbrated by Eugène's picture of his last meeting with Laura and repeated by Eugène's story after he sees the old picture.

When he finally finds the "bizarre" picture, it is hidden behind a curtain: "My heart beat violently since I felt that I had in front of me the object of my eager search [ardente recherche]. I threw myself at the curtain; I grabbed it, I pulled it, and the Devil's Betrothed fixed on me her penetrating gaze; but . . . but . . . this portrait . . . it was . . . it was . . . O God! It was the portrait of Laura" (176). The expression "the portrait of Laura" is ambiguous here: he either sees the representation of Laura or a picture of a woman who resembles Laura (and hence can be described as her portrait). The former interpretation will equate the painting "La Fiancée du diable" with Eugene's own picture of his last meeting with Laura—the only "portrait" of Laura we know about. Since subsequent to seeing this bizarre painting Eugène himself goes mad and dies, he is the double of the picture's painter, and the hell he sees depicted in the picture is the hell in which he will live as he is followed to death by the persecuting portrait.

The story we read, "Portrait du diable" (in which no portrait of the devil appears), is about a picture of Laura (from which the painter is absent). This picture, painted by the painter Eugène, is doubled by another picture, "La Fiancée du diable," in which the devil does not appear. This picture, we are told, tells a horrifying story, seemingly that of the picture's effect on its painter; and this story is replicated by Eugène's story.

Thus Eugène repeats the previous painter just as his painting repeats the older one. What is repeated in both pictures and stories is the loss and dispossession of the painter. This loss is inscribed in the paintings and in the story by absence—of Eugène, but also, indeed primarily, of the devil. The devil, the malignant agent that robs the subject of its subjecthood, is inscribed in this story only as an absence; he is, we can say, a figure for absence and loss, for a purely negative force that manifests itself through repetition.

The three stories by Hoffmann, Gautier, and Nerval all deal with a male portrait painter and raise the issue of his relation to, and presence in, the portraits he paints. As we have seen in the introduction, the painter's indexical presence in the portrait means that the portrait represents him, too. In the portrait of another person he can recognize himself—recognize his skill as a painter as well as his "vision" (which may be not purely artistic but fueled by identification or projection, envy or desire). The discrediting of representation that strives to be faithful to its individual subject derives from the notion that such representation denies the painter his vision and thus renders him invisible even to himself (as is the case, for example, in Haberland's portraits, "stolen" from mirrors). But Hoffmann's story, by staging an encounter with an older understanding of the imagination as reproductive (an oxymoron of sorts), shows, on the contrary, that when moved by desire it has the power to transgress social and natural laws, thus inscribing its producer in an image that is, nevertheless, a copy of the real (a real copy). Haberland, then, can be seen as both falling short of this reproductive imagination (he does not leave a trace in the copies he produces, maybe because he cannot truly desire a real person) and being threatened by it (the living portrait the mother produces of the man she loves is the double who threatens his own being).[8] Alternatively we can say that the figure of the double signifies both the power of the painter and his dispossession: if he can steal likenesses, someone else can steal his likeness too (as the double threatens to do); while he produces perfect likenesses, he himself is like a character in a novel, a "fictive" character. Whichever way we read it, Haberland's decision to devote himself to the ideal emerges from the threat the portrait of a real person poses to his sense of self. For him the only securely "real" subject is the one who neither has nor produces a double (and the two seem to imply each other), the one who neither paints portraits nor has his portrait painted.

Gautier's story can be read as exposing what Haberland tries to ignore: that the ideal to which he devotes himself is an artifact he himself produces rather than a divine source of inspiration. The story shows the process by which an absent real woman becomes an ideal, impossible object of desire, through the painter's act of representation. But though the story shows that, it also shows that the painter cannot be conscious of his being the dupe of his/the devil's magic of make-believe called art; only so can he continue to believe in, and mourn, the existence of the now lost ideal.

Nerval's story is somewhat different from those by Hoffmann and Gautier in that it shows the male painter's predicament as that of repeated loss—of recognition, of the love object, of self—that ultimately results in madness and suicide. The treachery of Laura's father, who usurps the place of the painter's father in the painter's heart with false recognition, is repeated by Laura's own refusal of recognition as well as of love. The picture of Laura he paints is a response to this loss, but, as we have seen, it also both repeats and prefigures loss. The repetition of dispossession shows that the painter cannot make up for his loss by representing it. Nerval's story of madness and suicide shows the portrait (the picture of Laura and the painting of "The Devil's Betrothed") to be the indexical representation of the painter; but rather than representing his vision or desire they tell proleptically the story of the painting's effect on him—the story of the painter's repeated dispossession. The way the painter's story repeats that of the painter of "The Devil's Betrothed" suggests that the devil missing from the painting is the painter, also missing from his own painting of Laura. The devil then stands for the painter, as was the case also in Hoffmann and Gautier. But whereas in the latter two the painter is both like the devil—a powerful magician who steals likenesses and creates trompe l'oeil—and the devil's victim, in Nerval's tale the painter is entirely dispossessed. For Nerval's painter (as for the woman painter of James's "Tone of Time"), representation is a repetition that does not make up for a loss—does not redeem or turn it into gain—since what is repeated in it is loss. The absence of the devil from the story and picture that bear his name is the figure for this loss that cannot be made good, the pure negativity of repetition, madness, and death.

As I argued in the introduction, the portrait was considered an inferior form of art because it aimed at representing "a mere individual." Such a judgment depends on the notion that the individual is, as Joshua Reynolds put it, "a defective model."[9] The attempt of the painter to go beyond the mere individual would be, then, an attempt to go beyond what is defective and lacking and represent what is absolute or essential. The painter's tale in Poe's "Oval Portrait" presents the most extreme version of this attempt.

As we have seen, this attempt is at the expense of the woman, the "mere individual"; the painter's power over the woman is inextricably linked to his disinterested devotion to "art," understood as the search for essence and truth.

The three stories discussed in this chapter take some distance from the painter's attempt to represent the ideal, through parody, irony, and framing. The power of the painter lies, rather, in his ability to create doubles—copies that appear real, *are* real—an ability that is also attributed to both woman (the mother in Hoffmann's story) and the devil. Though the ability to create a perfect semblance of the real is a source of considerable power, as is evident from the analogy between the painter who produces it and the devil, it does not have the cultural prestige of the attempt to transcend the real (indeed, it is denigrated as mere trickery and deception) since it is dissociated from the search for truth or essence. Moreover, the (male) painter is seen here as both a powerful devil and a powerless victim of diabolic deception—both the producer and the product of representations (which may be another way of accounting for the devaluation of this view of the artist).

The dissociation of the power of the portrait painter from the search for essence and truth means that the portrait does not go beyond the "defective" real, hence does not make up for what is supposedly lacking in the real. At the same time, the portraits in these stories are not simply faithful re-productions of the real. That the painter creates "doubles" (Hoffmann), that the phantasmatic figure of the ideal woman is produced by the painter's drawing of a coffee pot (Gautier), or that his paintings prefigure what will happen (Nerval) all mean ultimately the undoing of the hierarchical relation between the "real" and its representation: rather than being a representation of a preexisting subject, the portrait is a double or a simulacrum, or can be seen as producing its subject. The texts by Balzac and James analyzed in the next chapter will allow us to further explore this permutation.

CHAPTER 4

On Portraits, Painters, and Women: Balzac's *La Maison du chat-qui-pelote* and James's "Glasses"

With the exception of James's "The Tone of Time," all the stories I have discussed in the previous chapters tell of a male painter who produces the portrait of a woman. This, of course, is not the only possible configuration (indeed, the stories I will be discussing in the last three chapters of the book all present us with different scenarios), but it is a very common one, and we find it also in the two stories that are the subject of this chapter, Honoré de Balzac's *La Maison du chat-qui-pelote* and Henry James's "Glasses." What sets these two stories apart from those by Poe, Hoffmann, Gautier, and Nerval is that they are realist dramas that show the social function and power of the portrait qua representation (an issue also discussed in chapter 2). The difference between these two texts and Poe's story is especially revealing: unlike Poe's allegorical tale of the painter in his turret room, Balzac's and James's stories situate both painter and subject in a well-defined social setting and represent also their interaction and relations with other characters. This has considerable implications for the way the gender relation between painter and sitter is represented.

Since man is routinely seen as an active subject and woman as a passive object, portrayals of a woman by a man (and the stories that represent such portrayals) are often read as reaffirming woman's status as object. One should not omit, however, the other side of the equation: it is the act of representation that constitutes the man as a subject (who hence has the power to represent). In other words, what produces the gender asymmetry in these scenarios is not the "essence" of woman as object and of man as subject but the power to represent. That the power to represent has historically resided primarily in men is proven—if such a thesis needed proof—by the preponderance of male painters in portrait stories.[1] But Balzac's *La Maison du chat-qui-pelote* and James's "Glasses," I argue, open up the possibility that control over the means of representation may be contested. As stories that dwell on the social context in which the acts of portrayal take place and show the painter's artistic production to be inseparable from his interests and desires, they also show how, and under what conditions, the power to represent is gained, kept, or lost.

La Maison du chat-qui-pelote

Balzac's *La Maison du chat-qui-pelote* (1829) is the story of a beautiful woman, Augustine Guillaume, who is painted surreptitiously by an artist named Sommervieux, who has fallen in love with her and whom she subsequently marries; by the end of the novella, the portrait is destroyed and the wife dies shortly thereafter. The novella is usually read as "a cautionary tale of the dangers of marrying outside one's class,"[2] a view already expressed within the story by Augustine's father, the conservative, philistine merchant M. Guillaume (65; 53). There is no doubt that *La Maison* is a realist social drama in which class difference plays an important role; the interpretive question is what role the portrait plays in this drama. Most critics downplay the importance of the portrait; some ignore it altogether while others find that it detracts from the "real" drama.[3] And yet the importance of the portrait should be quite obvious. Although the text never establishes a causal relation between the destruction of Augustine's portrait and her death, one can argue that the climax of the novella is the destruction of the portrait, of which the death of Augustine herself is but a pathetic trace.[4] Nor does the portrait precede Augustine only in death: it makes an appearance at the Salon, and later at the Duchesse de Carigliano's, before she does.[5] The importance of the portrait, then, is manifested by its precedence over the represented subject, a precedence that does not bode well for Augustine, since it can be read as a sign of representation eclipsing its subject.

Critics who do discuss the portrait do so in the context of the relation between writing and painting.[6] As a result they are not sufficiently attentive to the specificity of the portrait—that is, its difference from other pictorial representations within the text: Sommervieux's painting of the interior of the Guillaume shop and the shop's signboard, a pictorial representation of its name, the "chat-qui-pelote." This difference is also quite obvious: at the end of the novella, the portrait of Augustine is destroyed while both Sommervieux's painting of the shop and its old signboard survive. More generally, the difference between the portrait and the other visual representations becomes clear when we look at the novella's plot, which is generated not by the pictorial representations of the shop (as the title might lead us to expect) but by Augustine's portrait.

NARRATIVE STRUCTURE AND VOICE: REPRESENTING REPRESENTATION

To understand the function of the portrait in the novella we need to look briefly at its narrative structure and narrative voice. It should be noted that the events told at the beginning of the *narrative* do not constitute the beginning of the *story*. The beginning of the story, told in a flashback, recounts how Sommervieux stumbles upon the shop, the "maison du chat-qui-pelote" of the title, "at dusk one evening" (47; 31), looks inside, and sees the entire family around the dinner table. At the beginning of the narrative, on the other hand, we see Sommervieux (characterized as an unknown young man) outside the shop "one rainy morning" (33; 16), trying to catch sight of Augustine, who eventually appears at her window. By the time of this scene, described on the first pages on the text, Sommervieux has already painted both the picture of the shop and Augustine's portrait; he and Augustine have already encountered each other in the Salon, where her portrait was exhibited (an encounter that took place more than eight months after Sommervieux first saw Augustine and the shop) and met four additional times (53; 37–38). Thus Augustine's appearance, as she stands framed by the window in the narrative's opening scene, is not the origin of the portrait but rather its repetition.

In the scene that constitutes the beginning of the story, Sommervieux's gaze penetrates the inside of the shop. This penetrating view is the origin of both the portrait of Augustine and the picture of the shop (which is a representation of its interior). By contrast, in the scene narrated on the first pages of the text, in which Sommervieux revisits the shop, we get a description of the shop's exterior: Sommervieux is still interested exclusively in the inside but cannot see through the shutters, curtains, and other obstacles that block his view. The description of the shop's exterior is carried out, then, by a narrator whose point of view differs from that of Sommervieux.[7] And since the scene in which the painter sees (and subsequently paints) the inside of the shop precedes temporally the scene in which the outside of the shop is described by the narrator, we cannot say that Sommervieux's view of the inside of the shop is an extension and continuation of the narrator's (following the typical Balzacian movement from outside to inside);[8] the two points of view remain divergent.

This divergence announces the existence in this text of two different and incompatible views of representation. In describing the outside of the shop, the narrator's point of view is that of a historian or an archaeologist—someone who is concerned with the traces of the past in the present. The shop building appears to him as a precious trace that might allow him to reconstruct what once was and is in the process of disappearing: "This venerable structure was crowned by a triangular roof of which no example will, ere long, be seen in Paris" (33; 16). The house is "a relic of the bourgeoisie of the sixteenth century" (33; 16), and in that sense represents its inhabitants, who attempt to retain traditions that are about to disappear. The passage of time has rendered it both dilapidated and incomprehensible: its "singularities" offer "more than one problem to the consideration of an observer" (33; 17), and its walls are said to be "decorated with hieroglyphics [bariolés d'hiéroglyphes]" (33; 16). The narrator's description deciphers and re-presents those traces.

The description by the narrator of the shop's outside (including the description of its signboard) thus suggests that representation is commemorative and supplemental. It is predicated on the assumption that representation re-presents and thus preserves what is past and lost, making possible knowledge and understanding of the past. Such a notion of representation does not necessarily depend on seeing reality as a fully present original and representation as its inferior copy; seen as a trace in a series of traces, representation allows the reconstruction of the historical process of change and loss. The narrator concludes his description of the signboard by telling us that the signboards of old shops are "the dead pictures of once living pictures [les tableaux morts de vivants tableaux] by which our roguish ancestors contrived to tempt customers into their shops" (35; 18).[9] Even though in this quote representation is designated as "dead" in relation to the "vivants tableaux" of the past, the passage as a whole makes clear that those living pictures, precisely because alive, are subject to time and therefore death, whereas the "dead pictures" subsist (though they too undergo change and thus require additional acts of representation).

For Sommervieux, by contrast, representation is neither supplemental nor a trace. As he gazes inside the shop, the family scene appears to him in its present plenitude as an aesthetically satisfying whole—that is, already as a tableau, or a static spatial arrangement of elements (47; 32). More precisely, under his painterly gaze reality becomes this composition. It is this idealized reality (idealized first of all in the sense that it is removed from the flow of time) that he aims to represent on the canvas, both in the picture of the shop and in Augustine's portrait. The narrator attributes to Sommervieux the painterly desire to "render nature [exprimer la nature]" (47; 32), but this desire seems to depend, paradoxically, on the erasure of difference between nature and art since what he re-presents is already in some sense a painting ("tableau naturel" [48; 32]). We are told that having returned from Italy, "the pompous land where art has everywhere left something grandiose," his eyes are thirsty for "real nature [la nature vraie]" (47; 32); more specifically, "his heart . . . craved one of those modest and meditative maidens whom in Rome he had unfortunately seen only in painting" (48; 32). However, the Augustine upon whom he stumbles appears to him not so much as "real" but as part of a composition ("la figure principale") in which he sees her as an "idol," "an exiled angel remembering heaven [un ange exilé qui se souvient du ciel]" (48; 32, 33) rather than as a creature of flesh and blood.[10]

REPRESENTATION AND VIOLATION

Because Sommervieux's idealization of Augustine transforms her from a creature of flesh and blood into an angel, her presence in the material and materialist environment of shop and family might be considered an exile. But Augustine's only possible sin (to warrant exile) is her "violation" by the intruding gaze of the painter. Here, the gaze that idealizes also violates since it turns a private scene into a work of art whose raison d'être, as we shall see, is to be exhibited. Watched unaware, painted and exhibited without her consent, Augustine, one might say, has her "likeness" stolen by the artist, who makes it the object of a public gaze.

In the Salon scene, Augustine, seeing her portrait as the object of public admiration and told by the triumphant painter that the portrait is the incarnation of his love for her (50; 35), recognizes herself in the "crowned work [tableau couronné]" (50; 34) —or, more accurately, mis-recognizes herself since the portrait is an idealized image —and falls in love with its admired painter. But her first reaction to the portrait is fear (50; 34). She feels as though a guilty relation ["pacte"] has been established, without her willing it, between herself and the painter (50; 35). The mixture of fear and "jouissance [rapture]"—her "étourdissement [bewilderment]," "enivrement [intoxication]," and "joie mêlée de terreur [rapture mingled with terror]"—makes her feel as if she were "under the power of the devil"; "This moment was to her like a moment of madness" (51; 35–36). The encounter with the portrait is thus experienced as a moment of loss of self.

The idea that representation involves loss of self through violation and exposure (for which Augustine feels half-responsible since she cannot but admire herself in the picture and thus retroactively condone the "stealth" of her likeness) presupposes both an opposition between inside and outside and a valorization of the inside. The latter characterizes the Guillaumes and opposes them to Sommervieux, who valorizes the outside. The dichotomy between inside and outside can thus be seen as underlying the opposition between bourgeoisie/commerce, on the one hand, and aristocracy/art, on the other.[11]

The description of the shop with its "threatening walls" (33; 16), windows that allow only a "doubtful light [un jour douteux]" (33; 17), "heavy shutters" (37; 21), and "strong iron bars" (38; 21) presents the shop as closed to and protected from the outside world. There is no attempt on the part of the shop's owner to advertise in any way its commerce; indeed, "many a passer-by would have found it difficult to guess the class of trade carried on by M. Guillaume" (38; 21). Nor does M. Guillaume's lifestyle broadcast his considerable riches. The Guillaumes rarely go out —Augustine and her sister, we are told, "very rarely suffered their eyes to wander beyond the walls of their hereditary home" (44; 28)—and M. Guillaume rarely indulges in the display of riches that entertaining his peers and neighbors would entail.

Whereas the Guillaumes stay in their dark shop, hidden behind blinds and curtains, Sommervieux first appears on the street, where he exhibits himself to the shop's occupants. What is emphasized in his characterization as an artist is not so much that he creates paintings but that he exhibits them. Indeed, exhibition is for him a mode of being; only twice does he stay hidden in the privacy of either his studio or his bedroom: when he paints the portrait of Augustine and when, after their marriage, he retires with her from the social world. In both cases, his withdrawal into a private interior space is marked as an anomaly. Sommervieux's drama is not governed by a conflict between love and art (or between life and art);[12] both the bedroom and the studio are instances of interior space and are opposed to an exterior space of both social relations and exhibition. Sommervieux's main scene of action has always been the salon (both artistic and social). And just as after eight months of work in the studio he displays his paintings in the Salon to the admiration of the crowd, so after a year of seclusion with Augustine he feels the need to go back into society, where, moreover, he tries to exhibit Augustine herself, hoping she will incite the same admiration as did her portrait. The portrait, which he had withdrawn from the Salon—from exhibition as well as from circulation and exchange—cannot remain hidden either and is brought out and used again to generate admiration for its creator.

HOW TO DO THINGS WITH PORTRAITS

Sommervieux's first appearance in the street shows him exhibiting himself as if he were a portrait or a statue: "His cloak, folded after the manner of an antique drapery . . . his black hair . . . dressed à la Caracalla, a fashion introduced . . . by David's school of painting" (35; 18–19). Sommervieux fashions himself into an art object, that is, an object of beauty displayed in order to be admired and desired. To please her husband, Augustine should have treated herself as if she, too, were such an object—in other words, as if she were her portrait. Sommervieux's growing indifference toward his wife is caused by her inability to do that. In the narrator's words, "At last Théodore could not resist the evidence of the cruel fact [d'une vérité cruelle]: his wife was insensible to poetry, she did not dwell in his sphere, she could not follow him in all his vagaries [ses caprices], his improvisations, his joys and his sorrows; she walked prosaically in the world of reality [terre à terre dans le monde réel] whereas his head was in the skies" (70; 56–57). Taken at face value, the difference between Augustine and Sommervieux is that between the world of materiality and the world of the spirit (as Andréoli has argued). Sommervieux is presented here as the epitome of the artist: a free spirit who follows his fancy rather than rules and regulations, experiences strong emotions, and is sensitive to beauty (in this case, poetry); Augustine, the merchant's daughter, is down-to-earth, has a limited sensibility, and is enslaved to rules (of religion). But the text does not fully support such a simple opposition. Augustine too has strong feelings, which Sommervieux fails to share; furthermore, as she attempts to educate herself in order to please her husband, she learns to appreciate and enjoy both music and poetry. The problem with Augustine is not that she is prosaic and crude but that she cannot use the sensibility and refinement she has acquired to dazzle the world

(73–74; 60). Likewise, the love that her beauty and melancholy inspire in others ("Ere long she was courted by the most fascinating men [les hommes les plus séduisants]" [73; 59]) is not sufficient to rekindle Sommervieux's desire, since in remaining "lonely and virtuous" (73; 59), hardly aware of the love and jealousy she inspires, Augustine denies these sentiments the status of visible signs of her desirability. This is why her fidelity displeases her husband (74; 60).

The opposition between the Guillaumes (including Augustine) and Sommervieux might therefore be rephrased as follows: both the Guillaumes and Augustine do not value display and its effects on others. Riches (for the Guillaumes) and love (for Augustine) have intrinsic value; exhibiting (or representing) them neither adds to that value nor has value in itself: "Augustine cared more for a look than for the finest picture. The only sublime she knew was that of the heart" (70; 56). In preferring a look to the finest picture Augustine pits her husband's (private) love for her against his commitment to his art, inseparable from its exhibition. She thus fails to realize what the text has shown —that she has been for him from the beginning a picture and that in order for him to continue to love her she needs to remain (like) her picture.

For Sommervieux (and, as we shall see, even more so for the Duchesse de Carigliano, with whom he has an affair), exhibition (and representation, which is both a means and a kind of exhibition) confers value. Even things that appear to be valued in and for themselves lose their value unless they are confirmed and reconfirmed as valuable by others. Exhibition or representation adds value to the thing exhibited by producing certain effects—admiration, envy, desire—and gives the person creating these effects power over others. Ultimately, then, the objects of display are not ends in themselves (or valued for what they are) but the means to an end: display and its effects.

This is the lesson Augustine should have learned (but did not) from the Duchesse de Carigliano. Although not a painter herself, the Duchess, like Sommervieux, fashions herself into an object of admiration, envy, and desire. As the scene between her and Augustine amply demonstrates, the Duchess lives in the public eye even in her boudoir, where she exhibits herself as if she were on stage.[13] Every pose she takes, every gesture she makes, is calculated to produce an effect that will establish or confirm her power over others.

Had Augustine proved a better pupil, she might have used the portrait to bring her husband back to her by, for example, giving it to another man (or, in a more general way, exhibiting it for the admiration of others), thus turning the portrait into a sign of her desirability. But by bringing the portrait back home to her bedroom Augustine does exactly the opposite. From her point of view—predicated on the valorization of a private self prior to and independent of representation—the return of the portrait is a moment of reappropriation. What was hers returns to her: the portrait is her soul, which was taken from her at a moment of exchange to which she was not an entirely consenting partner; it is a token of her husband's love, which under the marriage contract belongs to her and was given to another; it is her lawful property that had been taken from her. In bringing the portrait back home she attempts to bring what has been externalized back to the interior, to its point of origin, to return the representation to its creator and model—in essence, abolishing representation itself. Likewise, by dressing like the figure in the portrait she attempts to become again the person whose likeness the portrait represents rather than becoming a portrait herself (or letting the portrait take her place).

Sommervieux, however, depends on the admiration and envy of others to have his identity as painter and lover confirmed, and Augustine's portrait, displayed and admired, is the means by which this confirmation is achieved. For him, the return of the portrait from *chez* Carigliano is not the coincidence of object and representation, creator and creation, inside and outside, but his annihilation as both painter and lover. That he destroys the portrait in a fit of impotent rage directed against both the Duchess and Augustine (whom he apparently mistakes for an accomplice or a tool of the Duchess), instead of putting it to use in order to recover his power, suggests that he is no match for the Duchess. Unlike Sommervieux, who is limited by a residual attachment to an inner self—he draws the material for his paintings from a "scène de la vie privée" and needs to retire to the privacy of his studio to produce them—the Duchess, one might say, is able to give up entirely the "superstition" (or "illusion," to use the Balzacian term) of an inner, private self (that is, the self as origin and ground for representations rather than as constituted by them). Balzac's own ambivalence in this regard can be found in the narrator's clear sympathy toward Augustine, on the one hand, and his admiration for the Duchess, on the other. The latter, however, is inflected by a stereotypical gender bias that causes him to represent the female winner in the contest for power as an immoral coquette, whereas her male opponent, who even vows to take revenge through the manipulation of representations—"I will be revenged.... She will die of shame; I will paint her! Yes, I will paint her as Messalina [sous les traits de Messaline]" (89; 76–77)—is presented as an artist of genius.

MAGIC AND SIMULACRA

The scene in which the portrait is destroyed at the end of the novella echoes the Salon scene discussed above: in each a character experiences the sudden encounter with the portrait as a moment of madness ("folie" in the case of Augustine [51; 35]; "démence" in the case of Sommervieux [90; 77]), that is, as a loss of self. But these scenes also evoke supernatural or uncanny doings that seem out of place in the realistically depicted world of nineteenth-century Paris (which is one of the reasons that critics tend to deny importance to the portrait): seeing the likeness that has been "stolen" from her unawares, Augustine feels possessed, as if under the influence of a demon (51; 35); faced with the returned portrait, Sommervieux feels a mad rage (90; 77) akin to that of a creator confronted with his now hateful creation.[14] Augustine's death can itself be read as resulting from the destruction of her portrait. Such a reading may suggest a belief in sympathetic magic, according to which to destroy an effigy is to harm the person it represents. But whereas in sympathetic magic the power of the effigy derives from the belief that representation partakes of the thing represented (a belief we also find in the ritual use of images, as we shall see in the discussion of Gogol in chapter 7), in the world of the Duchesse de Carigliano (in other words, the world Balzac describes without entirely sharing its values) the power of the portrait depends on loosening the link between the subject (the represented subject but also the painter) and a growing parade of simulacra.

At the end of the novella, the impersonal narrator of the opening description has somehow morphed into a friend (maybe one of those fascinating men in love with Augustine) who deplores the fate of the young woman and mourns her death (90; 78). But the elegiac tone may indicate more than the sorrow of a secret lover.

The narrator does not share the Guillaumes' (and Augustine's) notion that representation has no value; their view is misguided since it fails to take into account time as a constant agent of change and loss.[15] But although the narrator's view is that the objects of representation are subject to time (and, in this sense, are historical), he also holds onto the idea that representation is grounded, even as he describes a world where such grounding appears more and more questionable. The brave new world Balzac contemplates in this early text is not only that of a new kind of commerce, characterized by the seductive display of merchandise, aggressive publicity, and the circulation of capital—a commerce that eventually will destroy the likes of the Guillaumes (as Zola will show in *Au Bonheur des dames*). It is also, more generally, a world in which signs are seen as no longer grounded in their referents, a world in which representations have power precisely to the extent that they do not correspond either to the objects represented or to the sentiments and opinions of their producer, and whose workings he will show most explicitly in his depiction of the world of journalism in *Illusions perdues*.

"*Glasses*"

"Glasses" (1896) is the story of a painter who paints portraits of a beautiful woman who, by the story's end, usurps his place by turning herself into her own portrait. It is also the story of a beautiful woman who becomes blind because she refuses to wear glasses. The relation between these two narrative lines is not one of cause and effect: neither the painting of the portraits nor the exhibition of one of them is the cause of Flora's blindness. Some of the (few) critics who have dealt with this story have suggested that these two narrative lines in fact tell the same story: since the opposition subject/object is commonly expressed as the opposition seeing/ being seen, both Flora's becoming blind and her being painted and displayed as an image to be gazed upon tell the story of her objectification.[16] According to this reading, Flora's triumph at the end of the story is illusory; it shows, rather, "her collusion with her own objectification," her becoming "herself an instrument of male domination."[17] It is, of course, true that all the characters in the story, including Flora herself, take for granted the status of woman as an object to be seen, even to be sold; the status of man as "seeing" and possessing the power to dominate is, however, more problematic, as Sharon Dean suggested long ago when speaking of the story's "myopic narrator." Nor is it obvious that the plot of the story reproduces without any change the power relations in place at its point of departure (that is, that it reinforces and naturalizes rather than modifies them).

A BEAUTIFUL FACE: WOMAN AND ART AS COMMODITIES

Flora Saunt is a woman with a very beautiful face; indeed, she has/is nothing more than a beautiful face, as the narrator's description of his first meeting with her makes clear: "I had been struck by the beauty of a face that approached us" (*Complete Tales* 9: 318).[18] This beautiful face is from the start an object offered to the sight of others— "everyone seemed to linger and gape," says the narrator (319)—and Flora is very much an active agent in this display. Yet even though, according to the narrator and his friend, Mrs. Meldrum, she worships her own beauty, Flora is not a narcissist since she does not consider her beauty to exist for her own enjoyment (or even contemplation) but rather for that of others.[19] That Flora's beauty resides exclusively in her face (we are repeatedly told that she has no figure) reinforces this point since the face is the one part of one's body one cannot see—unless, of course, with the help of a looking glass, which is conspicuously absent from this story about glasses. What takes the place of the mirror is the portrait, which, unlike a looking glass, makes Flora and her beauty an object for the contemplation and desire of others. Since Flora is solely a beautiful face to be looked at by others, there is no difference between her and her portrait. Flora herself subscribes to this conflation when she insists that her portrait, exhibited in the Academy, bear her full name, inviting an identification of herself with the portrait. Her would-be suitor, Dawling, for his part, "had fallen in love with a painted sign" and is satisfied by "possessing" an image of Flora's face (330). Flora's image is here "the real thing," since the "real thing" is nothing but an image.

Flora's portrait is displayed in the Academy not only to be viewed but also to be sold. Dawling, who is quite indifferent to "the element of art" (329), comes to the painter's studio simply "to purchase" (330). The painter's acceptance of this commodified view of art is manifested, among other things, by his long stay in America, the country of capital rather than of taste and culture. The portrait, the "gem of the exhibition" (331), is, then, a commodity that shows woman herself to be a commodity. The view that woman is an object to be seen as well as an object of exchange is shared by all the characters in the story, regardless of their other traits. Mrs. Meldrum attributes such an attitude to Flora's noble suitor, Lord Iffield, whom she considers a "regular beast" (357) and "brute" (358), when she comments that, in breaking his engagement with Flora, "He had conducted himself like any other jockeyed customer—he had returned the animal as unsound" (360). But Dawling—who is, according to Mrs. Meldrum, "the very pearl of men" (348)—expresses the same attitude: "I would take her [Flora] with leather blinders, like a shying mare" (343). The narrator himself declares that he is ready to make "a high bid for a good chance to paint" Flora (319) and suggests to Dawling, who has come to purchase a portrait, that he should "deal directly with the lady" (330). Moreover, Flora's identification of herself with the portrait suggests that she, too, recognizes that it is she (not merely her image) that is being displayed for sale.[20] She has fully internalized the view that her beauty is a commodity in the marriage market and is intent on playing it for the highest stakes. She worships her beauty as her sole weapon in a campaign for social advancement.

THE WEAPONS OF THE WEAK: BLINDNESS AND TRANSGRESSION

In interpreting Flora's becoming blind and her becoming a portrait as two ways of revealing her willing objectification, critics have neglected to pay attention to the transgressive character of her actions. "Glasses" is not simply the story of a woman who refuses to wear glasses out of vanity and as a result goes blind; rather, Flora's blindness, we are told, is the result of her refusal to obey the decree of the "greatest man" (the oculist [350]).[21] In other words, although in all she does Flora consciously assumes the subordinate status that her society imposes on women (and, more specifically, on "English gentlewoman" [319]), she tries to exercise some control over her life, that is, over her display and circulation. The stiff resistance she encounters can give us some sense of the seriousness of the challenge she offers.

Flora's effort to control her display and circulation is made against time, and time is here measured by the deterioration of her eyesight and the dwindling of her capital.[22] Her "folly" resides in her belief that she can manage these two treasures herself. As a young woman with no parents or guardians to guide her during the "awkward age" of premarital adulthood, she is considered by others to be in need of protection. What alarms her friends is that she herself does not feel that need and, in fact, declines the help of any would-be guardians. The point here is not the danger to her sexual innocence (as it is, for example, in *The Awkward Age*); the narrator disparagingly claims that "she was kept innocent by her egotism" (331). What takes the place of the danger of sexual misconduct is the danger of financial irresponsibility. Flora "had been left with just money enough to turn her head; and it hadn't even been put in trust," as the shocked Mrs. Meldrum, speaking through the narrator's free indirect discourse, exclaims indignantly (or perhaps enviously) (322). As a result, both the narrator and Mrs. Meldrum are convinced (or perhaps wish?) that Flora's life will end badly. But Flora never appears helpless and never appeals to others to take care of her. This does not prevent her, however, from using the image of the "lone orphan" for her own advantage: "It was as a lone orphan that she came and went, as a lone orphan that she was the center of a crush" (331). Even when swindled by the unscrupulous Hammond Synges, she manages to turn this misfortune to such an advantage that it appears as though she staged it herself: "The neglect of the Hammond Synges gave relief to this character [of the lone orphan], and she paid them handsomely to be, as everyone said, shocking" (331).

Thus, the vanity and silliness that the narrator and Mrs. Meldrum attribute to Flora have to do with her confidence not only in the power of her beauty (which the narrator considers to be great) but also in her ability to manage on her own her display as an image and to control her circulation as a commodity. The narrator and Mrs. Meldrum, on the other hand, advocate absolute passivity for women; they believe that the fact that Dawling loves her should be reason enough for Flora to take him. Betty, who was foolish enough to decline Dawling (because she, like Flora, has an exaggerated sense of her own value), has "dished herself by her perversity" (335) and will be punished by never being looked at again; Flora will fare no better. At one point the narrator is even "almost disposed . . . to protest that if [Flora] had so little proper feeling [toward Dawling] her noble suitor [i.e., Iffield] had perhaps served her right" by jilting her (359).

Flora's confidence in her beauty and in her ability to manage on her own does not mean that she is or feels socially secure (her resorting to dissimulation shows she is not); she is fully cognizant of her gender disadvantage. Her choice of Iffield is due not simply to his social status as a Lord but also to the other connotation of "lord" as the one who dominates. And as Iffield demonstrates, masculine domination (or what Eve Sedgwick calls "entitlement") is not possessed but, rather, is produced through relations with, and the approval of, other men. The few times we see Iffield (in Folkestone, when he declines to be introduced to the narrator's mother, in the shop at Christmastime) he is with other men or another man. Unlike Dawling, who travels in Italy with his sisters, or the narrator, who keeps company with his mother, Iffield goes to India to shoot tigers—and presumably not with women. But it is also important to note that if Iffield appears as a villain and a brute (that is, marked by a negative valuation of male domination), it is because he remains, like "the greatest man" (the oculist), outside our reach. We don't even know who the oculist is, and Iffield, although known by name and physical appearance, has no direct relation with either the narrator or Mrs. Meldrum (who provides the narrator with information about things he does not experience directly). The positions of male authority, presumed to be grounded in objective, disinterested knowledge (the oculist), and of male domination (Iffield), are sustained by not being directly represented.[23] The narrator himself would have been the figure of highest authority had he remained invisible (as a third-person undramatized narrator), but as an embodied, represented character, he does not have the status of the "Master." Among the characters that are represented (including the narrator), we do not find a clear opposition between active, seeing, dominating man and passive, blind, dominated woman, but rather a struggle where power (which is here primarily the power to represent) can be gained and lost.

MEDIATING DESIRE

The main line of the story, leading from the moment Dawling falls in love with Flora upon seeing her portrait to his eventual marriage to her, suggests that portraits qua representations have the power to shape and mediate desires. Iffield, who stares impertinently at the narrator at Folkestone, indirectly pays him homage by "snapping up" (331) Flora's portrait from the exhibition before the private viewing is over. This difference in attitude suggests that the narrator acquires social power by creating and circulating representations that both shape others' desires and are recognized by others as desirable. Thus although the painter-narrator shows dismay at Dawling's disregard for the portrait as art, he is also fully aware of both the power of commodified art and the power that accrues to him as a painter.

Since the power to represent is here the power to mediate desire, it is not separate from the narrator's role as a go-between. But whereas the prestige of art conceals to some extent the nature of its mediation, the narrator's more direct form of mediation can be seen for what it is—interested meddling—and is often presented negatively; this, however, suggests all the more its power. Indeed, although the different characters have different views of what the narrator is trying to achieve by his interference in the affairs of others, they all seem certain that his intervention will have a negative effect on themselves. Both Dawling and Mrs. Meldrum, at crucial moments, withhold information from the narrator (357, 369), and Mrs. Meldrum explicitly says that she was afraid of his interference (357). When she comes and "confesses" everything to him, Flora herself shows him "all her terror of the harm [he] could do her" (351), despite considering him "the most disinterested" of all her friends (349)—a clichéd view of the artist that the story as a whole undermines.

Not only is the narrator's meddling far from disinterested, but his position of power as the one who possesses the means of representation also does not place him outside the circuit of desire. The narrator suggests various times that he might have become one of the men vying for Flora's attention, but he immediately retreats from pressing or even entertaining such claims and declares that "from the very first, with every one listening, I could mention that my main business with [Flora] would be just to have a go at her head and to arrange in that view for an early sitting" (322). Both the narrator's need to make this point publicly and his reluctance (similar to Dawling's) to "deal" with the original suggest that he, too, is uncertain about his claim, and his social and sexual insecurity is expressed on the first pages of the story by his gratuitous sneering at the Jews with their big noses (317). Presumably, he counts on his position as a successful painter to stand out in the crowd of Flora's admirers.[24] Or he may be using his artistic interest in her as an alibi for a variety of other possible reasons he might have for not pursuing her as a lover. But, whether it functions as a substitute or an alibi, his painting of Flora is far from a disinterested activity. Thus, though the position of mediator confers upon the painter considerable power, he does not occupy a masterful position above the fray; entangled in the world of lack and desire, his power is never secure enough and it is not guaranteed either by a social position nor by his "essence" as a "man."[25]

In his role as mediator and go-between the narrator attempts (and ultimately fails) to control a set of interpersonal relations involving both Flora and Dawling. In these attempts he is seconded by Mrs. Meldrum. Although Mrs. Meldrum is certainly not an object of desire for the narrator, he can imagine her as a woman who might be desired by a man. After all, he offers Dawling "a hint to offer Mrs. Meldrum his hand" and is sure that, had Dawling proposed, she "would not have pushed him over the cliff," explaining, "Strange as she was to behold I knew of cases in which she had been obliged to administer that shove" (353). It would also be imprecise to say that for him Mrs. Meldrum is not a womanly woman.[26] Although in his description of her the narrator insists on all the traits that make Mrs. Meldrum appear masculine, he also attributes to her the supremely feminine mark of "the voice of an angel" (318).[27] But the important point is the complete unanimity between Mrs. Meldrum and the narrator (which critics on the whole have failed to note): both admire Dawling; both think Flora is mad not to take him but also try to prevent Dawling from pursuing her (probably because each desires Dawling for him/herself). They are also united in their concern for the narrator's mother. All this, as well as the merging of Mrs. Meldrum's speech with the narrator's discourse through the frequent use of free indirect style, suggests that she is in a sense an extension or amplified version of him. She provides him with information he needs since she often knows more than he does (333), and he does not appear threatened by her superiority in this respect. She also criticizes Flora much more bluntly than he does (saying, for example: "She's not worth talking about—an idiot too abysmal" [320]), thereby allowing his negative feelings to be expressed vicariously, without compromising him.[28] At the end of the story Mrs. Meldrum, too, loses her position of influence in relation to both Flora and Dawling.

THE NARRATOR'S STORY

"Glasses," however, is not simply the story of a beautiful woman who goes blind or of a man who falls in love with a portrait and ends up marrying the lady; it is also, and as importantly, the story of the narrator-painter's complex relation to the woman and her suitor, both of whom he paints. The end of the story juxtaposes the narrator's failure (as a painter, as a mediator) to Flora's and Dawling's triumph.

The narrator's interest in Dawling and his interest in Flora are presented as parallel and mutually exclusive. After he first encounters Dawling, the narrator refrains from inviting him to the studio because he knows Flora will be there; when Dawling starts sitting for him and becomes, as he puts it, "the interesting figure in the piece" (336), Flora no longer comes to his studio, and the narrator even goes as far as repudiating her beauty, claiming it is superficial and boring. The narrator also makes clear the way in which the opposition beauty/ugliness functions along gender lines.[29] Flora's beauty defines her; she is nothing but a beautiful face. Her beauty, therefore, cannot function as a sign for some other attribute; hence the narrator criticizes her beauty for its lack of depth and complexity (331). Dawling, on the other hand, is not beautiful, but in his ugliness the narrator sees the superficial cover (sand) of a soul: "I was really digging in that sandy desert for the buried treasure of his soul" (337). Furthermore, nothing is said about Dawling's portrait being exhibited or sold; it thus appears distinct from the commodified art associated with the representation of women (Flora, but also the "nymphs and naiads" the narrator paints in America [361]).

The narrator agrees with Mrs. Meldrum that Dawling is "the salt of the earth" (334)—and this in spite of Dawling's awkward (even ridiculous) behavior, the dreariness of his intellectual occupations ("figures of rural illiteracy" [362]), and the possible uselessness of his knowledge. The narrator's need to point out that, unlike Dawling, he "hadn't had an Oxford training" suggests that he is conscious of, and even resents, Dawling's social and intellectual advantage over him. This would explain his bizarre remark about "the great man at whose feet poor Dawling had most submissively sat and who had addressed him his most destructive sniffs" (336). Although the narrator's use of a quote from Gibbon to comment on Dawling's "variety of inclination" (334) is probably ironic, it still conjures up the specter of an emperor who managed to reconcile literary production with procreation—"By each of his [twenty-two] concubines, the younger Gordian left three or four children. His literary productions were by no means contemptible"[30]—an achievement that, according to the narrator, neither Dawling nor he himself can match. In trying to convince Dawling to stay away from Flora the narrator tries to convince Dawling to be like him—that is, to be someone who admires female beauty but attempts to possess it only through the production (or purchase) of images. He is quick to pronounce Dawling "permanently lame" (336), and his commiseration with him, like his pronouncement that Flora is "dead" (e.g., 363), can be read as a mixture of resentment and wishful thinking.

If the narrator admires Flora's beautiful face as an object to be painted, he also presents her to us as an artist. The scene in which he sees her with Lord Iffield on the cliff in Folkestone (chap. 3) presents Flora as part of a picture or composition she herself produced: it is she who set herself with her back to "the pretty view of Sandgate and Hythe" (324) in such a way as to make herself the main "attraction" (324), "the charming figure-piece submitted to [the two men's view]" and to the narrator, who watches them watching (325). Once he becomes bored with Flora's beauty, however, the narrator compares her to a bad artist who has no knowledge of shades and contrasts ("values") and lays on colors "like blankets on a cold night" (331).[31] Finally, in the last scene, where she appears to him more desirable than ever before, he acknowledges her mastery in having produced herself as an image of infinite beauty: "The expression of the eyes was a bit of pastel put in by a master's thumb" (368). To the extent that the narrator feels any desire toward Flora (a painterly desire), this desire appears to correlate with his view of her as a successful artist, and so a rival.

Such a rivalry explains the narrator's relish at the idea of Flora's disfigurement and humiliation. After the scene in which he claims he has "seen everything"—Flora has revealed to him "her secret" (the secret of her engagement and the secret of her failing eyesight); having come "to triumph" she very soon "put herself completely in [his] hands" (349) and "almost sank on her knees" (351)—the narrator delights in telling Mrs. Meldrum what Flora should have done: "She might have kept her [eyesight] if she had profited by God's mercy, if she had done in time, done years ago, what was imperatively ordered her; if she hadn't in fine been cursed with the loveliness that was to make her behavior a thing of fable. She may keep them still if she'll sacrifice—and after all so little—that purely superficial charm. She must do as you've done; she must wear, dear lady, what you wear!" (350). The beauty of Flora's face, her sole weapon— "My face is all I have" (351), she has just confessed—is dismissed as a "superficial charm," which it would cost "so little" to sacrifice. And yet, when Flora in fact follows this advice—and so much so that he mistakes her for Mrs. Meldrum (putting his own eyesight in question)—he is horrified.

How can we understand this contradiction? The narrator's horror and disgust at the sight of Flora in glasses resembles Flora's own discomfort and fear at the sight of the bespectacled Mrs. Meldrum (345): he sees Flora as Flora sees Mrs. Meldrum (a parallel that explains his confusion between the two). Dawling explains Flora's reaction to Mrs. Meldrum as identification: in Mrs. Meldrum "she sees herself, she sees her own fate" (345). By analogy, then, the narrator's violent reaction to Flora in glasses would mean his identification with her. But Flora is also a double/rival: she, too, attempts to make up for her weakness (her inability to "possess") by taking into her own hands the means of representation, that is, the means of shaping others' desire to possess, and in so doing she threatens to usurp his place. His relish at her projected disfigurement thus expresses his anticipation of victory over her.

But this victory never takes place. When the narrator sees Flora at the opera after an interval of three years in which he "had thought of her as buried in the tomb her stern specialist had built," he finds her "perfectly alive again . . . altered only, as it were, by resurrection" (363). His wonder at her "transfiguration" soon gives way (when he thinks that she has seen and recognized him) to the realization that his past representations of her were a failure; he feels "professionally humiliated" (365). He determines that she must once more sit for him, but after the encounter at the opera he never sees her again, let alone paint her. Flora has usurped his painterly power both to "fix for ever, rescued from all change" (368) an image of perfect beauty and to display it in public to the admiration of all, by producing and displaying such an image herself: "The expression of the eyes was a bit of pastel put in by a master's thumb; the whole head, stamped with a sort of showy suffering, had gained a fineness from what she had passed through" (368).[32]

We have no account of how the marriage between Flora and Dawling finally came about. Although the narrator's surmise that "She had taken him when everything had failed; he had taken her when she herself had done so" (367) sounds reasonable, it is also an account that makes the marriage a failure on both their parts (she took him and he was taken *faute de mieux*). The triumphal air of both Flora and Dawling in the last scene does not support such an interpretation (and even the narrator does not suggest that they are simply pretending). Moreover, in this last scene Dawling also appears different. For the first time he dissimulates (when the narrator asks him why he didn't write to him about his marriage). His face is now a "windowless wall" (370), as if lacking its "good green eyes" (329, 345): he now appears (like Flora) without eyesight or (again like Flora) like a smooth surface, offering no access to his "soul." If Dawling is "feminized" by his union with Flora, this feminization is not presented as a defeat or victimization. It is, rather, the painter-narrator who has changed from a powerful, feared mediator into a *terzo incomodo*.

This defeat might also explain why this painter/narrator presents himself to us "pen in hand" in the story's opening paragraph: if his painting of Flora has proved to be a failure, by writing about it he can still hope to achieve a success that will make up for that failure. But the metaphor he chooses for his story—"a row of colored beads on a string" (317)—betrays his own lingering sense of failure. It recalls the pearls Flora wears in the last scene: the way she fingers them, the narrator says, is a "sharp image of the wedded state" (367)—that is, an image of her secure social standing. The narrator's need to reassure himself that "none of [his] beads are missing" (317) is, by contrast, a measure of his insecurity, so that the story meant to overcome (or gloss over) his failure also betrays it.[33]

I began my analysis by stating that the two stories by Balzac and James follow a common scenario in which a male painter produces a portrait of a beautiful woman. However, whereas at the end of *La Maison* Augustine dies following the destruction of her portrait, at the end of "Glasses" Flora has turned herself into her own portrait. Augustine's death at the end of *La Maison* suggests that her valorization of the inside, understood as the belief in an inner, private self prior to representation, cannot survive in the world of Sommervieux and the Duchess. In "Glasses," on the other hand, Flora accepts from the beginning the equation of herself with her portrait; her triumph at the end of the tale is due to her determination to exercise some control over her display and circulation.

In both texts, the woman's portrait takes precedence over, or usurps, the place of the real woman: the portrait, as representation, somehow gains primacy rather than being seen as subordinate or inferior (as a copy is to an original). This precedence, however, does not derive from the portrait's ability to preserve the likeness of a particular person beyond his or her actual presence or natural life—that is, the portrait's ability, amplified by its status as a work of art, to immortalize its sitter (as well as its producer). Rather, the precedence (and power) of the portrait in these texts derives from a growing notion that there is no subjectivity outside of or prior to representations. Subjectivity, then, is vested in signs rather than residing in an essence beyond the realm of signs or prior to them.

In *La Maison*, Augustine cannot accept this "truth," while the Duchess, who embodies the world of spectacle, triumphs. Since it is not grounded in what she essentially is, however, her triumph is far from definitive and can quickly be reversed in a subsequent round. The world that Balzac depicts is, as we know, a world of constant oscillation, of ups and downs, ascents and descents, "splendeurs et misères." Flora's triumph in "Glasses" would make her similar to the Duchess were it not for the one important difference of her blindness. But, as we have seen, Flora's failing vision does not impair her agency; on the contrary, her blindness, which results from her own choice not to wear glasses in defiance of the advice of "the greatest man," is a mark of her refusal to be passively obedient. In the world of "Glasses," a clear-cut opposition between acting (seeing), powerful male subjects and passive (seen) female objects who lack this power, does not obtain.

At the same time, the elegiac tone at the end of Balzac's novella suggests a nostalgia for the disappearing world Augustine embodies. And although Augustine's view is opposed to that of Sommervieux, in comparison with the Duchess, Sommervieux himself is characterized by a residual attachment to an inner self. Moreover, the narrator's nostalgia extends to a pre-Guillaumes era when representation was not merely grounded but in fact unnecessary (see note 9). Similarly, in the commodified world of "Glasses," the narrator-painter still harbors an attachment to an art that would reveal the hidden treasure of a "soul" or an inner self. This suggests nostalgia for a world in which subjectivity is independent of and prior to appearances (or representations); it also suggests that the new regime the stories (in my analysis) depict is not entirely new and that the old regime it supposedly replaces subsists (or, alternatively, is in fact produced by the new regime as its lost, mourned past). Both stories then show the coexistence, in the same time-space of the story, of two opposing articulations of the relation between subjectivity and representation. This coexistence can be understood to mean that subjectivity and representation are not discrete categories, each closed upon itself, separate from and opposed to the other, but rather are always dependent on each other, implying and inhabiting each other. And while the idea of a past where this was not the case can be rejected as illusory, the historical dimension of the question should not be dismissed: Balzac and James can be seen as registering a sociohistorical change in power relations (along gender but also class lines) through which the idea that subjectivities do not exist prior to or independent of representation gains traction. This way of reading the relation between subjectivity and representation brings to the fore the importance of the power to represent while at the same time making the case that this power does not inhere in some subjects, is not an essential trait of being, for instance, male.

CHAPTER 5

Portraits of the Male Body: Kleist's "Der Findling," Hardy's "Barbara of the House of Grebe," and Wilde's *The Picture of Dorian Gray*

The three stories I will be discussing in this chapter—Heinrich von Kleist's "Der Findling" (published 1811); Thomas Hardy's "Barbara of the House of Grebe" (1890); and Oscar Wilde's *The Picture of Dorian Gray* (1891) are not usually read together.[1] But when read as stories about portraits (which is not the way the first two are usually read), they show surprising similarities. Each text features a full-body representation (rather than a representation of the face alone)[2] of an idealized male figure (portraits in the case of Kleist and Wilde, a statue in the case of Hardy); in all three, a man occupies the position of object, rather than subject, of both vision and desire; in all three, the portrait/statue is kept hidden rather than being exhibited; and in all three, the portrait/statue is more than a representation, is treated as if it were the represented subject itself.

As we shall see, all three stories focus on the viewers' relation to the portrait. In the introduction, I have argued that it is pre-nineteenth-century portrait stories that focus exclusively on the portrait's viewer: in most of them the portrait's subject is dead or absent and the painter is never mentioned. But although Kleist's and Hardy's stories resemble pre-nineteenth-century portrait stories in this respect, the experience of the viewers they (as well as Wilde's text) register is far from the simple one of recognizing the true subject of the portrait (and thus resolving or dissolving the residues of a past conflict). Nor do these stories display the typical scenario of realist fiction, featuring a male gaze whose "object of fascination" is a woman's body.[3] In other words, in these stories the focus is not on the nexus of scopophilia, epistemophilia, and the body, where "[m]an as knowing subject postulates woman's body as the object to be known, by way of an act of visual inspection which claims to reveal the truth—or else makes that object into the ultimate enigma."[4] Rather, in all three texts the subjectivity of the viewers (male or female) is shaped in relation to the portrait through acts of seeing that cannot be reduced to recognition or defined as search for truth. And though a subject's relation to an idealized image is often read in terms of narcissistic identification and mimetic desire, I will argue that such an interpretation does not fully account for what takes place in these texts.

Seeing Resemblance in Kleist's "Der Findling"

There are two narrative strands (or, as Terence Cave puts it, two subjects, in the musical sense)[5] in Kleist's "Der Findling." The first has to do with the tradesman Piachi, who, having lost his only son, Paolo, to "a pestilential sickness" (199; 211) while away from home, brings back with him Nicolo, a foundling/orphan from whom Paolo caught the deadly disease, adopts him as his son, places him in his countinghouse, marries him to his wife's niece, and finally hands over to him all his possessions. The second subject has to do with Piachi's young wife, Elvire: as an adolescent she was rescued from a fire by a Genovese nobleman named Colino who, wounded in the act of rescuing her, died after three years of illness. Elvire keeps hidden a full-body portrait of this nobleman, to which she appears tied by an erotically charged veneration. Nicolo discovers her secret as well as a resemblance between himself and the painted nobleman and devises a plan to "get at Elvire's spotless soul" (212; 223)—as the text euphemistically puts it—by taking the place of the nobleman in the portrait. At this point, the first subject returns in an inverted form: Piachi comes back home to find his wife fainted and Nicolo in a compromising position. Whereas at the beginning of the story he saved Nicolo's life and then took him home with him (in what can be seen as acts of excessive generosity since at their first meeting he knew that Nicolo was infected with the contagious disease, and he later agrees to take him home though he has been the cause of Paolo's death), now, in a series of acts of increasing violence, he first tries to expel Nicolo from his home and, when this fails, savagely kills him and then refuses to ask for absolution for his crime so that he will be able to pursue Nicolo in hell.

The relation between the two subjects remains uncertain: on the one hand, Nicolo's attempt to rape Elvire can be seen as just one more example of his thanklessness toward Piachi and his wife (as the reference to Tartuffe suggests [213; 224]); on the other hand, Kleist's choice to link Nicolo's erotic aggression toward Elvire to the resemblance between him and the nobleman in the portrait results in a monumental piece of coincidence and pure chance that calls attention to the fragility of the connection between the two strands. But the sheer implausibility (or contrived nature) of Nicolo's resemblance to Colino's portrait also invites us to look carefully at the experience of seeing resemblance.[6]

If we think of "Der Findling" as a story about subjectivity, which the presence of the portrait invites us to do, we can say that in the first narrative strand, dominated by Piachi, subjectivity is primarily a matter of social role, is produced by occupying a preexisting slot, thus replacing someone and/or being oneself replaced or replaceable.[7] This is conveyed by the long list of substitutions that, as critics have noted, mark this part of the story:[8] Nicolo literally takes the place in the carriage made vacant by Paolo's death and then takes his place as Piachi's son; Piachi himself took Elvire as his wife after the death of his first wife, and she married him after the death of the nobleman she loved. Piachi has Nicolo replace a clerk in his countinghouse and marries him to Constanza with the hope that she will take the place of Nicolo's mistress, Xaviera.[9] Since we are told little else about these characters, these placements seem to fully define them, and so the characters appear as the more or less arbitrary holders of preexisting places. The relations among Nicolo, Elvire, and Colino, however, cannot be understood in this way, and the reason for the difference is precisely the existence of the portrait. Thus Nicolo cannot take Colino's place because this place is already taken by an image, the portrait; and what governs the relation between Colino, Nicolo, and the portrait is an experience of seeing resemblance (no matter how mediated and even illusory it might be) rather than the need to fill up a vacant place or replace an inadequate occupant. Resemblance, which is the central issue in this strand of the narrative, and its relation to subjectivity, prove, however, to be far from a simple matter.[10]

There is no mention in "Der Findling" of the painter who produced the portrait of the young man in Genovese costume whom Elvire worships in secret. Colino, the presumed subject of the portrait, is dead and gone long before the story opens. The drama that unfolds around the portrait is, then, that of its two secret viewers—Elvire and Nicolo—and it revolves around the viewers' problematic experience of seeing resemblance. As we have seen, this drama does not begin to unfold until midway into the story. The change from one narrative strand to another is accompanied by a change in narrative point of view: the narrator who, up to that point, limited himself to reporting external facts, now reports also Nicolo's thoughts, feelings, and wishes.[11] Thus the part of the story that tells of Nicolo's relation to Elvire and the portrait also shows Nicolo's coming into being as a subject of/in the narrative.

Nicolo's experience of seeing resemblance between himself and the man in the portrait Elvire adores is never direct: it always occurs *après coup* and through the mediation of others. When he faces the portrait for the first time, the description of what he sees—"the life-size portrait of a young knight, illuminated by a candle of its own, behind a red silk curtain in a niche in the wall" (207; 219)—does not include any details of the depicted man's face, figure, or clothes. It is as though Nicolo sees a blank. Faced with his double or his mirror image, Nicolo fails to recognize (or misrecognize) himself.[12] He confronts a self that is as yet unknown to him. As the resemblance between him and the portrait becomes gradually visible (first to others and then, through them, to himself), Nicolo, as we shall see, assumes this self.

The resemblance between Nicolo and the portrait is first perceived, and repeatedly experienced, through the mediation of clothes and, more precisely, clothes that are put on as a disguise. This accounts for the puzzling fact that Nicolo's resemblance to the man in the portrait—who is the object of Elvire's secret worship—is not noticed by Elvire for a long time; it is apparently never noticed by Piachi (who, we are told, knew the nobleman himself, though he may not have seen the portrait).[13] Elvire first notices the resemblance when she sees Nicolo, by chance, as he comes back from the carnival ball dressed in the costume of a Genovese nobleman, just like the figure in the portrait—a costume he has chosen also by chance. Nicolo here "becomes" Colino's portrait and does so before he (and the reader) even know that such a portrait exists. What we call chance is here the reversal of cause and effect: it is because of his choice of that costume that Nicolo will eventually assume the place and identity of the man in the portrait rather than the other way around.

A year will pass before Nicolo discovers the existence of the portrait and sees it for the first time but, as mentioned above, without seeing any resemblance between himself and the portrait—indeed, without seeing anything at all (it is rather the portrait that is "staring fixedly at him" "with its large eyes" [207; 219]). He "sees" a resemblance only later on, when Xaviera and her daughter Klara come to see the portrait and Klara makes a remark that brings back to his mind the scene in which Elvire saw him in his costume and fainted. He sees resemblance only through the mediation of others, *après coup*, and through the similarity of clothes rather than that of facial or even bodily features. The same is true for Nicolo's mistress, Xaviera: she is dumbfounded by her daughter's declaration that the portrait resembles Nicolo, but the resemblance becomes gradually visible to her "when she imagined [Nicolo], as it was easy for her to do, in the Knight's costume he had worn a few months ago when he secretly escorted her to the carnival" (208; 220).

The only person who detects a resemblance between Nicolo and the portrait immediately and not through the medium of clothes is Xaviera's young daughter, aptly (though ultimately, ironically) named Klara; as soon as Nicolo raises the curtain that covers the portrait she exclaims: "God, my father! Whose else is it but you, Signor Nicolo?" (208; 219). The clarity, certainty, and immediacy of Klara's response set her apart from the other characters in the story:[14] unlike Xaviera, Elvire, and Nicolo himself, she apparently sees a resemblance not (or not only) in clothes and general appearance. Her exclamation "God, my father!" when she sees the resemblance, and Nicolo's joking (and not entirely clear) answer to her that the portrait resembles him as much as she resembles the person who thinks he is her father (208; 220) suggest that what she sees might determine the identity of the foundling Nicolo by assigning him a father. But this "promise" is never fulfilled in the story; Klara's clarity is a false route. Just as the resemblance in names between Nicolo and Colino (which Nicolo discovers also by chance and which Elvire does not seem to have noticed before) cannot prove a family relation between them (Colino is only a nickname twice removed from the nobleman's real name, and an anagrammatic relation between names does not prove kinship), so the resemblance between Nicolo and the figure in the portrait does not end up grounding Nicolo's identity biologically. If the portrait does not tell us who Nicolo is (say, the illegitimate son of Colino and Elvire), it is, nevertheless, the object around which his sense of self crystalizes.

When the resemblance between himself and the portrait is pointed out to him by Klara, Nicolo is confused and embarrassed, as if the revelation of resemblance uncovers or implies something secret or shameful—his desire to occupy the place of the painted lover. However, this desire did not exist before Klara's remark and his memory of Elvire's fainting revealed to him the resemblance: it comes into being only as a result of this revelation. Thus we again find a reversal of cause and effect showing the self (as well as desire) to be not a cause but an effect (of chance, of the mediation of others).

Once Nicolo "sees" the resemblance between himself and the man in the portrait, he assumes this identity, in the sense that he takes the painted man to be literally himself: he considers the portrait as an image of himself in the carnival costume.[15] This would mean either that his own portrait was miraculously produced unbeknownst to himself (so that his identity has been "stolen" from him) or that the portrait uncannily anticipated his donning of the costume, determining rather than representing it. Similarly, when he "idly toy[s]" with the six letters of his name and discovers to his great surprise "the combination that spelled the name Colino," he sees the anagrammatic relation between the names as "more than a coincidence": it is a "property [Eigenschaft]" of his own name of which he was up to now unaware (210; 221), and hence, if Elvire calls the painted image "Colino," she in fact is calling his own name. In both cases, the resemblance Nicolo "sees" (and that might well be a pure coincidence) consists of inessential, general, external features: his resemblance to the portrait is to the body, that is, to the contours and general form rather than to particular, individual features; it is mediated by clothes—external to the body—and, more precisely, to clothes worn in order to hide rather than reveal identity. The resemblance of the name depends on an anagrammatic relation to a nickname. In both cases, Nicolo takes this chance, external, general, inessential resemblance to be essential and particular—which is precisely what it means to say that he is assuming this identity.

It is important to note that we never get a direct description of the man in the portrait. As we have seen, in the scene in which Nicolo confronts the portrait for the first time we are told only that it is "the life-size portrait of a young knight" (207; 219). By contrast, in the last scene of Nicolo's narrative, when his identification with the man in the portrait is complete and he is ready to occupy his place by creating a *tableau vivant*, imitating the painted man, we get an indirect but full description: we are told that he puts on "the cloak, collar, and plumed hat of Genovese cut just as the portrait showed . . . taking a staff in his hand and striking the very same pose as that in which the young patrician was portrayed" (212; 223). It is only from this description of Nicolo's imitation of the portrait that we can deduce what the man in the portrait (and the "real" man) look like. Though we are told that the costume Nicolo dons now is the same as the one he wore a few months before, when he went with Xaviera to the carnival, the description here is more detailed (in that scene we are told only that he was "dressed in a plumed hat, cloak, and sword" (204; 215–16). And that description is more detailed than the one we get of the portrait's original, when he came to Elvire's rescue, where all we are told is that he was "a young Genovese from a patrician family" and that he appeared wearing a cloak (202; 214). Thus Nicolo's imitation of an imitation (a *tableau vivant* that imitates a portrait) is presented to us as fuller, more detailed, thus more "real," than either the portrait or its original. Put differently, the portrait as the object of identification through which the subject constitutes itself as a subject is shown to have been produced retroactively, through the subject's growing identification with it.[16]

Nicolo's identification with the image of the man in the portrait and his desire to take the place of the image is mediated by Elvire's worship of it; conversely, his coming into being as a desiring subject destroys Elvire's relation to the image and thus causes her death. The text refers twice to Elvire's relation to the portrait as idolatrous or idolizing ("the stranger she idolized in secret [in heimlicher Ergebung vergötterte]" [209, 221]; Nicolo "awaited Elvire's adoration [Vergötterung]" [212; 223]). We can take these expressions figuratively, as meaning simply "excessive devotion"; alternatively, we can see them as indicating a specific relation to images or a particular way of seeing. Given the role the portrait plays in shaping Nicolo's identity and his complicated experience of seeing resemblance, this direction seems worth pursuing.

Broadly speaking, idolatry means taking the sign for the referent or the representation for the represented subject, collapsing the difference between them. Calling Elvire's relation to the portrait "idolatrous" would mean that for her the portrait is not merely a substitute—a sign for its absent subject—just as an idol is not a substitute for the god but the god itself. Her calling the portrait "Colino" (as Nicolo hears her doing when he spies on her [207; 218]), as well as the erotic nature of her relation to it (Nicolo sees her through the key hole "in an attitude of ecstasy" and suspects that she is with a lover [207; 218]; she undresses before opening the curtain that hides the portrait [212; 223]) suggest that she treats the image as if it were a real person. Unlike a real person, the image is, of course, immobile, fixed, and unchanging, but then Colino himself, who lingered half-dead for three years, was already like the image in that respect.

When Nicolo impersonates the image in the portrait (first unknowingly, when he returns from the carnival, and then deliberately when he stages the *tableau vivant*), he causes Elvire to lose consciousness; she recovers after the first scene but dies as a result of the second in which Nicolo not only wears the same clothes as the man in the portrait but also imitates his posture and puts himself in the place of the portrait. What, then, does Elvire see in that scene?[17] We cannot say that she simply mistakes Nicolo for the painted figure (misrecognizes him, takes him for the image): if that were the case, she would not have fainted. But neither can we say that she recognizes Nicolo: if that were the case, she would have realized that a trick was being played on her. Her exclamation—"Colino, my love"— echoes her "whisper[ing] lovingly the word 'Colino'" earlier in the tale (207; 218), suggesting that she thinks she sees the painted figure but obviously with some difference, hence the fainting. Since the portrait has been covered with a black cloth by Nicolo and since Nicolo places himself in front of the covered portrait, she sees a figure that resembles the figure in the portrait but is outside the portrait (without a frame, closer than usual). But if the figure is no longer part of the portrait, it is not quite a real person either since it is in a frozen pose, the pose of the painted image. While her idolatrous relation to the portrait equated the painted image with the person Colino, the Colino she imagines she sees in this scene is neither the portrait nor the original: it is a Colino who repeats with a difference his own portrait. While he/it is different from the portrait, he/it is still not quite the original since he/it models himself/itself on the portrait. With this noncoincidence, the whole system of representation on which Elvire's idolatrous love depended crumbles and she dies.

As we have seen, Nicolo's progressive identification with the image in the portrait—his growing resemblance to it—is partially motivated by Elvire's love for the image in the portrait and manifests itself as a desire to take the place of the image as Elvire's object of desire. His relation to the image in the portrait, then, can be understood within the double logic of narcissistic identification and mimetic desire. Elvire's relation to the portrait, however, does not fit within this paradigm. For her the portrait is neither a rival nor an object of narcissistic misrecognition nor yet an enigma to be solved, an object to be mastered. And yet the image does play a role in shaping Elvire's subjectivity. Critics have pointed out the striking difference between Elvire's ecstatic, erotic relation to the portrait and her everyday character, which is rather cold and impersonal. It is as if in the space of her shrine and face to face with the fixed image of her lost lover Elvire assumes a different kind of self through an erotic relation to the image. Elvire is not the one who produced the image (she is no Pygmalion), nor does she try to change or control its appearance. But through her erotic love for the image, she endows it with interiority (attributing to it the ability to hear, to feel). The image becomes "animated" while it also stays fixed and unchanged and thus serves as a prop (rather than a model) for her identity and sense of selfhood.[18] Nicolo also "animates" the portrait but through an act of imitation that destroys the portrait (and with it Elvire). Piachi's violence against Nicolo, the rival who attempts to take his place, remove him from his home, obeys the same logic as Nicolo's destruction of the portrait. Thus though both Nicolo's and Elvire's subjectivities are shaped in relation to the image of the male body, Elvire's case suggests the possibility of a different relation to this image, other than that of narcissistic identification and imitation.

"Barbara of the House of Grebe" and the Defacement of the Stone Mirror Image

The eponymous heroine of Hardy's "Barbara of the House of Grebe" is courted by her parents' aristocratic neighbor, Lord Uplandtowers, but she is in love with a handsome commoner, Edmond Willowes; they elope and get married. Barbara's parents soon forgive them and send Edmond on the Grand Tour with a tutor, to provide him with a gentleman's education. While in Italy, Edmond heroically saves lives in a burning theater but is seriously wounded and disfigured as a result. When he comes back to England and shows himself to Barbara, she is appalled; he leaves her, and though he promises to return within a year, he never comes back. As in Kleist's "Der Findling," here, too, the absent man is replaced by his image—in this case a full-body statue Edmond has commissioned while in Italy. Barbara, who after some years has given in to her noble suitor's persistent courting and married him, hides the statue in a little shrine and spends the nights lovingly communing with it. Her husband eventually discovers her nightly activities and, convinced that this idolatrous love interferes with his chance to have a son and heir, decides to cure Barbara of her love by causing the statue to be maimed as Edmond himself was and forcing Barbara to face the maimed statue until she renounces her love for him/it.

In this story, as in Kleist's "Der Findling," the common scenario of rivalry between two men over the love or possession of a woman is recast as a rivalry with an image that is taken to be more than a representation, is equated with its subject. Thus in both texts the "mimetic desire" that pits the two men as doubles/rivals of each other is entangled with the doubling of mimetic representation, the creation of a "likeness" that takes the place of the subject. In Hardy's story, Lord Uplandtowers plays the role of Piachi (he takes the place of the dead Edmond as Piachi took the place of the dead Colino) as well as that of Nicolo (he competes with the statue for Barbara's love). But whereas Nicolo's attempt to take the place of the man in the portrait is predicated on his growing perception of a resemblance between him and the image, Lord Uplandtowers, who does not resemble Edmond, tries to take the place of the statue not by becoming (like) the statue but by destroying the statue's beautiful appearance, turning the statue into a double of the mutilated Edmond. Whereas Kleist's story deals with the way resemblance to an image is constructed and produces a subject, Hardy's story deals with the ways in which the creation and destruction of a statue, its veneration and desecration, all obey the same logic, the logic of mimesis.

Though at the end of the story the narrator claims that Edmond's beauty "was the least of his recommendations" (276), during the entire preceding tale Edmond's main attribute is his beauty.[19] He is described as "one of the handsomest men who ever set his lips on a maid's"; his clothes "set off a figure that could scarcely be surpassed" (254). Edmond's beauty, then, is of both face and body. But the body takes precedence over the face when the sculptor, from whom Edmond commissions a bust (in response to Barbara's request for a miniature portrait), decides to produce a full-body statue. The move from painted portrait to sculpture is, among other things, a move away from representation focused on individuating detail since sculpture is much less likely to include particularizing features (wrinkles, warts) than painting.[20] The move from bust to full-body statue has a similar effect. The artist's decision is motivated by his desire to "get a specimen of his skill introduced to the notice of the English aristocracy" (256); a full-size body would not only give him more scope to display his skill but is also more likely to attract customers since it is not restricted to the particular (face) but also represent the general (body). And, indeed, the narrator characterizes Edmond's statue as "a specimen of manhood almost perfect in every line and contour" (267–68). Through the near perfection of "line and contour"—of the body's outward form—manhood itself is made visible. Conversely, the mutilated Edmond is so changed in form that it seems to Barbara as if "he was metamorphosed to a specimen of another species" (262).[21] Hardy here reiterates the paradigm that associates form—understood as what gives meaning to meaningless matter or substance—with the idealization of man as "the human."

But the statue does not simply represent a particular body as a specimen of manhood or the human. Statues are like bodies, occupy the space of bodies, but they are freed from whatever dangers we know or fear the body can undergo. As Kenneth Gross puts it, "Statues are bodies to which nothing can happen . . . complete surfaces without the troubling depth or interiority of bodies"; "statues are comfortingly without hidden insides."[22] As a representation of the body's surface the statue can stand for the "bodily ego," itself a projection of the body's surface, which is at the basis of identity formation,[23] while also providing an "idealized stone mirror" (Gross 17) that is, a phantasmatic view of the body as impenetrable, invulnerable. Thus Edmond's statue, as a representation of a male body "almost perfect in every line and contour," both transcends particularity and presents the human body as a closed, inviolable surface; emphasizing outward surface and form, it disavows the material substance of the body, figured as its inside.

The statue of Edmond is not, however, the only statue in the story. Lord Uplandtowers is repeatedly described as a statue, although the ground for this analogy is not his outward appearance (which is never described). What is emphasized in his description is his lack of feeling, his resistance to being moved, acted upon. His main characteristics are "doggedness" and "determination" (248), an "irresistible incisiveness" (265), "insistence" (251), impassivity (249), an equanimity that cannot be disturbed (249), lack of passion, impulse (248), or even energy (250). Unmoved, he is unmovable or immobile. The narrator talks about the "sculptural repose of his profile" (249), his "still countenance" (265), his "calm" (250), his "frigid despair" (251); his movements are marked by "mechanical stiffness" (256). His "severity on the bench towards poachers, smugglers, and turnip-stealers" (265) shows his unyielding disposition (which will manifest itself more clearly later in the story in his cruelty toward Barbara).[24] Always there and always the same, unmovable both physically and emotionally, Lord Uplandtowers is a living statue that, unlike both Edmond and his statue, is indestructible. His imperturbability and impassivity mean that he indeed lacks interiority, and it is this lack, rather than a perfection of appearance or form (of Edmond, of the statue), that makes him indestructible. Thus the reassuring view of a statue-like, inviolable body, a perfect surface without troubling inside, is proven illusory and doubly so: the statue and the statue-like Edmond are maimed beyond recognition, and the lack of inside in the statuesque Lord Uplandtowers is anything but reassuring.

As rivals for Barbara's love, Edmond and Uplandtowers are presented as doubles, same and opposite. Both are in some sense (like) statues; both become Barbara's husbands; both force upon her (Edmond gently, Lord

Uplandtowers brutally) the view of a mutilated body/statue. Whereas Uplandtowers is an aristocrat, Edmond is a commoner, whose beauty is from the start presented as what makes up for his lack of class.[25] Lacking Edmond's beauty, Lord Uplandtowers has the statue's endurance, which both Edmond and his statue lack.[26]

As doubles, Edmund and Lord Uplandtowers can be mistaken one for the other, take each other's place. When Barbara's father discovers Barbara's disappearance, he first thinks it was Lord Uplandtowers who abducted her but then concludes "'tis t'other, 'tis t'other" (251). When Barbara waits by the roadside for Edmond (who is coming back from Europe) to arrive in the post-chaise, it is Lord Uplandtowers's chariot that arrives instead (259). At the very beginning of the story, in a statement that collapses the point of view of the narrator with that of Uplandtowers, we read that on the very night of her elopement with Edmond, Barbara seemed "preoccupied—almost, indeed, as though she had been waiting"—not for Edmond but for Uplandtowers (249). When Edmond finally arrives home after the accident, Barbara is still under the impression of her recent encounter with Lord Uplandtowers so that "his [Lord Uplandtowers's] voice and image still remained with her, excluding Edmund, her husband, from the inner circle of her impressions" (260).

As Barbara tells her parents in her letter, she decided to elope with Edmond since she felt "closing around her the doom of marriage with Lord Uplandtowers" (252), but the narrator speculates that Lord Uplandtowers resolved to win Barbara only after her elopement (248). The elopement may have caused what it was supposed to prevent; it certainly did not prevent doom, only postponed it so that Lord Uplandtowers's estimate that "'Tis only a matter of time" (250) proves right. But the "detour" through Edmond has produced the statue, and it is with the statue rather than with Edmond himself that Lord Uplandtowers battles to win Barbara. The opening pages of the story call attention to Lord Uplandtowers's failure to see (and thus possibly confront) Edmond before he elopes with Barbara: although he notices the coach in which Barbara and Edmond will elope (249) and later sees a carriage leaving the ball (250), he fails to understand what he sees. Rather than confronting the real Edmond in a rivalry over Barbara's love, Lord Uplandtowers, in taking the place of the dead Edmond, has to compete with the statue, which also has taken Edmond's place and which Barbara treats as if it were her husband.

The role of the statue in the story—indeed its very presence—depends on Barbara's investment in Edmond's beautiful appearance. This dependence becomes clear when Edmond leaves on his grand tour. In his absence, Barbara starts forgetting "his features" (256) and therefore asks him to send her his portrait (256). Reading his letters, she can perceive his mental development and improvement, but this does not help keep her love for him alive, since it is his beauty (rather than his character, his inner self) that she loves; with his beauty not visible to her (and others), she has nothing to support and justify her choice of him (255). The object of Barbara's longing is thus not Edmond's presence but his physical appearance, which she cannot recall on her own.[27]

That what is at stake in the story is appearance rather than presence is made clear in the sequence of three crucial scenes. The first one is that of Edmond's return from Europe after the accident. Here Edmond is present, but his appearance has been destroyed. In the second, that of the arrival of the statue, the situation is reversed: after many years of uncertainty Barbara receives "absolutely conclusive tidings of her Edmond's death" (267). It is at this moment, when the absolute and final absence of its subject is no longer in doubt, that the statue, a faithful replica of Edmond's beautiful external appearance, arrives. The third scene, in which Lord Uplandtowers reveals the mutilated statue to Barbara, repeats the scene of Edmond's appearance after the accident. In order to cure Barbara of her love for the statue, Lord Uplandtowers does not remove it—make it absent—but rather maims it, creating a faithful replica of Edmond's destroyed appearance. The emphasis on appearance suggests that the story is structured not around the opposition presence/absence but rather around visible appearance (beauty of surface and form) and its relation with a disavowed inside.

Barbara's investment in Edmond's perfect external appearance is what makes the role of the statue possible and explains why Edmond's statue—pure appearances—is equated with his person (rather than being considered as a mere sign that refers to an absent or invisible person). We should note that Lord Uplandtowers never saw Edmond in "life" (or his image while he was alive); he sees him for the first time as a statue and thus the statue for him is not, strictly speaking, a re-presentation. His comment when he sees the statue for the first time: "Phoebus-Apollo, sure" (268), sarcastic and clichéd as it may be, designates the statue as an idol, thus both collapsing subject and representation and idealizing (divinizing) the beautiful appearance. For Barbara also the statue is Edmond. While the mutilated Edmond is for her "this new and terrible form, that was not her husband's" (263), a "sad spectacle" that "had never been her Edmond at all to her" (267), the statue is Edmond: when she sees it for the first time she tells Lord Uplandtowers, "I am looking at my husb—my statue" (268).

Edmond's mutilation is the destruction of his beautiful appearance. We hear about the extent of Edmond's maiming piecemeal: in his letter to Barbara he indicates that he has lost one eye; the scene of his meeting with Barbara mentions the mangled hand. When Lord Uplandtowers undertakes to repeat the mutilation of the body on the statue he finds out that after the accident Edmond had "Neither nose nor ears, nor lips scarcely!" (270). Edmond's maiming, then, means two things: first, what is destroyed is the face and a hand, the two parts of the body that most clearly identify a person as a particular individual (rather than fitting a general human form);[28] second, the maiming causes the destruction of parts of the body that, through the senses, mediate between the body's outside surface and its inside, allow the inside to be affected. This damage, and especially Lord Uplandtowers's words, cannot but remind us of the passage in Psalms 115, verses 4–8, describing idols: "They have mouths, but do not speak; eyes, but do not see. They have ears, but do not hear, noses, but do not smell. They have hands, but do not feel; feet, but do not walk; and they do not make a sound in their throat" (see also Psalms 135, 16–18). Edmond, on the contrary, has hardly a mouth, only one eye, a mangled hand, and neither ears nor nose; but he can speak, see, hear, and feel. The mutilated Edmond is thus not only so different in appearance from his former self as to be barely recognizable; he is also presented as the opposite, the "negative," of idols and divinized statues.

The very fact that we learn the full extent of Edmond's mutilation when Lord Uplandtowers decides to disfigure the statue suggests that the mutilated body is primarily a negation (or parody) of the (body as) statue.[29] The destruction of the outer envelope makes the mutilated Edmond appear no longer as "a specimen of humanity" but as "a human remnant" (262) or a member of another species; the removal of his most individuating features did not result in a "transcendence" of the particular but in a monstrosity. But if Edmond's mutilated body is the negation of the body-as-statue, his statue itself is not simply a replication of and replacement for his beautiful appearances. The statue is also what effaces, negates, or disavows the image of the mutilated figure: "The mutilated features of Willowes had disappeared from her [Barbara's] mind's eye; this perfect being [i.e., the statue] was really the man she had loved, and not the later pitiable figure" (268). If Barbara's investment in Edmond's perfect outward appearance denied the vulnerability of the body (seeing it only as a beautiful surface, "contour and line"), the mutilation of the beautiful body, destroying its outer envelope (burning the skin), shows the permeability of the line dividing inside and outside and thus puts in question the integrity of the body. The statue serves to disavow the evidence of the eyes—the vulnerability of the body; it serves to exclude and reject the mutilated body, the abject.

Edmond's perfect body is disfigured by an accident. When he first appears in front of Barbara, he wears a mask to cover up the mutilation, a mask that imitates the face as it was before the wreck. His beautiful appearance is also replicated in a perfect statue that gets mutilated, a mutilation that imitates the body as it was after the wreck. Both the mask that covers up the disfiguration and the mutilation of the statue that repeats it, imitate life: the mask is "coloured so as to represent flesh" (261) just as the mutilated statue is "tinted to the hues of life" (271). Creating the statue, refacing the mutilated figure, and defacing the statue are all acts of imitation or mimicry that hide or bring out (hide and bring out) what is both known and disavowed:[30] the body's openness to the outside, its vulnerability (and thus the vulnerability of the image of the self predicated on the form of the body).

Lord Uplandtowers does not mutilate the statue himself; he obtains from Edmond's tutor a "sketch of the disfigured head" (270) and hires an "ingenious mechanic and painter" to perform the changes on the statue (just as Edmond engaged a sculptor to make the statue). Under Lord Uplandtowers's directions, the maiming of the body, caused by fire, is imitated, reproduced on the statue by a chisel (the instrument used to create the statue). Lord Uplandtowers explains his actions by saying, "A statue should represent a man as he appeared in life, and that's as he appeared" (271). But Lord Uplandtowers does not create (or commission) a new statue representing Edmond "as he appeared in life" after the accident; rather, he mutilates the existing statue, treating it as if it were the real body by inflicting on it the same damage as that suffered by the body. The maiming of the statue animates it: it was "tinted to the hues of life, as life had been after the wreck" (271). The statue becomes a maimed body.

Thus, though Lord Uplandtowers's maiming of the statue destroys the object of Barbara's love, it obeys the same logic as her love. Both the maiming and Barbara's love of the statue involve treating the statue as if it were a real person (rather than a representation), that is, treating it as if it were alive or giving it life, animating it. While Lord Uplandtowers gives life to the statue by maiming it, Barbara does so by caressing the statue and speaking to it as if expecting it to respond, thus attributing to the statue the ability to hear and feel (that is, attributing to the statue the inside it does not and is not supposed to have). But the reverse is also true: the statue is just a statue, and in treating it as if it were a living person one turns into a statue oneself. Thus Barbara clasping her arms around the statue has the "appearance of a second statue embracing the first" (269). Likewise, Lord Uplandtowers's "animation" of the statue shows him to have no heart, to be less than a man, a statue.

Barbara's love of the statue is represented as the worship of a god, since she creates a little temple where she can commune with it (268). Lord Uplandtowers mimics Barbara's veneration of the statue too: just as she had turned a recess in her boudoir into a "tabernacle" and there placed the statue behind a closed door, so does he create "a little shrine" out of "a tall dark wardrobe" (272) where he places the statue after the mechanic-painter, following his directions, "set to work upon the god-like countenance of the statue" (271). Barbara's act of veneration is echoed by her husband's act of desecration. Both betray the same contradictory attitude toward the statue: it is both (like) a living body (can hear, feel, be maimed) and its opposite (it is an idol, a god; it has no inside, cannot be affected, penetrated, violated). Having mutilated the statue (undoing what the sculptor did, imitating the damage to the real body), Lord Uplandtowers repeats/parodies Barbara's actions by creating a mock tabernacle for the defaced god.[31] He also forces Barbara to see the mutilated statue in order to "cure" her of her love for Edmond/the statue, thus repeating/reversing Edmond's asking Barbara to look at his mutilated body ("Look up Barbara . . . view me completely" [262]) in order to see if she loves him still.

If the arrival of the statue allows Barbara to experience, in relation to this image, an intense affective life missing from her previous experience, the mutilation of the statue entails both the destruction of the "stone mirror image" and the return of the mutilated body, that is, the return of the abject, of what has been denied and disavowed. Forced to view this monstrous statue-turned-body, Barbara becomes less than human—an object, an abject creature. Enslaved to Lord Uplandtowers's imperturbable, indestructible solidity (his statue-like being), she loses all sense of self. She bears him twelve children, but all but one, a girl, die. She herself dies without ever recovering her former self.

Barbara's strong reaction to Edmond's changed appearance can be easily understood; Edmond himself "foresaw as quite possible" the effect that his "forbidding appearance" would have on her (264). Barbara's horror at the sight of the mutilated statue is more complex. One reason for her horror is that the mutilated statue reminds her of the first horror, that of seeing the mutilated body. In addition, since the statue has been equated with its subject, she "sees" the mutilated body again (rather than simply being reminded of it). But another reason is that the divided belief that underlies Barbara's relation to the statue (it is and is not the real person, is and is not a statue) had to be kept secret, in the sense that it could not be avowed without coming undone since it is predicated on contradictory beliefs that negate each other.[32] Mutilating the statue did not destroy this divided belief since, as we have seen, it depends on it (or betrays it). But taking the mutilated statue out of its secret hiding place into the open, forcing Barbara to face it in the presence of another, means exposing not only the mutilation of the statue but also, and more importantly, the avowed/disavowed belief that constituted Barbara's relation to it.[33] It destroys the system of contradictory beliefs that subtended her defining affective relation.

As we have seen, Lord Uplandtowers's desire to possess Barbara, which may be in part motivated by her elopement with Edmond, shows him to be Edmond's double and rival. Uplandtowers's rivalry with Edmond is then transferred to Edmond's statue. In maiming the statue, Lord Uplandtowers intends to undo Barbara's love for the statue, which, in his mind, interferes with his chance of having a son and heir. Thus Lord Uplandtowers's relation to both Edmond and the statue can be understood within the logic of mimetic desire understood as the desire to be the other, by taking the other's place and possessing what the other possesses. But whereas Nicolo, in Kleist's story, "destroys" the portrait by trying to become one with it (identification), Uplandtowers does not try to become like the statue and thus gain Barbara's love; rather, he is intent on destroying the statue, exposing its vulnerability, exposing and destroying Barbara's relation to it—all through acts of imitation. Imitation here appears as a purely negative force, the force of sheer negation.

Three Men and a Portrait: Wilde's The Picture of Dorian Gray

As a story about a portrait, *The Picture of Dorian Gray* depends on two commonplaces concerning this art form: the idea that the portrait preserves the image of its subject against the ravages of time (which it inverts) and the notion that a great portrait reveals the secret or "soul" of its subject (which it literalizes). It is the combination of these two ideas in their inverted/literalized form that produces the main conceit of the novel: that the portrait, as Dorian himself puts it, is a "diary" that shows his "soul" (147, 146), registering day by day the effects of his actions, while his own appearance remains unchanged.[34] The shift (never explained in the text) from Dorian's initial wish that the portrait grow old instead of him to the portrait becoming the site where his "sins" are inscribed, is also the result of the combination of these two commonplaces in their inverted/literalized form.[35] Though the portrait thus conceived may appear to us magic or supernatural, we should note that this is only the rhetorical effect of Wilde's deployment of his signature figure—the paradox—here generating a narrative out of statements contrary to received ideas, conflicting with our expectations.

The inversion of the common view of the portrait is performed within the text through Dorian's wish to exchange places with the portrait—a performative use of language, partaking of what Dorian will later on call the "subtle magic" of words (22). With the accomplishment of the wish, the portrait's relation to Dorian is no longer that of re-presentation. Whereas in Kleist's and Hardy's stories a portrait/statue takes the place of an absent, dead man (so much so that it is treated as if it were that man), in Wilde's story both man and portrait are present (though one is visible and the other is hidden). But though both man and portrait are present, neither one is identical to himself or itself: the man is (also) a portrait—has the portrait's attributes—while the portrait is (also) a man—has man's attributes. The "normal" doubling through representation (with the attendant possibility that the representation will take the place of its subject) is here disrupted by the inner division of both the subject and the portrait. As we shall see, the iconic or mimetic aspect of the portrait (copying, doubling) is inflected in Wilde's text by nonmimetic shaping (influence), indexical traces, as well as inner divisions.

The picture of Dorian Gray is a full-body portrait, though this feature is partially concealed in the text. In the descriptions of Dorian's beauty and of his resemblance to the portrait as well as in the descriptions of the changes undergone by the portrait as a result of Dorian's actions, the emphasis is mostly on the face (eyes, lips, hair). It is only in the account of the painting of the portrait Basil gives Dorian in chapter 9 that the importance of the body is spelled out. Before painting Dorian's portrait, Basil painted several pictures using him as a model, primarily for mythological figures. Through the highly prestigious medium of historical paintings (prestigious because not associated with imitation of the real), where the representation of the full body is authorized by convention, Basil is led to paint a full-body portrait of Dorian, with unexpected consequences: "I had drawn you as Paris in dainty armour, and as Adonis with huntsman's cloak and polished boar-spear. Crowned with heavy lotus-blossoms you had sat on the prow of Adrian's barge, gazing across the green turbid Nile. You had leant over the still pool of some Greek woodland, and seen in the water's silent silver the marvel of your own face. And it had all been what art should be, unconscious, ideal and remote. One day, a fatal day I sometimes think, I determined to paint a wonderful portrait of you as you actually are, not in the costume of dead ages, but in your own dress and in your own time" (110). In itself, the mention of clothes would not necessarily imply a full-body representation: it could be one of face and bust alone. But the sustained analogy with the mythological paintings, the mention of armor and cloak as well as bodily actions such as sitting and leaning, strongly suggests that in painting Dorian in his own clothes, Basil paints a full-body portrait. Having painted Dorian "in his own dress," without "the mist or veil" of ancient clothes, Basil is struck with the "wonder of [Dorian's] own personality thus directly presented to [him]" (110–11)[36]— his personhood manifested through the image of his body. For Dorian, too, the portrait is a revelation of the body: "This portrait would be to him the most magical of mirrors. As it had revealed to him his own body, so it would reveal to him his own soul" (103). If Basil's fascination with Dorian is the result of a "face to face" encounter (10), his art betrays this secret fascination through the representation of the body when it is no longer "ideal and remote." It is only as a portrait of the full body that the picture of Dorian Gray can be the site of Basil's secret love; it is only as a portrait of the full body that it can accomplish Dorian's secret wish to exchange places with the portrait (and these two secrets are presented as one and the same when both Basil and Dorian think that the secret of the other is the same as his own).

The three men whose story the novel tells occupy the three character positions of a portrait story: a painter (Basil), a sitter (Dorian), and a viewer (Lord Henry). But the apparent neatness of this allocation is blurred in several ways. To begin with, since the novel starts at the point where the portrait is just about finished, the story it tells is primarily that of the portrait's effects, that is, it puts all three characters in the position of viewers.[37] But Basil's assertion that "every portrait that is painted with feeling is a portrait of the artist, not of the sitter" (9) and Wilde's own assertion in the preface, that "It is the spectator, and not life, that art really mirrors" (4) suggest that all three men might also be considered the portrait's subjects. Lord Henry's faux-naïve surprise at Basil's assertion that he has put too much of himself into the portrait ("I didn't know you were so vain. . . . You are not in the least like [Dorian]" [6, 7]) reminds us, however, that if both sitter and painter may be present in, or revealed by, the portrait, it is not in the same way: unlike the sitter's, the painter's presence in the portrait is indexical rather than iconic. The indexical presence of the painter is usually thought to manifest itself through his style, understood as technique. However, Basil's specification that it is a portrait "painted with feeling" that reveals the painter suggests that his presence in the portrait has to do with more than brush strokes, or, alternatively, that style itself is the expression or product of feeling. And indeed Basil claims that Dorian is "much more for me than a model or a sitter.... His personality has suggested to me an entirely new manner in art, an entirely new mode of style" (13). Dorian, Basil adds, "is never more present in my work than when no image of him is there" (14). Though this assertion can be read as an attempt on Basil's part to disavow his fascination with Dorian as a person (or with his body), it also indicates that as a "new mode of style" Dorian too is present in the portrait indexically. And while his iconic presence in the portrait can be dismissed as simply an "accident," the mere "occasion" (9) that, according to Basil, the sitter provides the painter, his indexical presence as the source of the painter's style makes him coextensive with the portrait.[38] Moreover, the portrait's status as a mimetic representation of its subject now appears less obvious since Dorian's presence in the portrait as a "new mode of style" means that the portrait is shaped by Dorian's influence on Basil (as well as by Basil's love for him).

Lord Henry's relation to the portrait is also complicated and not only because, according to Wilde, as a spectator (of both life and art, of life as art) he is in some way "mirrored" by the portrait. As Basil is putting the finishing touch on Dorian's portrait, Lord Henry talks and his voice and words have a powerful effect on Dorian: "The few words that Basil's friend had said to him [Dorian]—words spoken by chance, no doubt, and with wilful paradox in them—had touched some secret chord that had never been touched before, but that he felt was now vibrating and throbbing to curious pulses" (21). This "fresh influence" (21) produces "the most wonderful expression" on his face—"the half-parted lips, and the bright look in the eyes" that Basil declares to be "the effect he wanted" and that he captures on the canvas (22). Just as Dorian influences the manner or style in which the portrait is painted, Lord Henry influences the way Dorian appears in the portrait. If Lord Henry is "mirrored" in the portrait, then, it is because his influence on Dorian is inscribed in the portrait: just like Basil he is present in the portrait indexically rather than iconically (that is, not really by being mirrored). Thus the portrait of Dorian Gray, perceived or recognized as a mimetic representation, a likeness, of its subject, is in fact the product of "influence," that is of a shaping that is not a copying, not a doubling. Produced by all three men who leave their traces on it, the portrait is the site where their intersubjective relations (of influence and desire) are inscribed.

When Basil declares the portrait finished, Dorian is invited to look at it: "Dorian . . . passed listlessly in front of his picture and turned towards it. When he saw it he drew back, and his cheeks flushed for a moment with pleasure. A look of joy came into his eyes, as if he had recognized himself for the first time. . . . The sense of his own beauty came to him as a revelation" (27). Though Dorian perceives the change he undergoes as coming from within him, both his recognition of himself and the self he recognizes are produced by Lord Henry's shaping influence. Lord Henry's chance words do not reveal to Dorian a preexisting hidden self; rather they shape this self.[39] Under this shaping influence, Dorian now recognizes himself in the painted image, itself shaped by Lord Henry's words as well as by his own influence on Basil and by Basil's love. In the same way that Dorian influenced Basil's art so that in this new art Basil can recognize his love for Dorian, Lord Henry influences Dorian, who can then see his newly discovered/produced self in Basil's painting. The portrait then represents both the Dorian Basil loves and a somewhat different Dorian, who, through Lord Henry's influence (which Basil considers to be corrupting), has come to know himself as different. The portrait thus raises the question of who is the "real" Dorian, not as a question of the relation between the real and its representation but as a question that cuts across, and undoes, the separation of and opposition between the real and its representation.

Looking at Basil's portrait, Dorian, influenced by Lord Henry's words, experiences a joyful self-misrecognition that can be called narcissistic. But Dorian is different from Narcissus, who falls in love with his image and wants to join it even at the cost of death. Dorian, by contrast, wants to exchange places with the portrait, which is quite a different thing: rather than wishing to unite with the image, he would like to keep the difference between them, only exchange their respective attributes. So while it is true that Dorian, influenced by Lord Henry, (mis)recognizes himself in Basil's portrait—sees himself as an unchanging image of beauty and youth (since this is what he is for both Lord Henry and Basil)—he is not in love with his image in the portrait: he is first jealous of it (28) and then is appalled by it. In spite of the frequent metaphoric use of "mirror" to describe the portrait (e.g., "This portrait would be to him the most magical of mirrors" [103]), the text also calls attention to the difference between mirror and portrait by featuring, besides the portrait, a mirror (given to Dorian by Lord Henry [210]). When Dorian recognizes himself in the portrait, sees himself as he is painted there, beautiful and young, the portrait assumes the role played by the mirror (of water or of glass) in the myth of Narcissus as well as in Lacan's elaboration of narcissism in his essay on the "mirror stage": the portrait gives him an idealized image of himself. A portrait can play this role because it captures a moment in time and arrests it, thus leaving the subject unchanged, immortal. But the portrait of Dorian Gray does not play this role of narcissistic mirror image since it does not keep his image as eternally young and beautiful. It is, rather, the literal mirror that reflects his unchanging beauty and youth. The mirror, both in the myth of Narcissus and in Lacan, also mimics the self, moving a hand when he does, etc., thus creating the illusion that the image is real, a double. A portrait normally does not have this attribute, but because of Dorian's wish, the portrait does change, registering (though not reflecting) his own change. Thus, after Sybil's suicide, there is "a touch of cruelty in the mouth" of the portrait (87) whereas in the mirror "no line like that warped his red lips" (88). In short, while in one sense the portrait does not function as a mirror (it does not give Dorian an idealized image of himself as eternally young and beautiful), in another sense it does (it registers the changes Dorian undergoes). The portrait is not the same as the mirror, but neither is it its symmetrical opposite. The portrait of Dorian Gray is situated between what is normally considered a portrait and a mirror.

Rather than being a Narcissus infatuated with his "mirror image," Dorian, for most of the novel, enjoys the perverse pleasure of contemplating these two different versions of himself (a difference he embodies).[40] When he says that "there will be a real pleasure in watching" the picture (103), the pleasure he evokes is not that of sameness with the image, of absorption or rapture, but that of measuring the image in the picture against the one in the mirror, and vice versa: "the very sharpness of the contrast used to quicken his sense of pleasure" (124). If part of the pleasure derived from this divided contemplation is that he feels all the more invincible—"like the gods of the Greeks, he would be strong, and fleet, and joyous" (103)—the other part seems very much like a masochistic pleasure of seeing his body degraded, seeing it being "punished" for his actions and passions,[41] while at the same time subjecting himself to the portrait's disapproving gaze (as when, after the death of Sybil, looking at the portrait is like "looking into a mirror after he had done some dreadful thing" [88]). Until the end, when the destruction of the portrait (following the shattering of the mirror) brings about his own death, Dorian is a subject split between two contradictory images (and their pleasures).

While Lord Henry's words disturb Dorian and upset him (though he also comments that words have their own sweet music [22]), his reaction to Basil's portrait is that of pleasure and joy: he sees in it the power of his beauty and youth. It is this power that he desires to preserve through his wish to exchange place with the portrait (a wish born out of Lord Henry's words, since they have made him aware both of his youth and beauty and of their ephemerality). Dorian's influence over others throughout his life demonstrates the power of the image he has become through this exchange. But in becoming his own portrait Dorian has not eliminated the portrait; the result of the exchange is, as I have mentioned earlier, that both man and portrait are present, but neither one is identical to itself. Man and portrait, subject and representation, are each divided within and inextricably linked to the other: while Dorian qua portrait presents a fully visible and yet indecipherable surface, the portrait qua Dorian is both hidden and revealing. In Wilde's text, then, subjectivity and representation are seen as inseparable from each other; it is no longer a question of which one comes first and determines the other since they are coextensive while each one also divides the other, and is divided by the other, from within. However, this split within subjectivity/representation is understood in the novel in two different ways: one—Basil's way—has to do with the dialectic of hiding and revealing, while the other—Lord Henry's way—involves a particular relation between ignorance and knowledge. It is this difference that accounts for what Dorian calls the "contrast" between these two characters (20). We can see this contrast in their symmetrical and inverted responses to Sybil's suicide and their opposing attitudes toward the rumors about Dorian's relations with young men; it is also brought out through the compositional symmetry between the two chapters in which Dorian meets with Basil, shows him the portrait, and then kills him (chapters 12–13) and the two chapters (19–20) in which Dorian meets with Lord Henry and then destroys the portrait, thus killing himself (or being killed by it).

Whereas Basil is associated with secrets and secrecy, Lord Henry is associated with "strategic ignorance."[42] Basil is concerned with secrets and their revelation; much as he would like to keep his secrets, he cannot *not* reveal what is inside him. He considers his love for Dorian a secret and would like to keep Dorian's name a secret, but he reveals both to Lord Henry. He is afraid that he has revealed his idolatrous love for Dorian, "the secret of [his] own soul" (9), in the portrait and therefore is determined not to exhibit the portrait—"not bare [his] soul to [the world's] shallow, prying eyes" (14); he also is determined never to tell Dorian of his love for him. Eventually he both decides to exhibit the portrait and confesses his secret love to Dorian. He reveals not only his secrets but also his very investment in secrecy: he tells Lord Henry that he "has grown to love secrecy" (7) and that he creates secrets about his whereabouts. He is interested in Dorian's "soul" and the way in which Dorian's own "secrets" have become known. But Basil also believes that there can be no secrets: "Sin is a thing that writes itself across a man's face. It cannot be concealed" (143).[43] Therefore, while he does not dismiss or ignore the rumors that circulate around Dorian, he also believes that Dorian can have no secrets since his appearance belies any such idea. Basil both reveals himself and fears discovery, creates secrets and tells them, has secrets but believes it is impossible to have them, credits rumors and denies their ground. His whole being is defined by the structure of the "open secret," the secret that leaks or gives itself away, where subjectivity is understood as an interiority that has to be kept secret in order to be protected but also has to be revealed in order to be acknowledged (or, alternatively, where the marks that are supposed to make identity—and more precisely sexual identity—legible are both written on the body and invisible).

Had the portrait only grown old while Dorian remained young (as he had originally wished), there would have been no secret even if the portrait had remained hidden: the secret would have remained hidden, nothing would have revealed it, and hence it would not have been a secret. But the portrait becomes the site where Dorian's "sins" (passions, actions) are inscribed; these actions have effect on others, whose behavior betrays this effect and produces rumors; he himself has memories of his own behavior and of his relations to others that he cannot avoid. The hidden portrait does not absorb all this; it does not protect him entirely, does not keep his secret entirely secret: and this is precisely the definition of the portrait and subjectivity as "open secret."

Whereas Basil is afraid that he involuntarily revealed his secret in his portrait of Dorian and therefore does not want to exhibit it, Lord Henry advertises his supposed immorality through his conversation. But though his conversation is considered by everybody (including Basil) to be cynical and corrupting, Basil, for one, does not believe that Lord Henry's words actually express his opinions. Though Lord Henry's long speech to Dorian promoting the "new Hedonism" (21) appears as his personal credo (he repeats the phrase "I believe"), there is no reason to take this declaration at face value rather than reading the speech as the rhetorical piece of seduction and attempt at influence that it is. He himself neither lives according to this credo[44] nor thinks it is important whether he believes in what he says or not (12). Passages describing Basil often depict facial expressions that reveal his inner feelings or thoughts: he smiles with pleasure (6), looks worried (19), bites his lips (19, 31, 72), stares with amazement (28, 108), turns pale (28), frowns (16, 71, 149), speaks "with a strained touch of pain in his voice," "with sorrow in his voice" (105, 146), has "a puzzled expression" (148). By contrast, though at times we have access to Lord Henry's thoughts and feelings, his "musical voice" (21),"subtle smile" (22), "dreamy, languorous eyes" (22) or "meditative manner" (74) are hard, if not impossible, to interpret: they do not "reveal" him. Nor does his behavior, since it is governed by the conventional, external calculus of decorum. Basil puts it in a nutshell when he tells Lord Henry: "You never say a moral thing, and you never do a wrong thing" (8). "Wrong," in this context, clearly does not mean morally wrong (since Basil considers him immoral and sees his influence as corrupting) but inappropriate; he abides by his own dictum that "One should never do anything that one cannot talk about after dinner" (203). Lord Henry thus remains inscrutable without, however, having secrets.

The association of Lord Henry with shaping influence and with exteriority (as opposed to Basil's association with representation and interiority) means that in this novel voice—with which Lord Henry is often associated—is not connected with the soul or with interiority, as it commonly is: it is the material aspect of the voice that has its effect on Dorian.[45] And when voice is associated not with music but with language, words themselves are seen not as a vehicle for a content or meaning (that lies inside or behind them) but as providing form. Words, Dorian says, have power ("a subtle magic") because they "give a plastic form to formless things" (22). Words do not represent a preexisting reality or truth but give shape; their power (or magic) is that of their ability to influence rather than copy. The "corrupting" power of words lies not in a particular (secret, hidden) content they "represent" but in their lack of grounding.

Lord Henry, who influences Dorian, was himself influenced by a certain yellow book that he passes on to Dorian later on in the novel. Lord Henry thus sees his own influence on Dorian as the repetition of the influence that once marked him (22). Despite being influenced himself and influencing others, Lord Henry presents influence as always bad, since the influenced person "becomes an echo [both a copy and a trace] of someone else's music, an actor of a part that has not been written for him" (20). He preaches that rather than being influenced by others one should "realize one's nature perfectly" (20). The contradiction between being influenced and realizing one's nature is resolved by presenting influence as the holding of a mirror that allows the other to discover and assume his yet unknown self (that is, treating an index as an icon). In other words, the view of words and images as "mirrors" or copies produces the illusion of a self prior to the influence of words and images, prior to their shaping—producing, performing power.

Lord Henry's strategy of "knowing what not to know" does not mean complete blindness. When in their last meeting Dorian tells Lord Henry about his intention to become good, Lord Henry knows that he has not really changed. What he does not know—is not allowed to know—is Dorian's secret. Basil hears the rumors about Dorian; Lord Henry either does not hear them or does not concern himself with them. At the end of the novel he tells Dorian: "The world has cried out against us both" (207), but this does not seem to concern him or to make him question Dorian's perfection. For him Dorian remains to the end the incarnation of perfect beauty, youth, and innocence—for him he remains as he was on the first day he saw him (206). He understands this sameness as a victory over time rather than as having to do with the purity of the soul, with interiority.

Dorian resembles Basil in that they both have secrets and fear exposure; each mistakes the other's secret for his own; each tells the other his secret. They both disappear occasionally and behave in a way that causes rumors (5, 202, for Basil; 124, for Dorian). But Dorian also can be seen as complicit with Lord Henry, since he actively protects the latter's willed ignorance. Dorian does not show Lord Henry the disfigured portrait so that the secret he shares with Basil is not disclosed to Lord Henry, who, indeed, never sees the portrait after the first sighting in Basil's studio. Though Lord Henry tells Dorian that "All through your life you will tell me everything you do," and though Dorian seems to agree, since he tells Lord Henry that if he ever commits a crime he will confess it to him (51), Dorian does not tell Lord Henry either the secret of the portrait or his murder of Basil. In a meeting with Dorian after he has killed Basil, Lord Henry tells Dorian that he "should like to know some one who had committed a real murder" (196) and that he cannot imagine Dorian committing a crime (203). The irony of these comments highlights his (willed) lack of knowledge. Of the three men, Lord Henry is the one who survives, and it is, one may argue, his "strategy" of knowing what not to know (which Dorian helps him sustain) that allows him to survive. When in attempting to destroy the portrait Dorian also kills himself, he shows that he was inseparable from the portrait as the site of secrets; but the novel, like Dorian, protects Lord Henry against this knowledge (that is, sustains its representation of him as the one who does not/should not know). A scene in which Lord Henry sees Dorian's dead body, "withered, wrinkled, and loathsome of visage" (213) is inconceivable.

In *The Picture of Dorian Gray*, the relation between Basil and Lord Henry is initially one of rivalry over an object of desire; each tries to keep Dorian for himself and remove the other. Basil refuses to reveal Dorian's name to Lord Henry for a long time and doesn't want Lord Henry to meet him (16). When they do meet, he tries to get Lord Henry to leave the studio (19) and asks Dorian to stay with him rather than going to the theater with Lord Henry (31). Later on, when the three go together to the theater to see Sybil Vane acting, Henry pointedly tells Basil that there is only room for two in the carriage (77). But the rivalry between Basil and Lord Henry over Dorian's attention does not develop into a full-fledged plot and, after the initial confrontation between the two, it no longer plays any role in the novel. Dorian's violence against Basil is not caused either by rivalry or by identification: for Dorian, Basil is neither an ideal self nor a rival. Lord Henry sees Dorian as an ideal self (and claims that Dorian sees him as his ideal—"I represent to you all the sins you have never had the courage to commit" [77]), but the relation between them seems free of either rivalry or aggression. And as to the picture: when Dorian feels that the portrait is his rival—"every moment that passes takes something from me, and give something to it" (28)—he desires to change places with it, not to annihilate it (it is Basil who wants to destroy it in that scene and Dorian who begs him not to [29]).

Dorian's wish to exchange places with the portrait animates the portrait, and hiding it casts it as the equivalent of Dorian's hidden interiority; the portrait comes to life, it is "this monstrous soul-life" (212). As in Hardy's story, here, too, we find a hidden/visible, disavowed/avowed interiority. Dorian himself, having become his own portrait, appears as unchanged and unchanging exteriority (as the portrait in Kleist's story appears to Elvire). But the separation between Dorian (unchanging exteriority) and his portrait (hidden/visible interiority) is illusory: subject and representation are both coextensive and traverse each other so that destroying the portrait entails the destruction of its subject.

All of Dorian's actions at the end of the novel are under the sign of repetition as undoing. Through the assault on the portrait the original wish is undone: the real body is revealed as subject to time and bearing the traces of Dorian's actions while the portrait keeps its pristine beauty. Dorian attacks the painting with a knife—committing the very action he prevented Basil from carrying out at the beginning of the novel while also imitating/undoing the production of the picture, which was carried out with a palette knife. He kills himself with the same knife he used to kill Basil, thus murdering the murderer, repeating/paying for that murder.[46]

While Dorian hopes that through these repetitions he can "kill the past" (212) and thus restore things to what they were before he made the wish, his acts of repetition and imitation serve only to undo or erase what has been done; they appear as the expression of a negative power to unmake what has been made, to destroy rather than restore or construct. This concatenation of purely destructive acts of repetition and imitation at the end of the novel stands in stark difference to the emphasis on non-mimetic shaping and influence in the production of both the portrait and the subjectivity of the three men inscribed in it.

In the three texts examined in this chapter, a representation of an idealized male body becomes the site of identity construction or production for its multiple viewers. Unlike the representation of the face, which allows us to recognize an individual as individual, the representation of the body does not in itself individuate (to use Louis Marin's formulation, [see note 2]). The portrait of the body, specifically of the male body, is then a portrait that tends towards transcending the particular, representing the general or universal or essential. This is clearest in Hardy, where the statue of a beautiful male body, giving the form and contours of this body, is said to represent the human, stand for the species. This would not be the case either with the face (of a man or a woman) or with a woman's body, commonly regarded as representing the enigma of woman rather than the form of the human.

In Kleist's story, too, the gradual filling up of the portrait suggests that the image that is "given" is that of a general form, devoid of particular features. Though in Wilde's text the body is individuated inasmuch as it is the object of Basil's desire, the utterly conventional description of Dorian's beauty, suggests a certain abstraction. The evacuation of the image of particularizing traits (through the choice of the body rather than the face, of a man's body rather than a woman's, of the outer form of the body, of conventional description and lack of detail) is what defines the portrait/statue in these texts and enables it to function the way it does.

But while this may mean that in these stories the form of the male body is presented as the ground for the production of subjectivity (suggesting complicity between the aesthetic ideal of transcending the "mere individual" and phallocentrism), the stories also complicate the status of this image as ground. The viewer's relation to the image in these stories is one of identification and desire through which the image itself (and not only the viewer's subjectivity) is constructed or modified. Thus in Kleist's text, identification can happen only through the mediation of others who point out its suitability for identification, and it produces both the subject and his "mirror image" through a long process in time; there is nothing spontaneous—natural or immediate—about it. It is only through this mediation and repeated acts of projection and adjustment that the image becomes the right one, the mirror image. In Wilde, the portrait represents several subjects in their intersubjective relations; rather than reflecting either one of them as a mirror, the portrait is shaped by all three, who are also shaped by it and by each other. Thus in both texts the givenness of the image is questioned; what is the ground of identification is not quite a ground since it is also the product of the process it supposedly grounds.

In these texts, then, the portrait/statue does not function as a mirror (full of individuating detail). And though in its generality it may appear as the equivalent of a "real other"—another human being in whom the subject-to-be recognizes/misrecognizes itself—it is only an image. Unlike the mirror, it is a *real* image—it is not virtual, it is a physical, material object (it can be slashed, mutilated); unlike the real other, it becomes animated only through the viewer attributing to it an interiority. The status of the portrait/statue as a "real image" determines the viewers' relation to it while the image itself is transformed—becomes more than an image—through this experience.

Moreover, though all three texts represent subjects in relations of rivalry, identification, and desire predicated on imitation (mirroring, doubling), they also foreground other forms of relating to the portrait/statue: Wilde's text foregrounds influence and shaping rather than imitation as governing intersubjective relations and in both Kleist's and Hardy's stories the women's relation to the portrait/statue is that of "propping" oneself on an image (rather than imitating it or modeling oneself on it).

Thus all three texts present us with a relation between portrait/statue and viewer that is much more dynamic, mediated, temporal, and reciprocal than we might have expected and that includes forms of shaping that are not imitative. By describing identification as a simultaneous production of subject and image and by foregrounding mediation and the role of influence, shaping, and "propping," these stories invite us to consider, through the use of the portrait as a "real image," other possibilities for the construction of subjectivity "in the field of vision" than narcissistic identification and mimetic rivalry. [47]

CHAPTER 6

Portraits, Parents, and Children: Storm's "Aquis submersus" and Sand's "Le Château de Pictordu"

Many portrait stories are based on a scenario that Maurizio Bettini called "the lover's story," where the lover paints the beloved (the ideal, the muse) because he is in love or, conversely, falls in love because he paints. We have seen versions of this scenario in several stories—for example in Balzac's *La Maison du chat-qui-pelote*, where Sommervieux's friend, finding him hard at work on Augustine's portrait, concludes that the painter must be in love, or in Hoffmann's "Die Doppeltgänger," where the young painter Haberland falls in love with Natalie because he paints her. James's "The Tone of Time" also features "a lover's story," where a woman paints the portrait of the beautiful man she loved and lost, but neither the portrayed man nor his portrait play there the role of muse or ideal that the women did in Balzac's or Hoffmann's story. Indeed, the story of the painter and his real/ideal beloved woman is a specifically male story and not only because throughout the ages the majority of painters (and especially the majority of painters to enjoy recognition) were male. Rather, it has to do (also) with the fact that though as objects of representation women have often been made to stand for the ideal, as artists they have just as often been associated with a servile (or mechanical) imitation of the real and were considered "as *congenitally incapable* of transcending immanence to attain the ideal."[1]

Another scenario we find in portrait stories and that I have discussed briefly in chapter 3 (in the reading of Hoffmann's "Die Doppeltgänger") has to do with the relation between portraits, parents, and children.[2] Portrait stories that deal with the relation between a parent and a child are often stories about transmission: of traits but also of authority, knowledge, the past. In patriarchal societies, the transmission that counts is the one from father to son, and, as we have seen in Hoffmann's story, the mother is often considered as a mere carrier of the paternal heritage: she has nothing of her own to transmit. Indeed, as Jean-Joseph Goux has argued, the father's position as "the guardian of transmission" has much to do with "the mythical archeology of conception" from which the very opposition between matter and idea derives and according to which the mother provides unformed matter whereas the father provides "pattern, a model . . . constant ideal form"—in other words, that which can be transmitted.[3] Likewise, Freud's theory of the family romance uses the difference between father and mother in conception to explain idealization or the lack thereof: the uncertainty that surrounds paternity means that the father can be "worked" by the imagination, transformed and translated into a higher social status and, more generally, idealized, whereas the certainty of maternity means that the mother is seen as what is inescapably given; she is coded as material, bodily existence that no imagination can transform.[4] Thus the same gendered distinction between ideal and real that we find in the lover/painter story also subtends certain understanding of the child-parent relation.

The two stories I discuss in this chapter—Theodor Storm's "Aquis submersus" (1876) and George Sand's "Le Château de Pictordu" (1873)—revolve around the relation between a parent and a child. In Storm's story, we have a portrait of a dead child, painted by his father; in Sand's story, we have a daughter who paints the portrait of the dead mother she has hardly known. Both stories deal with the question of transmission in a way that problematizes the paradigms delineated above: Storm's story puts into question genealogical transmission and the power of the father, while Sand's story de-idealizes the father and represents a successful transmission from mother to daughter. The stories are very different from each other—thematically and formally. It is thus the difference between a paternal and a maternal transmission that will provide the point of comparison between the two texts. Since both stories problematize the paternal order, they also raise the issue of class affiliation determined by paternal descent; I will discuss the relation between class and the power to represent at the end of the chapter.

Portraying the Fault of the Father: Storm's "Aquis submersus"

"Aquis submersus" has at its center the portrait of a dead child. The frame narrator tells how, in his childhood, he was fascinated by the portrait and wished to know more about its subject. The portrait also has an inscription—C.P.A.S—the full meaning of which escapes him. Only as an adult does he find out that the first half of the inscription stands for "culpa patris," that is, it assigns the responsibility for the child's death by drowning (A.S.: aquis submersus) to the father-painter. How should we understand, however, "culpa patris"—that which portrait, inscription, and the manuscript in which the father-painter tells his life all seek to convey? Though "culpa" means both guilt and fault, critics have dealt primarily with the question of the painter Johannes's guilt, that is, his moral responsibility and his remorseful awareness of having committed an offense. But in the inscription, "culpa" indicates a cause rather than an effect: a fault—a weakness, defect, or error—that brought about the drowning of the child; this meaning of "culpa" is on the whole neglected by critics and was dealt with only in terms of a "tragic flaw."[5] My analysis, by contrast, will center on the fault of the father as a structural lack: the father's perennial absence and failure to protect his son, his powerlessness. This does not mean that guilt plays no role in the story but that we have to understand personal, moral guilt in relation to the structural fault of (or in) the father. In what follows I will argue that "the fault of the father" as well as the relation between portrait and inscription, painting and manuscript, frame and narrative, can be understood in terms of the logic of the supplement (or the *parergon*): a surplus, added to what appears complete, revealing a lack in that to which it was added (or for which it was substituted).[6]

FATHERS AND SONS

The main narrative of Storm's "Aquis submersus" takes place in the seventeenth century, and its protagonist and narrator is the painter Johannes, who learned his art in Holland under the well-known portraitist Van der Helst. This is the golden age of Dutch painting and, more specifically, of portraiture. It is at this historical moment that "portrait"—which up to then meant "'pictorial imitation' of any kind"—becomes officially, in the writings of André Félibien (1619–1695), a term reserved exclusively for the depiction of human beings. Moreover, "verifiable resemblance"—which was not a characteristic of portraits until the late Middle Ages—becomes at that time an essential criterion for portrait painting.[7] As the art historian Joanna Woodall has shown, portrait painting in Holland of the seventeenth century was also closely related to "the enrichment and enhanced confidence of elites outside the hereditary noble order."[8] The portrait painter provides the nonhereditary elite with the means of defining and presenting their economic success and social status (suggesting that success and status are not fully visible on their own and need a supplement, in this case, of painting, to make them visible and thus acknowledged and recognized); in so doing, the successful portrait painter himself acquires economical status and social prestige.

When Johannes returns to Holstein after a five-year stay in Holland, he resembles his patrons and their portraits: he has "a good supply of traveling money and a bill of exchange on a Hamburg bank," and he is "sumptuously attired" (386; 116). As he explains to Katharina, the daughter of his former patron Herr Gerhardus, "over there in Holland, there an able painter is regarded as the equal of a German nobleman" (418; 142). By contrast, on the estate of the now dead Herr Gerhardus, Johannes confronts the hostility and contempt of Katharina's brother, the Junker Wulf; of the brother's friend, the Junker Kurt; and of Katharina's mean chaperone, Bas' Ursel, who are all firm defenders of the hereditary world order, based on bloodline. But the opposition between Holstein and Holland is only apparently that between a hereditary world order and a world order defined by individual achievements and possessions. On the one hand, Herr Gerhardus has taken Johannes under his protection after the death of Johannes's father, who, though not a nobleman, was Herr Gerhardus's intimate friend. Herr Gerhardus's daughter, Katharina, considers Johannes more worthy of her love than the Junker Kurt; when Johannes tells her that he is "not a nobleman and may not court [her]" (418; 141), she answers, "roguishly": "Not a nobleman, Johannes? I should have thought you were that, too! But—oh no! Your father was only the friend of mine—that probably does not count with the world!" (418; 142). The Gerhardus house is, thus, a divided one. On the other hand, and more importantly, Johannes never considers himself a self-made man. Just as he depended on the patronage of Herr Gerhardus to become a painter, so does he depend for his success on his "dear Master Van der Helst" and other powerful patrons (386; 116). As patrons, Herr Gerhardus and Van der Helst are surrogate fathers whose function is to protect their son in the absence of the real father (and the word for "patron" in the German text is "Protektor"). Similarly, in the second part of the main narrative, the pastor will become, in Johannes's absence, a surrogate father and protector to his son. The surrogacy intended to supplement paternity defined by blood proves, however, to be as faulty as what it supplements. If the fault of the father is first and foremost his absence, and therefore his inability to protect his son, the surrogate fathers (Gerhardus, Van der Helst, the pastor) are no less at fault: they, too, are absent, dead, unable to protect. In this account of paternal relations, the death of the father does not liberate or empower the son; rather, it generates a need for surrogate figures who, however, fail too. Johannes's obsessive discourse of filial piety (he never refers to his own father other than as "my dear father" [386, 388; 116, 117, 118] or "my dear late father" [391; 120] and to his teacher always as "my dear Master Van der Helst" [386, 427; 116, 148]; he refers to Lord Gerhardus as "my noble, most gracious patron" (386; 116) and "my dear departed Lord Gerhardus [410; 135–36] voices also an implicit accusation leveled at the father for failing him, a failure he himself ends up repeating.[9] This is a world where the father is always guilty of having failed his son (rather than a world where the son feels guilty for wanting to take the father's place).

GENEALOGY AND PORTRAITURE

How are the father and the fault of the father related to portraiture? To the extent that portraits are likenesses, depicting the subject's individual traits (rather than representing the subject metonymically, through emblems, as they mostly did until the late Middle Ages), portraits can be said to function as an analogue, and hence as a support, for the hereditary system, since both transmit traits; both function on the principle of non-reciprocal resemblance, the kind of resemblance we find between original and copy.[10] The portrait galleries we find in so many nineteenth-century literary texts (and that we encountered in Gautier's "La Cafetière," and Wilde's *The Picture of Dorian Gray*) testify to a preoccupation with ancestry and descent. In an aristocratic society (and more generally, in patriarchal society), where the transmission of name, fortune, authority, and status is in the male line, it is the resemblance between father and son that is of importance and portraits can be called upon to make this resemblance visible. The portrait gallery at Herr Gerhardus's estate displays portraits of past lords and their wives but curiously the resemblances that are commented upon in the text are not those between father and son. As Johannes looks at the portraits, he notices *Katharina's* resemblance to the portraits of both Herr Gerhardus and his wife; it is to her, rather than to her brother, the Junker Wulf, that their traits were transmitted, and it is in her that they are preserved: she is her parents' living portrait.[11]

The other resemblance Johannes comments upon is that between the Junker Wulf and the portrait of the evil ancestress who, generations ago, cursed her daughter for loving beneath her state. As critics have pointed out, this resemblance cannot be explained by recourse to heredity: the ancestress, a wife of a Gerhardus, had only one daughter who died childless.[12] The ancestress and the Junker Wulf, the two people who represent uncompromising belief in the hereditary world order where class difference is grounded in blood, are themselves not related by blood. Thus, in Storm's story, the portrait gallery diverges from, or even challenges, the hereditary world order rather than supporting it, strengthening our sense of a crisis within the genealogical system: the Junker Wulf does not resemble his father—it is rather the lowly born Johannes who is truly Gerhardus's son; it is the daughter Katharina who resembles her parents; the resemblance between the evil ancestress and the Junker Wulf, evidenced only by the portrait (since they are separated by several generations), has to be explained by something other than heredity.[13] We should note, however, that, as events will show, though the hereditary world order is challenged and even in crisis, it has not lost its power: the Junker Wulf *is* his father's heir and retains power over his sister and over the "true" son, Johannes.

If portraits in this story do not transmit traits from father to son, what they do transmit is the fault of the father. The story links the fault of the father to portraiture most explicitly when Johannes undertakes to paint the portrait of his dead child, following the instructions issued by the pastor who has served as the child's surrogate father; both are guilty of the child's death since both were absent from his side and failed to protect him. While Johannes comments that the child's eyes resemble those of his mother, Katharina (440; 159), there is no mention in the text that the portrait of the dead child (whose eyes are closed) resembles either one of his parents. Thus the portrait does not transmit the traits of the child's parents (or, if it does, this is not what the text is concerned with) but rather, as the inscription Johannes adds to the portrait—C.P.A.S—makes clear, points to the fault of the father.

The very presence of the inscription suggests that the portrait, though complete, does not convey, or make visible, the meaning intended by its painter and thus needs to be supplemented. The inscription and its full meaning, however, are not immediately available. At first the child narrator does not even notice the inscription. When he does, he is told that the second part of the inscription—A.S—means "aquis submersus," (382–83; 113), but the only interpretation proposed for the first part of the inscription—"casu periculoso"—is discarded as inadequate. Though the child-narrator himself, "without thinking [ohne viel Besinnen]" translates it as "culpa patris," this interpretation is rejected by the voice of paternal authority (his friend's father), and this part of the inscription remains enigmatic for the narrator until he discovers the manuscript. The inscription that supplements the portrait needs to be supplemented by the manuscript. Thus the fault of the father, which creates the need for surrogates, has its analogue on the formal level where portrait and inscription each needs to be supplemented.

GENEALOGY AND AFFINITY

In Storm's tale, the hereditary relation is constantly challenged/supplemented by another relation, which we can call a relation of affinity (that is, of resemblance and attraction). This relation is not one of generation; rather, it is often described as produced by spatial proximity or contiguity, independent of blood relation. Though we see this relation operating in the main narrative (where Herr Gerhardus's true son is Johannes and where the Junker Wulf resembles an ancestress who is not a blood relation), it is most visible in the frame narrative and especially in the relation between the frame narrative and the main narrative. This relation is formally already one of supplementarity.

Both the main narrative and the frame narrative are in two parts. In the first part of the main narrative, Johannes tells of his return to Holstein to find his patron, Herr Gerhardus, dead, his enemy the Junker Wulf in charge, and his childhood playmate, Katharina, the promised bride of the Junker Kurt. While Johannes paints Katharina's portrait in preparation for her wedding, his love for her grows stronger and is reciprocated; it culminates in their night of love. Wounded by the Junker Wulf, Johannes is separated from Katharina. He leaves for Holland, where he hopes to gain enough money and support to marry Katharina, but when he comes back to Holstein, Katharina is gone and all his efforts to find her are in vain.

The second part of the main narrative takes place some four years later in a town by the North Sea, where Johannes has a commission to paint the resurrection of Lazarus; he is also commissioned to paint the portrait of the pastor of a nearby village. After several visits to the village, Johannes realizes that the pastor's wife is Katharina and the pastor's son is his own child. During his passionate (indeed, violent) encounter with Katharina, the child is left unattended and drowns in a ditch; Johannes paints the portrait of his dead child following the pastor's instructions.

The frame narrative doubles and reverses the two parts of the main narrative. In the first part of the frame, the frame narrator tells of the happy weekends he spent, as a child, in the house of his friend's father, the pastor in a village near the town by the North Sea where both he and his friend went to school. It is in the village church that as a child he saw the portrait of the dead child and, later on, the inscription on it. The narrator's friend, the pastor's only child, lives with his parents in the same house where the child in the portrait used to live generations ago (though the hospitality and warmth of the home of the narrator's friend is, as we shall find out, quite the opposite of the austerity of the dead child's home). The narrator does not mention his own parents, his own family, so it is as though his friend's home is the only home he has, as if he, too, were the pastor's son (or the pastor his surrogate father) and so he himself (and not only his friend) is like the child in the portrait. The child-narrator's sense of affinity with the dead child, the "irresistible" compassion he feels for the boy in the picture and his "fantastic longing" (381; 112) to know a bit more about him are both the result of a shared space. He sees himself in the dead boy and wonders whether the dead boy "might have once run about here [the house they share] in person" (382; 113).

The interest the frame narrator shows in the portrait of the dead child suggests that he identifies with him, and his intuitive translation of the inscription on the portrait suggests that he "knows" what caused the child's death; but it also suggests that he himself knows something of a father's fault. And indeed, if the child narrator of the frame narrative sees himself as repeating the dead child of the portrait (playing in the places he played, staying in the house where he lived), he also repeats the father's—Johannes's—acts without knowing it. His description of the village mentions the priest's field, the water ditch, the village church, the sexton's house—all places that are important in the second part of Johannes's story; it even refers to the garden near the village in the same way as Johannes does: the "palace garden" (compare 378; 109 and 442; 160).[14] Indeed, the *first* part of the frame narrative repeats and anticipates the *second* part of the main narrative where we see Johannes doing what the child narrator and his friend used to/will do: shuttle back and forth between the village, where the pastor's house stands, and the nearby town (where Johannes's brother and presumably the frame narrator's family live). Thus the frame narrator not only discovers and brings to light the story of Johannes and his son, but also repeats both father and son. However, since the frame narrative precedes Johannes's tale, we see *Johannes* as walking in the narrator's footsteps. The relation between past and present becomes reversible, generation gives way to a relation of affinity based on spatial proximity.

If in the first part of the frame narrative the child narrator's attraction to and affinity with the child in the portrait allows him to intuit the meaning of the inscription, in the second part of the frame, chance (or maybe the fact that he is "thinking about [his] own youth" [384; 114]) leads him to the house in town where he will find the manuscript telling of Johannes's life. This manuscript corroborates his earlier interpretation of the inscription and also tells him what neither the portrait nor the inscription did: that the guilty/faulty father is the portrait's painter. The manuscript is found in the house where, centuries before, Johannes lived with his brother and where the descendants of his sister still live. In it are objects related to Johannes's life (an oil painting, a little oak chest, the manuscript), which are transmitted, handed down, from one generation to another but are considered of no importance or value: the baker tells the narrator that he may take the manuscript with him home, adding: "It's just old papers; they have no value" (385; 115). It is the frame narrator who reads the manuscript that Johannes's heirs ignored and thus transmits it to us. It is thus the frame narrator who is Johannes's true heir, the one who accepts—and transmits—the heritage of fault/guilt that the blood relatives deny or ignore. The relation of affinity that supplements the hereditary world order makes visible the fault of the father that the genealogy ignores or hides.

Though the relation of affinity, like the genealogical relation, involves transmission, what is transmitted through it is not positive traits but rather the lack in the genealogical system. This is why this form of transmission is not one of preservation: as we shall see, the end of the story is under the sign of loss even though the story, against all odds, has been transmitted to us. But the lack of preservation has also to do with the way portraits function in this story.

As we have seen in previous chapters, a portrait can function as a substitute for its subject in the subject's absence and, by capturing the subject's likeness in a particular moment in time, arrest time and thus "immortalize" its subject. As Robert Holub has argued, Johannes's portrait of Katharina, painted in order to keep her image in her father's house after she leaves it to be married, the portrait he paints in Holland of a girl about to be married, the portrait of the village pastor commissioned by the parishioners to join the images of previous pastors—all can be seen as designed to preserve their subjects "against" death. The same is true for the landscape Johannes paints so that Katharina can have a view of her homeland while in Holland.[15] But the main portrait in the story—that of the child—and the drawing Johannes makes of Herr Gerhardus are different since they are portraits of the dead. Rather than representing a person who will eventually die while his/her image will subsist, thus "preserving" this person, keeping him/her alive, what we have here are representations of a dead person as dead, keeping him dead, eternalizing or preserving death.[16]

The importance for the story of the painting of Lazarus (the painting Johannes considers his best) derives precisely from this question of the portrait's relation to death. A portrait of a dead person as the resurrected Lazarus (which is what the brewer's widow commissions Johannes to do) would not only "preserve" that person but would also infuse the deceased "with new life," "nullify[ing] absence and death by re-representing and resuscitating" (Holub 129, 130). It would perform what it represents, would bring the dead man back to life, "resurrecting" him. But in the portrait of the dead child and the drawing of Herr Gerhardus, the dead are far from resuscitated; they are "preserved" as dead. In the picture of Lazarus, Johannes ends up producing a copy of the drawing he has made right after his patron's death. In the face of the dead Herr Gerhardus, Johannes sees a reproach for his own fault/absence: "From his shroud the dead man's face somehow looked at me in silent accusation [Aus seinem Lailach blickte des Todten Antlitz gleichwie in stummer Klage gegen mich]" (433; 153). The curious expression whereby it is the *face* that looks at him suggests that the eyes of the portrayed Gerhardus are closed: though brought back from the dead, he is dead.[17]

Treating the portraits of the dead as if they were no different than portraits of the living—as most critics dealing with Storm's story do—means failing to recognize the function of this subgenre (to register the death of a person rather than commemorating that person or immortalizing him/her) and what it actually represents (dead people lying on their deathbed, their eyes closed, their face sealed).[18] More importantly still, it means ignoring the way in which portraits of the dead challenge commonplaces about the relation between art and life, be it the view that art is superior to life, conquering, overcoming death, or the opposite view that art is inferior, "dead," merely pointing out to a life that always escapes it.

RESEMBLANCE, SUPPLEMENT, AND REALISM

In the house in town, the frame narrator finds himself in the same room where Johannes lived and wrote, and there he recognizes, in a picture hanging on the wall, the dead child from the portrait in the church. He tells us that while talking to the baker from whom he is trying to rent a room for a relative,

> My eye had fallen upon an oil painting hanging in the shadow of a wardrobe, which suddenly absorbed my whole attention. It was still well preserved and depicted an elderly man with a serious and mild gaze, in a dark costume such as had been worn in the middle of the seventeenth century by men of the better classes who were more occupied with public affairs or learned matters than with the military calling.
> Yet the old gentleman's head, as fine and attractive as it was and as felicitously as it may have been painted, would not have aroused this excitement in me; but the painter had put a pale boy in his arm, whose little, limply hanging hand held a white water lily—this boy I had long known. Here too it was doubtless death that had closed his eyes. (385; 114–15)

The resemblance that allows recognition is here not between a painting and its subject but rather between two paintings depicting a dead child: the portrait in the village church the frame narrator saw as a child and the oil painting he sees, as an adult, in the house in town. This invites us to compare the description of the child in the oil painting (quoted above) with the description of the portrait in the church, where we read:

> Among all these strange or even eerie things [seltsamen oder wohl gar unheimlichen Dingen] there hung in the nave of the church the innocent portrait of a dead child, a beautiful boy of about five, resting on a pillow decorated with lace and holding a white water lily in his small, pale hand. His delicate expression, as though pleading for help, spoke, alongside of the horror of death, of a last sweet trace of life [Aus dem zarten Antlitz sprach neben dem Grauen des Todes, wie hülfeflehend, noch eine letzte holde Spur des Lebens]. (381; 112)

Two salient features of the representation of the child in the church portrait are the position of the child, resting on a pillow decorated with lace, and the complex expression, fluctuating between life and death, the viewer reads in his face: while the child's face expresses—hence is alive—

the horror of death, it also seems to speak—as if alive, pleading for help, against death—of the last trace of life—that is, what remains after life is gone. In the oil painting, the child is taken out of his bed and put in the arms of an old man; his appealing, speaking expression gives way to eyes unambiguously closed by death. Given these differences, recognition seems to depend primarily on one feature or trait: the limply hanging hand, and, even more specifically, the white water lily it holds. The water lily is an ornament, a *parergon* in the sense that both Kant and Derrida give the term: Kant defines ornaments or ornamentation as "what is only an adjunct, and not an intrinsic constituent in the complete representation of the object" (Derrida 53). External to the human subject of the painting and in many senses inessential to the depiction of the dead child, the water lily is, by its very superfluity, the detail on which recognition of the boy as the same boy, identical to himself, depends.[19] By inviting the recognition of the boy in the oil painting as the same as the boy in the church portrait, the water lily creates a link between the oil painting that presents genealogical continuity—a grandfather holding his grandchild— and the portrait where the fault of the father is inscribed. The water lily makes that fault or lack visible: if one could recognize the true son or true father (that is, the subject of genealogy) simply by hereditarily/painterly transmitted traits, one would not need quasi-detachable signs such as the water lily to make recognition of the subject possible.

Whereas critics tend to read the water lily as an emblem that stands for the innocence of the child, Johannes has no such thoughts.[20] Having completed the portrait of his dead child, he feels as if something is still missing. He writes: "When I contemplated the empty little hands lying on the linen, I thought: 'You must at least give your child a little present!' And I painted into his hand on the portrait a white water lily, as though he had fallen asleep playing with it. Such flowers are rare around here, and so it might be a desirable gift [ein erwünschet Angebinde]" (452; 168). For Johannes, the water lily is not an emblem that stands for an essential trait; rather, it is an ornament whose main attribute is being rare, hence a desirable gift. The water lily fills in a lack—the empty hands—while at the same time it is in some sense an excess: an unnecessary ornament, an object that is added to the "real" scene Johannes sees and depicts. As a gift to the dead, it remains outside reciprocity and exchange. Therefore, though Johannes feels that he has to give his dead son something—that he owes him something—and though the water lily is the only thing he can give him, the gift makes the debt visible rather than erase it, leaving Johannes's

"Schuld"—his guilt, his fault—unpaid. This is another way in which one can read the water lily as the "trait" of the fault of the father.[21]

The frame narrator's understanding that, in the oil painting, it is the painter who put the dead child in the arms of the elderly man is correct since Herr Gerhardus had died before little Johannes was even born. Putting the dead child in the old man's arms repeats putting the water lily in the empty hand of the dead child. The dead child in the oil painting is a copy of the child in the church portrait, but the copied image is transplanted into a different context, the old man's arms, as if it too, and not only the water lily were a "quasi-detachable" object, a parergon.

As a painter, Johannes seems committed to realist representation, the faithful copying of a model present to the painter (or the copying of a copy). Though he objects to the Junker Kurt's considering him as "a machine by which a picture was painting itself on the canvas" (406; 132), his objection is not in the name of imagination and inspiration but rather in the name of his labor, his craft as a conscientious student of his master, and as someone who put to good use the investment of his patron. His art lies in the skill of composition and technique with which he depicts what he sees. But the picture of Lazarus already indicates that what one sees is not what is "objectively" there: the face of Herr Gerhardus that Johannes has conjured up is a copy of the drawing he made of his dead patron, but the expression of "silent accusation" (433; 153) on his face seems to have been added on. Clearly, it is Johannes's sense of his own "fault" that produces the expression of accusation on Herr Gerhardus's face. Similarly we can say that while Johannes depicts his son as he lies dead in front of him, holding nothing in his hands, his perception that the child's hands lack something and hence need to be filled already includes an act of interpretation, shaped by his own sense of lack (of power) and failure (to protect).

This may explain why the pastor (Johannes's double and antagonist), who has no use for art either as imitation of the real or as a product of the imagination, is moved to tears not by seeing the faithful image of the dead child he loved dearly but by the water lily that inscribes their shared fault/guilt.[22]

THE PICTURE IN THE FRAME

The relation between frame and main narrative is also broadly within the parameters of realist representation. The many details noted by the frame narrator—the portrait of the pastor in the village church, the oak chest he finds in the house in town, the linden trees—allow us to "recognize" the village and the house in town as the same ones described in Johannes's manuscript (just as the frame narrator "recognizes" the two paintings featuring the child as being of the same child). This contributes to the reader's sense that, though the two narratives are separate in time and told by two different people, they are representations of the same objective, external reality.[23] In other words, the similarity between copies would attest to the existence of the original—the same original—while also certifying each copy as a faithful representation. However, as we have already seen, removing the child from his bed and placing him in the arms of his grandfather as well as the painting of the water lily put into question both the sameness of the original (the referent) and the representation's faithfulness to the real.

The frame narrative and the main narrative appear particularly close to each other in the scene that describes the frame narrator reading Johannes's manuscript in the same room where Johannes wrote it and where some of the objects mentioned in his narrative are still present. But the way frame and main narrative corroborate each other is disrupted by the presence in the room of an oil painting that is not the same as the one Johannes had in his room while writing and that, moreover, Johannes could not have painted. Previous critics of Storm's story have systematically misread this nonexistent, impossible portrait, ignoring its difference from other portraits mentioned in the text. [24]

The painting, showing an elderly Herr Gerhardus holding the dead child in his arms—that is, representing something that could not have taken place in reality—is never mentioned in Johannes's narrative. Nor does his narrative ever mention a portrait of Herr Gerhardus as an elderly man (of which his image in the painting might be a copy). Johannes tells in his manuscript that he made a drawing of Herr Gerhardus right after he died and that he later copied this drawing unconsciously when painting the resurrection of Lazarus (433; 153). He also mentions that he copied the portrait of Herr Gerhardus as a young man ("in the most vigorous manhood" [401; 128]) from the portrait gallery in his estate and that the portrait he made later from this copy is by his side as he is writing the manuscript (402; 129). Neither one of these drawings, portraits and copies could have served as the model for the depiction of Herr Gerhardus in the oil painting, where he appears neither dead nor in vigorous manhood but as an elderly man. Thus the portrait that Johannes had at his side while writing the manuscript (Gerhardus as a young man) is not the same as the painting the narrator sees in Johannes's room while reading the manuscript (elderly Gerhardus with the dead child in his arms).

The narrator's recognition that the Herr Gerhardus about whom he reads in the manuscript is the same person as the one in the oil painting—he writes, "Here the first part of the manuscripts ends.... My eyes rested on the old picture across from me; I could not doubt that the handsome, earnest man was Lord Gerhardus" (431; 151)—this recognition is grounded in a painting absent from the manuscript. This absence is not simply an omission: Johannes starts his story right after Herr Gerhardus's death and ends it right after he painted the portrait of his dead child; his story therefore could not encompass the painting of a portrait of an elderly Herr Gerhardus or the copying of the portrait of the dead child into a painting featuring the elderly grandfather. Rather than corroborating the main narrative and thus affirming the origin of both in reality, the frame here adds what the main narrative cannot contain.

Thus the oil painting that represents genealogical continuity does not have a clear foundation either in reality or in other representations; its origin is never stated, it seems indeed to have no origin. If children resemble their parents (and especially, if sons resemble their fathers) in the same way that portraits resemble their subjects—that is, as a copy resembles an original—then the lack of origin for a painting featuring genealogical descent from father to son is the coup de grâce for both realism and paternal descent.

If in some sense the oil painting is in excess (of the real, of the manuscript), it also, and more obviously, represents a lack or an absence—that of the father. The oil painting represents a genealogical relation—Herr Gerhardus, Katharina's father, is little Johannes's grandfather—from which the father, Johannes himself, is absent. As we have seen, a painter can be present in his painting not only iconically (self-portrait) but also indexically, as the painting's cause or origin, expressed most explicitly through his signature. There is no mention of a signature in the painting's description; elsewhere, the narrator (who himself remains nameless) comments that the portrait of the dead child and that of the pastor "contained neither a name nor a painter's mark" (384; 114). The artist's name, the name of the father (the child's as well as the painting's) cannot be ascertained: "His name does not belong to those that are named; one would hardly be likely to find him in a dictionary of artists; even in his local region no one knows of a painter by his name" (455; 170). Rather than preserving the painter's name, the story and the painting transmit this absence or the fault of the father.

AQUIS SUBMERSUS

At the end of the main narrative, the frame narrator briefly comes back to tell us that all traces of Johannes's name and work have disappeared, and he ends with the words that also end the main narrative as well as provide the title for the entire story: aquis submersus. Though in this context "aquis submersus" refers generally to loss, it cannot be reduced to a lament over the passage of time and the transience of all earthly things. "Submerged in water" has a specific meaning in this story situated by the North Sea. After Johannes takes leave of his dead child and of the pastor, he hears the water: "I suddenly became conscious of something that I had never heard here before: that I was hearing the surf roaring from the distant shore. I met no one, I heard no bird calling, but from the dull surging of the sea I heard constantly, like a grim lullaby: *Aquis submersus—aquis submersus!*" (454–55; 170). What wipes things out in this story is not only time, which is present everywhere, but rather, more specifically, the water of the sea (as well as war). On his first visit to the village, the sexton tells Johannes about the great flood of 1634 that drove hundred of houses "into the fierce waters" and took many lives (437; 156). The pastor, on the other hand, after expressing his iconoclastic beliefs (his disapproval of images that help sustain "the illusion of dust [the body] . . . when the breath of God has left it," his objection to the image of Mary, which he removed from the church) moves on to what seems an unrelated topic: "He said vehemently: 'Did not the king summon the Dutch papists onto that destroyed island, only to defy the judgment of the All High with the human work of the dikes?'" He then returns to the topic of carving images of saints (438; 157). The iconoclastic pastor objects to both painted images and dikes. On one level, the connection seems to be the "papists" who both carve images and were brought to build the dikes. But on another level, the creation of images that represent the saints and the deity but also may be seen as taking their place—the creations of man taking the place of God the creator—is similar to the building of dikes where "human work" takes the place of divine creation as human beings try to protect themselves against a natural disaster that God has either ordained or failed to prevent—at any rate, failed to protect humans against it. Thus both sacred images and dikes in some sense usurp the place or power of God; or put otherwise, attempt to supplement it. The breaking of the dikes that brings about submersion by water shows that here again the supplement repeats the failure it was intended to mend.[25] By building dikes, humans acknowledge that God is not the all-powerful father protector of mankind, but their attempts to make up for His failure fail too.[26]

Sand's "Le Château de Pictordu," or the Missing Face of the Mother

George Sand's "Le Château de Pictordu" is the story of a young girl, Diane, who lives with her father, a fashionable portrait painter, and her stepmother. An accident brings her and her father to the half-ruined chateau of Pictordu. There Diane hears the voice of the Veiled Lady of the castle, who invites her in and, during the night they are forced to spend there, shows her the castle, transformed into a beautiful, living space. As she grows up and timidly pursues her desire to become a portrait painter herself, Diane is addressed again by the voice of the Veiled Lady, who finally reveals herself to be her dead, forgotten mother. Now Diane's desire to be a portrait painter becomes one with her quest to find her mother: in painting the portrait of the mother she hardly knew, Diane gives her mother a face and thus "finds" her while at the same time showing herself to be an accomplished portrait painter.

Part of Sand's *Contes d'une Grand-mère*, "Le Château de Pictordu" is a didactic fairy tale of a woman's access to art through the medium of the maternal voice. In telling this fairy tale and addressing it to her granddaughter (and through her to young women in general), Sand herself can be seen as anticipating and repeating the address of the mother (in her various manifestations) to the story's heroine, and hence assuming the mother's voice.[27] As the heroine of a Künstlerroman, however, Diane can also be read as a figure for Sand herself (though, as we shall see, a highly idealized one). The story is dedicated to Sand's granddaughter Aurore Sand, who, by her name, stands for (or repeats) both the woman—Amantine Lucile Aurore Dupin—and the writer—George Sand. In occupying simultaneously (though on different levels of the text and with different modes or degrees of figurality) the position of grandmother, mother, daughter, and granddaughter, Sand both tells and enacts a story of maternal descent and successful maternal transmission.

Such a story is not common in Sand's oeuvre and is especially different from the one she tells in her official autobiography, *Histoire de ma vie*, where she joins her own biographers in diminishing, if not outright denying, any legacy from her mother. As Naomi Schor notes, despite her denunciation of her biographers' "favoring of the more glorious paternal branch of her family tree" (with the result that "what is handed down across four generations is viewed as primarily the paternal legacy, with the maternal genetic pool serving simply as a source of renewal through crossbreeding"), Sand ended up repeating her biographers "matricidal gesture, first by devoting a disproportionate part of her text to her father's story and second by revealing the seamier sides of her mother's life, the blots on the maternal escutcheon."[28] Schor also claims that "Sand's idealist aesthetics draw their affective impetus from the idealization of her dead father" (165) and, following Freud's theory of the "family romance," argues that the reasons for that are structural rather than anecdotal: the idealization of the father is facilitated by the uncertainty of paternity whereas the certainty of maternity links the mother to the given, the real, and the material. Rather than being an object of idealization, the mother tends to become debased. Ultimately, according to Schor, the only mother that can function for Sand as the "sponsor of idealism" is an adoptive mother.

I will argue that in "Le Château de Pictordu," Sand's idealism is the result of her attempt to de-materialize the real mother so that she can become a source of inspiration and transmission. The story therefore departs considerably from the common scenario described above: the heroine's father is far from idealized, though he is not rejected either; it is the real mother rather than an adoptive one who is the object of idealization and, more specifically, it is through the mother's voice that Diane finds her vocation and becomes a successful portrait painter. That this can happen is partially due, of course, to the story being a fairy tale; but this should not be a reason to discount it since fairy tales can be seen as one form of utopian writing, describing things not as they are but as they should be, and Sand's fairy tales especially so since they often have a didactic function.

DAUGHTERS, FATHERS, AND MOTHERS

The story generates much of its meaning through relations of similarity and difference among its characters. To begin with, Diane, the heroine, is contrasted with Blanche, the young daughter of the Marquis de Pictordu, whom she meets when the coach accident that initiates the story leads her and her father, M. Flochardet, to the half-ruined chateau. Both Diane and Blanche have lost their mother and live with their father. The opposition between them is first of all one of class: between the aristocratic (but poor) Blanche and the middle-class (quite rich) Diane. But aristocracy here stands more generally for blind faith in patriarchal values: the motherless Blanche is committed to the aristocratic fetishization of descent through the male line; she has inherited and fully internalized her father's senseless pride in his name and is happy to marry an insignificant man because he is "a Pictordu, a true one, of the elder branch" (102; 290). She herself is just the means by which the father's name is perpetuated; she thus serves as a spokesperson for the valorization of a purely paternal descent where the mother has no active role (and thus can be seen as an embodiment of the biographers' view of Sand's genealogy to which I referred earlier on).

Paradoxically, though both Blanche and her father are proud of their old name, they have no understanding of or interest in the past—the half-ruined chateau and the artifacts that still survive in it hold no charm for them. Though they inherit from the past, the true "guardians" of the past are the doctor, M. Féron, who serves as a surrogate father for Diane, and Diane herself, who from the very first moment is drawn to the half-erased wall paintings in the chateau and intuits their aesthetic value. Thus in Sand's story, as in Storm's, the transmission of the past does not occur through the male bloodline.

The other structuring opposition in the story is that between two sets of parents. In a stark dichotomization we expect and accept in fairy tales, we have two opposing sets of parents: Flochardet's friend and neighbor, the doctor M. Féron, who oversees Diane's education and provides for her future, and the dead mother, through whose voice Diane is able to find her vocation, are the good parents. They are contrasted with the real father, the painter Flochardet, and the vain and shallow stepmother, Madame Laure, the bad parents.

Diane's father, M. Flochardet, is described thus by the narrator:

> Monsieur Flochardet was not more than forty years old. He had a handsome face, was amiable, rich, well-brought-up, and a very pleasing, elegant person. He had made a good deal of money painting portraits, finely finished and very fresh, which the ladies found a good likeness because they were always pictured as beautiful and young. To tell the truth, all Flochardet's portraits were alike. He had in his head a very pretty type which he painted again and again, modifying it very little. He only endeavored to render faithfully the dress and the hair of his models. These details were the only original traits of the figures [L'exactitude de ces détails constituait toute la personnalité des figures]. He excelled in imitating the shade of a dress, the movement of a ringlet of hair, the airiness of a ribbon. . . . He was not without talent. He even had a great deal of talent in his line [dans son genre]. As for originality,

genius, the perception of life as it really was [le sentiment de la vie vraie], these were things which must not be demanded of him. But then he was an undisputed success. (44–45; 227–28)

Rather than being inspired by a "vision" from within, by an idea (or ideal) to which he would seek to give form, Flochardet is driven by "a very pretty type," the type of beauty that, though "in his head," is in fact (as we find out later), the fashion at the moment (and Flochardet himself acknowledges that he is "fashion's blind servant"). This clichéd type he reproduces endlessly and almost mechanically: he has no originality, no genius. But if in painting his subjects' faces Flochardet is not following a noble, original aspiration toward an ideal of beauty, neither does he paint them realistically: unlike an unnamed "great master who would have had the impertinence to reproduce a wart or show a wrinkle" (45; 228), Flochardet removes all individual marks, considered as flaws, from the faces in his portraits; his fame derives from flattering his subjects by painting them "embellis et rajeunis" (45). While idealist aesthetics condemns the depiction in portraits of such particularities as warts and wrinkles as slavish imitation of the real that fails to grasp the subject's "soul," his/her character or "essence," in Flochardet's portraits the omission of such details yields nothing but standardization and anonymity. But though he does not paint the faces of his subjects realistically, Flochardet is still a realist artist in one important respect: he imitates faithfully and with great skill his subjects' clothes and hairdo: "L'exactitude de ces détails constituait toute la personnalité des figures." The clichéd ideal of beauty he imposes on his subjects makes them all look alike; their individuality (or personality) resides in their accoutrements, objects of consumption and display, which are painted with an extreme attention to detail we may well call fetishistic. The clothes take the place of the person, who has disappeared under the equalizing power of a cliché. Thus the idealized representation of the face is here a cliché dictated by fashion rather than an ideal that expresses the originality of its painter, and realistic representation serves not to highlight the individuality of each subject but, rather, is manifested in the fetishization of details of material objects where "reality" now appears to reside. The critique of Flochardet as a portrait painter could not have been any harsher.[29]

Flochardet's second wife is in many respects the right wife for him—though this is something that is never made explicit in the story. She is interested in what he paints best—clothes and hairdo—and shares his (implied) belief that it is clothes that make the person and hence are more important than their bearer. Unlike Diane and the doctor, they both believe that painting is sheer "work," rather than a vocation, and that work of all sorts is mere necessity, to be avoided if possible. Flochardet's neglect of Diane's education and his insistence that she should not concern herself with painting to earn money also accord with his second wife's view that women's only goal in life is to be decorative.

But while Madame Laure is subject to constant and open critique in the story, the similarities between her and Flochardet remain unmarked both by Diane (who loves her father dearly) and by the narrator (who openly criticizes Flochardet as a painter). Since the story is presented as a fairy tale, we tend to attribute all of Madame Laure's faults to her being a stereotypical evil stepmother. Thus the figure of the stepmother enables both Sand and Diane to be critical of the father's values without, however, criticizing or disapproving of him directly. Whatever else the daughter does, she does not explicitly condemn her father, does not dethrone him. As we shall see, this does not mean that she accepts the father's judgment and abides by his law.

Eventually Diane will see both her "fathers" as lacking, and this will, paradoxically, neutralize the critique of both: "Diane knew that the doctor, who had some good critical ideas, understood nothing of the method in painting [n'entendait rien à l'exécution].... She knew also that her father had a method entirely opposed to the theories of the doctor, that he could never judge favorably what was outside his own style, and without meaning to be was quite capable of being unjust.... What ought she to think of her father's talent which the doctor criticized with so much apparent justice? And what ought she to think of the criticisms of the doctor who was incapable of holding a crayon or of drawing a line?" (80; 265–66). Whereas in Storm's story, the "lack" in/of the father—his absence and powerlessness—is repeated in/by his surrogates, here the lack in the father figures means that they complement each other: Diane learns much of her technique by watching her father paint and develops her taste and understanding with the help of the doctor.

But though both fathers contribute to her becoming a painter, ultimately their teaching can come to fruition only through the voice of the mother. Diane does not consider her fathers as obstacles on her way to fulfill her dream (the doctor actively and judiciously supports her), nor does she dismiss them altogether; and yet without the intervention of the mother she cannot reach her goal. The relation between the role of the mother and that of the father is mapped, as is often the case, on the opposition between what is given by nature and what is acquired by learning, each here complementing the other. The ability to paint is presented as an innate talent (the real father thinks Diane does not have any, and the doctor says that she is a born artist [67; 253]), but it is also an art that needs to be learned. Learning itself, however, is not sufficient, and it needs the intervention of the mother to be put to good use. But then, again, the "gift" of the mother is not outright—it cannot be actualized without an effort on the part of its recipient. We have to remember that if "Le Château de Pictordu" is a fairy tale, it is also a Künstlerroman, a genre that always tells the story of an effort (rather than of outright gifts).[30] Thus the strict opposition between what is given (by nature) and what is acquired (by education) is undermined, with the result that the mother partakes of both. The real mother does not stand for what is inescapably given and hence can be the source of her daughter's ability to create.

Nor is the real mother presented as the archaic figure with whom the daughter seeks to merge. The mother first appears through the figure of the Veiled Lady, whose home is the chateau of Pictordu and at whose invitation Diane and her father enter the chateau. The part of the chateau where father and daughter stop is the pavilion of the baths, modeled after Roman baths and named "Le Bain de Diane." Thus Diane is "chez elle" in a chateau that is also the home of the figured mother: this, then, is her maternal "home." By having Diane discover her maternal home at the very beginning of the tale, Sand suggests that this cannot be the end/goal of Diane's quest. And indeed, once Diane's quest reaches its end (when she discovers/creates her mother's face by painting her portrait), she has no use for Pictordu any more, has no desire to possess it. The appearance of the maternal figures does not lead to a return to the home/womb, a regressive fusion with the mother, and loss of difference.

FROM VOICE TO FACE: THE PORTRAIT

Both the statue of the Veiled Lady that Diane hears inviting her in and the painting of the dancer that becomes animated and detached from the wall of the chateau are faceless: the lady is veiled and the dancer's face has been obliterated. The obliteration of the face here is not the result of standardization and stereotyping, as in the father's portraits, but rather of the passage of time and the work of the elements. Seeing the faceless, broken, or fragmented figures requires one, as M. Flochardet puts it, to "view them with the eyes of faith" (65; 250), which he himself is incapable of doing. Thus the faceless figures function already as an invitation to Diane to create by herself the missing face of her mother, imagine it rather than take it as a given.

The association of the voice of the faceless Veiled Lady with that of the missing, forgotten mother comes about through the mediation of the stepmother, who also affects Diane through the medium of the voice. In chapter 5, Diane overhears her stepmother maligning her mother, saying that she, Diane, "takes after her mother, who was a common person and more occupied looking after her kitchen than in making a good appearance and having good manners [bon air et bon ton]" (70; 256). "Common," that is, of lower-class origin, and at home in the kitchen—here is the mother de-idealized, "materialized" (though we should note that what is opposed to this supposed materiality of the mother is conventional behavior, "bon air et bon ton" rather than a lofty ideal). This view of the mother is not only discredited (since it comes from the shallow and vain stepmother); casting it as the impetus for Diane's search for her mother's face indicates that her creation/discovery of her real/ideal mother is meant as a rebuttal of the view of the mother as material and debased.

The stepmother's harsh words cause Diane to consciously feel, for the first time, the loss of her mother. Her anguished call—"Mamma! Mamma"—produces a response: "Diane, my dear Diane, my child, where are you?" (72; 258). Following the voice, Diane continues to hear but cannot see her mother. Later on, a veiled figure, whom she recognizes as her "good fairy" and who identifies herself as the mother—"your mother? . . . I am she" (74; 261)—finally appears; she is faceless. She tells Diane: "you will see it [my face, *ma figure*] the day you give it back to me [Tu la verras le jour où tu me la rendras]" (76; 261).

Diane is now on a quest to give her mother her face and thus confronts the problem of painting a portrait. She feels unequal to the task because she knows that she cannot paint like her father. She tells the doctor: "I look at how my father sets about improving his models, for it's certain that he beautifies them. . . . In my mind, I paint them as they are, and it's clear to me that if I knew how to paint, I'd do it just the contrary to the way papa does it" (81; 267). Since Diane presents herself here as a painter who paints things as they are, copying the real—a common view of the female artist—the doctor, who wants to help her in her search for her mother's face, tells her that her father has "a very good half-miniature of [the] mother, and very like her" (81; 268) and that he will get it for her. The implication is that Diane will be able to find the mother's face by copying the portrait, copying a copy.

The doctor also tells Diane that the half-miniature portrait was not painted by her father and that the latter does not like it "because its style is the opposite of his own. He does not show it to anyone and maintains that it isn't like her at all" (81; 268). The reason for hiding the portrait is not, then, the common one: a secret concerning the dead mother, her materiality/sexuality, her being the opposite of the ideal woman—a whore or an adulterous wife—as it is, for example in Sand's *Le Péché de Monsieur Antoine*.[31] Rather, in hiding the portrait, Flochardet hides his own inadequacy as a painter in the place where traditionally his skill counted most: the painting of the beloved woman as the ideal, the muse, whose beauty is the source of his art and whose portrait is the expression of his genius.

While the doctor gives Diane the half-miniature portrait of the mother, formerly hidden by her father, the mother/Veiled Lady, appearing to Diane in her dream, tells her to look for her (the mother's) likeness among the graved stones and pieces of mosaic that cover the ground of Pictordu: "Try to find my face," she tells her; "It should be there; it's your task to recognize it" (82; 269). Diane finally finds "a transparent cornelian stone, on which was cut in dim white an ideally beautiful profile [un profile d'une beauté idéale]" (83; 269). The voice declares that yes, "It is indeed I, your muse, your mother," but before Diane can lift the fairy's veil, she disappears, and with her the cameo (83; 270). What Diane is left with, then, is the memory trace of an ideal beauty she saw in a dream. It is this ideal vision that she will end up drawing.

Diane, indeed, does not look at the miniature portrait. Rather than copying it, she draws "mechanically," while thinking about her mother.[32] When she looks at what she has drawn, she recognizes in it the image from the cameo of her dream, which is also the face of the Veiled Lady who now appears to her without a veil (91; 278). But the drawing is also (like) the portrait of her mother, though, as the father puts it, "very much more expressive and better done. The likeness is more noble and truer" (90; 277). Summoning again in her mind the "ideal figure" of her dream, Diane looks at the miniature portrait for the first time and recognizes in it "the same face she had drawn. It was the muse, it was the cameo, it was the dream, and it was her mother." A synthesis has been achieved between representing the real as it is and capturing the ideal: "It was reality found through poetry, sentiment and imagination" (92; 279).

Diane's painting of her mother's portrait is a literalization of prosopopeia, the rhetorical figure whose function is "to confer a mask or a face" and which Paul de Man introduced into literary discussion in his essay "Autobiography as De-Facement." A short detour into de Man's essay will allow us to sharpen our understanding of Sand's textual strategy in this tale. De Man sees prosopopeia as the trope of autobiography but also argues that autobiography is not a genre or a mode but "a figure of reading or of understanding that occurs, to some extent, in all texts" (70). That figure is the "mutual reflexive substitution" between "the two subjects involved in the process of reading," a substitutive exchange that in fact "constitutes the subject." In autobiography—a text in which "the author declares himself the subject of his own understanding"—this specular structure is interiorized, and thus thematized (70). Since, however, this "specular moment" reveals "the tropological structure that underlies all cognition," the interest of autobiography is that "it demonstrates in a striking way the impossibility of closure and of totalization (that is the impossibility of coming into being) of all textual systems made up of tropological substitutions" (71). Prosopopeia, as the figure of (or for) autobiography, is defined by de Man as "the fiction of an apostrophe to an absent, deceased, or voiceless entity, which posits the possibility of the latter's reply and confers upon it the power of speech. Voice assumes mouth, eye, and finally a face.... Prosopopeia is the trope of autobiography, by which one's name ... is made as intelligible and memorable as a face" (75–76). However, the specularity of the moment of giving face means that "by making the death [*sic*] speak ... the living are struck dumb, frozen in their own death" (78).

In Sand's story, prosopopeia functions quite differently since voice, face, and name cannot be seen as part of one chain of substitution where each term functions as the signifier or the signified of another term. The voice initially comes from the statue of the Veiled Lady who first addresses Diane. Face does not follow, is not "assumed," or derived from voice. Diane herself, when awake, is puzzled about the ability of the faceless statue to speak, "How had she talked? She had no mouth, she had no face [elle n'avait pas de figure]" (53; 236). But the voice remains faceless until Diane gives it a face; and then it fades out. Voice and face remain separate. As to name: it is never made "intelligible as a face" since the mother's name is never given. Diane herself does not attach much importance to the name. Looking at the perfect, engraved face of young Bacchus she found in Pictordu, she does not read in that face the name of its author/painter. On the contrary, as she prepares to paint her first portrait, she addresses the face, saying: "Dear little god ... you have helped to reveal life in art to me. Inspire me, now! Teach me the secret of truth which a great unknown artist has put into you. I am willing to be unknown as he is, if like him I leave behind something beautiful like you" (100; 287). Name and face are and remain separate too.

Thus in Sand's text, Diane's prosopopeia does not entail the series of substitutions that de Man finds in the texts he analyzes. There is a prosopopeia, a giving of face, but the face does not derive from voice and does not imply a name. One consequence of this lack of alignment among terms is that the two subjects involved in the prosopopeia are not in a specular relation (that would constitute them as subjects): the living subject confers a face on the dead, but the dead has voice that precedes the face. The lack of specularity is related to the difference in emphasis in Sand's text: at issue in her text is not an act of understanding or self-understanding (and its failure) but an act of creation defined as a positing of what is (also) real. Or, as J. Hillis Miller puts it in another context, a creation that "against reason, [is] both constative and performative."[33] The text then is overtly and explicitly rhetorical and assumes the consequences of its own rhetoricity (for example, lack of totalization: voice, face, and name do not constitute a whole). The shift in emphasis away from cognition is most explicit in the scene in which Diane sees the sunrise (to be discussed below) and where the light of the sun definitely does not stand for Diane's coming to know (herself or her mother): we are not within "the cognitive, solar system of specular self knowledge" (de Man 78). It is worth noting, however, that though the emphasis on rhetoricity can be hailed as demystifying, showing language to produce the referent it represents, it also, by the same token, undermines the text's claim to truth and knowledge and thus risks diminishing its authority (a situation similar to the one we have discussed in the conclusion to chapter 3). Thus Sand has to negotiate between rejecting/adhering to the Law of the Father and losing/retaining the authority that this law confers.

Aesthetics and Ethics

During the night Diane spends in Pictordu, the Veiled Lady makes it possible for her to see what others cannot see—the chateau in all its beauty. The chateau stands for the art of the past—it belongs to "le temps des Valois" (the Renaissance), which itself harked back to the Greco-Roman tradition. That only Diane can see the beauty of the chateau suggests her intuitive appreciation for an art that her father and the society of his time fail to appreciate; Diane's coming to her own as an artist will coincide with a change in taste that brings (a new version of) this art back to life. But the chateau does not stand only for an aesthetic ideal. What Diane sees during the night and the others cannot see is "things as they should be [les choses telles qu'elles doivent être]" (52; 235). The ideal, opposed to daytime "reality," to what everyone sees, to what is commonly accepted, is here not simply an aesthetic ideal; rather, it also answers a moral imperative.

When Diane for the first time consciously feels the loss of her mother (after she hears her stepmother maligning her), her nurse tells her that the death of the mother is "a misfortune which [she] must overcome for [her]self by always being as good and as well-behaved as if she [the mother] were looking at [her]" (73; 259–60). In other words, the loss of the mother has to be made up for by internalizing her gaze, and this is what produces both morality and good manners. But the mother here has no gaze since she is faceless; she will have a face, and thus a gaze, only when her daughter gives it to her. On the other hand, Diane is already "toujours bonne et sage." In fact, she is a perfect child, a perfect daughter, reasonable, cheerful, undemanding, caring for others—the ideal, idealized child. By the end of the story we (as well as Diane) realize that the maternal voice is in fact an internal voice: as the voice puts it, it is a "maternal spirit [âme] who watches within you and over you [qui veille en toi et sur toi]" (110; 298); after all, everything Diane saw and heard was the product of her own dreams and imagination. Positing a voice that is subsequently understood as maternal is but a way for Diane to articulate (and authorize) her own sense of "things as they should be." The mother's voice is thus both the cause and the effect of Diane's moral sense, just as the mother's face is both found and produced by her. In this tale, then, a woman has a strong moral sense whose origin is not a censorious or punishing gaze (the superego, the paternal law) but rather her relation with a mother who is both real and imagined.

Whereas Diane's association with the maternal moon is emphasized in her first visit to Pictordu (where she finds herself in the baths of Diane and observes the waxing and waning of the moon), the last chapter, describing her last visit to Pictordu, is under the sign of the sun. Going to see the sunrise from the top of a mountain, Diane has an epiphany: "For the first time Diane experienced the intoxication of color" (112; 300). Though the sun of the end contrasts with the moon of the beginning, Diane does not see in the sun the father, the logos, reason or law—all common metaphorical meanings of the sun. Rather, her discovery of color allows her to differentiate herself from her father, whose faulty vision now becomes clear to her: "Her father had often spoken to her of *neutral tones*. 'Father,' she cried involuntarily, as if he had been there, 'there are no neutral tones.

I swear to you that there aren't any!'" (112; 300). Leaving the mountain, Diane, who up to now has not used oil paint, feels that "she would be able to paint without ceasing to draw" (112; 301); the traditional opposition between color (matter) and the drawn line (that which gives form and hence meaning) is overcome. Finding her own vision and acknowledging her difference from her father do not mean giving up either drawing or what she has learned from her father. Differing from the father (rather than trying to imitate him) does not mean rejecting him.

The discovery of color is the last step in Diane's apprenticeship in art, which is also a moral education. The last time the maternal voice speaks to Diane, she tells her that there is no conflict between her artistic aspirations and her sense of moral obligation toward others. Diane links her acceptance of her moral obligations toward her father and stepmother to her discovery of color. Addressing the voice for the last time, she says: "You told me to return smiling to the prison of duty. I promised you, and behold, today I have made an intoxicating conquest in art. . . . I have acquired a new power" (113; 301). Here, as elsewhere in Sand, the desire of the individual (here to become an artist) is not separate from the concern for and care of others (and Diane will later on help other young women become artists).[34] But if Diane remains a woman who cares for the welfare of others, as well as a dutiful, loving daughter, it is not because she is forced (or chooses) to subordinate herself to her father's law. Rather, following the voice of the created/discovered mother, she finds her own mode of artistic creation (different than his) and sees it as inseparable from an ethical commitment. It is this moral commitment to others, so different from her father's moral neutrality, that binds her to him.[35]

As a portrait story, "Le Château de Pictordu" shows Diane achieving the perfect "double vision" articulated by Henry James (which I discussed in chapter 2): the portrait is literally that of the artist's "vision" (a tracing of an image she saw in a dream) while at the same time it is also a true likeness. While the portrait's resemblance to the half- miniature attests to its likeness to the original—the real subject—its superiority over the half-miniature shows the temper and quality of the artist's effort (to use again James's vocabulary). The presence of the artist in the portrait, however, does not diminish or problematize the portrait's status as a true likeness. The didactic nature of the fairy tale allows us to read this achievement allegorically rather than simply as the result of "magic" (what is possible in fairy tales but not in reality): it stands for the possibility for a woman to both create and discover her mother—idealize the real mother—and for that mother, therefore, to become her muse, what enables her to create. At the same time it is of course telling that Sand cannot represent this possibility except through a fairy tale.

That the mother is absent and faceless means that with all her reality she is not entirely given; she is both discovered and created by her artist daughter. She is not, and should not be reduced to, simply matter. Or, alternatively (though Sand does not say this), matter itself should not be seen as simply given; it is, rather, produced by a layered history of acts of positing. Thus, it can and should be the subject for new and contestatory acts of positing, creating and/as discovering.[36] The absent, faceless mother who manifests herself only as a voice is also, of course, Sand the narrator, who thus encourages her daughters-readers to create/discover *her* as their enabling muse.

Written at the same time period, though in countries with different sociopolitical histories, "Aquis submersus" and "Le Château de Pictordu" register a "crisis of paternity" brought about by challenges to hereditary power, following the French Revolution. The painters in both these texts are contrasted with representatives of the landed, hereditary nobility to which they themselves do not belong and whose authority they question. The two stories, then, are concerned (in different ways and to different degree) with the way class relations inflect the power to represent. We have encountered the question of class already in other texts. It was clearly articulated in Balzac's novella, where the aristocratic painter Sommervieux was opposed to Augustine and her merchant family; we have seen it in James's "Glasses," where Flora's and the painter-narrator's precarious social standing is opposed to that of Lord Iffield, and in "The Tone of Time" in the role the portrait is supposed to play in establishing Mrs. Bridgenorth's social standing. It is present also in Hardy's story in the opposition between Lord Uplandtowers and the commoner Edmond Willowes.

A comparison with Balzac's text can shed some light on Storm's. In Balzac, the difference between Sommervieux and the Guillaumes is articulated through a series of binary oppositions that together create a coherent paradigm. Besides the basic oppositions artist/merchant and aristocracy/bourgeoisie, this paradigm includes the oppositions outside/inside, light/darkness, freedom/rules, artifice/simplicity, spirit/matter, among others. The attributes on each side of the opposition are consistent with each other, and so the opposition has internal coherence. Defined by one or the other set of terms, Sommervieux and the Guillaumes occupy clear and coherent ideological positions that render their actions intelligible and account for the difference between them, including the power differential (determined also, in the case of Augustine, by gender).

In Storm's story, things are less neatly parsed. The conflict at the center of the first part of the story is due to the class difference between the painter Johannes and the Junkers Wulf and Kurt. Johannes's lowly birth was not an impediment to his success as a portrait painter in Holland, where his skill and hard work gained him recognition among the nonhereditary elite he painted and who themselves had come to power through their skill and hard work. By contrast, the Junkers on the Gerhardus estate hold him in contempt both because of his lowly birth and because he is a painter: he is a hired hand, a manual laborer; worse yet, his hand is likened to a machine. As a "realist" painter who attempts to faithfully represent what is in front of him, who is concerned with the practical sides of his profession—getting his easel set, commissioning the frame, getting paid for his work—rather than with inspiration or even aesthetics, and whose claim for recognition is predicated on the merit of his labor (his body) rather than his imagination or spirit, Johannes is all too immersed in the material world so that his being a painter reinforces rather than modifies his low-class origin. From this perspective, a painter who strives to transcend the real, who rather than copying "manually" or "mechanically" creates through his vision and imagination, could be viewed as attempting to remove himself from the material, associated with lower class, and thus achieving a higher social status. But though Johannes has social aspirations, he is not this kind of painter. At the same time, the Junkers who oppose his low birth with their aristocratic descent are not associated with culture, sentiments, light, and the spirit; on the contrary. Since what defines their aristocratic status is a firm belief in "blood," they are constantly associated with the body and the material: food and drink, animals (the bloodthirsty dogs). It is rather the lowly born Johannes, as well as Herr Gerhardus and Katharina, who valorize an affinity of the spirit that does not depend on blood.

In the second part of the novella, the main conflict is between Johannes and the austere pastor. The pastor, who was formerly a soldier, who looks more like a soldier than like a preacher (434; 154), has become a soldier of God (435; 155). Though he is of lowly birth, he is similar to the Junkers, who are associated with physical violence and with the invading army of Sweden. At the same time, his religion is a clear negation of things of the earth, and therefore of both the body and of art. His opposition to art is that "art has always dallied with the world" (438; 157), that is, art according to him promotes the flesh, the material, rather than the spirit. But the pastor's desire to annihilate both art and the body and his rejection of the material is associated not with a spiritual dimension but with violence (the destruction of the image of Mary, his assistance in the burning of the dead woman presumed to be a witch); hence his similarity to the Junkers, in spite of their class difference. Thus the coherent ideological position that allowed Johannes to thrive as a painter in Holland comes apart when he goes back to Schleswig-Holstein and is confronted first with the Junkers and then the pastor, and this may account for his ultimate failure to survive as a painter: though he showed great promise, all his works are lost and his name is forgotten.

In Sand's story, as in Storm's, the belief in an aristocracy defined by blood is discredited (here through the figure of Blanche de Pictordu), and the superiority of a nobility of the spirit or of the mind is affirmed, primarily through the figure of the doctor. But in Sand the class opposition does not result in a conflict. Though Diane thinks Blanche is misguided in her aristocratic pride, she ends up helping her improve her financial situation (thanks to knowledge she has acquired from the doctor). The class question emerges, rather, in the attempt of the stepmother to badmouth the dead mother by presenting her as belonging to a lower class—being "common." The association of materiality (in this case, the kitchen) with both the lower class and women means that Sand's attempt to dematerialize the mother entails refusing to consider the possibility of her being of lower class. Likewise, Sand's vindication of the mother as both real and ideal means that her narrative has to stay away from the body. Though the description of the figures Diane sees in her first visit to Pictordu mentions their arms and legs—their full body—these are left behind when the disembodied voice of the mother tells Diane to find the mother's face. In other words, the only way for Sand to posit the mother as a source of transmission and inspiration is to bracket any reference to her class origin and her body; though she invites us to rethink the mother's materiality she herself cannot do it.

CHAPTER 7

Gogol, "The Portrait"

Gogol's "The Portrait" (1835; 1842) is a double story, told backward: in its second part, it tells of an old painter who paints the portrait of a mysterious, diabolic moneylender, with terrible consequences to himself and others; in its first part, it tells of a young painter named Chartkov (Chertkov in the 1835 version), who, many years later, buys this same portrait and his life is changed for the worse.[1] The story presents in an especially forceful way two of the commonplaces about portraits: its entire plot depends on the idea that a portrait "extends" a person's life, re-presenting him or her after death. At the same time, the harm that the portrait causes to both painters is explained in part through the common understanding of portraiture as a "worldly," degraded art.

But Gogol's story is also very different from all the other stories I have discussed in this book. Neither the old painter's encounter with the moneylender nor Chartkov's encounter with the portrait and his subsequent career in society produce the kind of intersubjective relations and plots we have found in other portrait stories. This is because, as critics have argued, the world Gogol describes in his works is one devoid of interpersonal relations (no love intrigues, no family relations, no friendships).[2]

"The Portrait" can be read as revolving around one relation: that of rivalry, manifesting itself as the feeling of envy.[3] Envy here is not so a much a desire to possess an object that belongs to another (or that another desires); rather, it is spite and resentment at the success of others and the desire to ruin it. The emphasis, moreover, is on the way this feeling affects its subject, rather than on the interpersonal relation with the envied other or others. It thus remains curiously "intransitive" (not interpersonal). At the same time, this envy affects everybody who comes into contact with the moneylender or his portrait so that rather than being a personal feeling, it appears general or even abstract.

The paradox of a portrait—a form of representation centered on a particular individual—generating a plot that is general and abstract can be explained by the main conceit of the story: that the diabolical moneylender who is the subject of the portrait is the "money devil," an allegorical representation (that is, an abstraction) of the evil of money—the universal equivalent par excellence.[4] The story about this portrait, I will argue, is a story about the relation between money and representation, about money as representation.[5]

Portrait and Money

The idea that a portrait can extend the life of its sitter is expressed clearly when the moneylender, in the story's second part, asks the painter to paint his portrait since he feels he is about to die: "I want you to paint my portrait. I don't know, but I may possibly be dead soon. I have no children and I don't want to die completely. I want to live. Can you paint a portrait that will look alive in every detail?" (149). Whereas in other tales, painting a portrait is often seen as endangering its subject, bringing about its death, this is not quite the point in Gogol's story.[6] It is true that the moneylender dies, but it is precisely the knowledge that he is about to die that prompts him to have his portrait painted: the portrait will extend his life. Thus, when the old painter decides not to finish the portrait, the moneylender begs him to continue, "pleading that his fate and his continued existence in the world depended on it" (150). And indeed, the portrait, even though unfinished, succeeds in extending the subject's presence beyond his natural life, as the evil effect the moneylender has had on all those who entered in contact with him continues after his death through the portrait. The painter is but the first to be affected by the portrait's power, which extends that of its original in time and space, affecting all those who possess or even view it.

The spread of the moneylender's evil influence through the medium of the portrait suggests an analogy between money and portraiture. This analogy is thematized in the first part of the story when Chartkov discovers the gold coins hidden in the frame of the portrait: the evil effect the portrait has on him is the evil effect of money. Such an analogy between portrait and money is not surprising given that money has always been a medium for portraiture. The function of the portrait of a ruler on a coin is that of representing *in absentia* the authority and power of the ruler who issued the coin (or of the community he represents) since it can be used—indeed, so that it could be used—far away and after the death of the person represented on it. The portrait of the moneylender functions in the way portraits on coins (and on paper money) function: they extend the power of their portrayed subject in time and place by abstracting it. It is important to note, however, that in Gogol's story, while the moneylender's power is extended by being abstracted, the portrait is also equated with its subject: the portrait *is* the moneylender, not simply his representation, since it has the same effect on those who come in contact with it as did the moneylender himself. The indexical relation of the portrait to its subject is neither severed nor weakened by its extension in time and space. Indeed, this is one of the peculiarities of the portrait as an indexical sign: whereas in other cases (such as that of the weather vane, for example) the indexical sign is co-temporal and co-spatial with what it signifies, the very function of the portrait is to overcome this limitation and to render present the absent subject (or an aspect of this subject).[7]

There is a difference between the story's two versions as to whether or not the power of the portrait will perpetuate itself endlessly. In the first version, the maleficent portrait is metamorphosed, at the end of the second part, into an insignificant landscape, whereas in the second version it disappears, having been probably stolen from the auction house while everybody was engrossed in listening to the narrator's tale about the old painter. Critics agree that the overall difference between the first and second version is that the former emphasizes the supernatural, while the latter is more realistic.[8] It therefore makes sense that in the first version, where the old painter literally identifies the moneylender as the Antichrist, a proper act of exorcism, performed at the right time—"when fifty years had passed, at the time of the new moon" (1, 277)—would eliminate the evil power of the portrait. In this version, the events involving Chertkov, told in the story's first part, must have taken place at a certain point between the main narrative of the second part (the story of the old painter) and its frame narrative (the appearance in the auction house of the old painter's son, who narrates this story). The end of the second part, with the portrait morphing into an insignificant landscape, is thus also the end of the story. On the other hand, in the rational/realistic world of the second version, where the portrait disappears through a banal theft, the portrait would continue to circulate and spread its evil.[9] In this version, the relation between the different parts of the story is less certain. If one assumes that the first part, dealing with Chartkov, follows the frame narrative of the second part, the portrait that disappeared from the auction house will eventually end up in Chartkov's hands so that its circulation and efficacy have not been arrested or exhausted. But even if we assume that the order of the parts is the same in the second version as in the first, the portrait's circulation will continue since it has merely disappeared rather than changed into an innocuous landscape. Thus in the "real," "rational" world, the power of the portrait, like that of money, cannot be obliterated.

The story, however, suggests an analogy not only between portraits and money but also, more specifically, between portraits and moneylending (or usury). When he asks the old painter to do his portrait, the moneylender explicitly refers to his being childless, suggesting that the portrait serves as a substitute for children, is an artificial rather than a natural way of extending one's life. Ever since Aristotle, lending money with interest—usury—was considered an unnatural breeding, opposed to natural procreation. As scholars have pointed out, the word Aristotle used to indicate interest yielded from moneylending—*tokos*—means both offspring and usury: money "bred" through usury is an unnatural offspring.[10] In the first version of the story we are told that the old painter, who was often in need of money, could have had it by borrowing from the moneylender or by painting portraits; he is about to ask the moneylender for a loan when he is asked to paint his portrait (1, 262). Thus an analogy is established between taking a loan and painting a portrait. The evil that the portrait produces should be attributed, then, not only to the portrait's sitter—the diabolic moneylender—whose life is extended through the portrait but also to the painter's willingness to portray him (or to borrow money from him) and to the very act of portraying, which, like usury, is seen as an unnatural breeding or production. It is significant that after he atones for the sins he committed under the influence of the moneylender/portrait, the old painter paints a picture representing the

Nativity, thus opposing supernatural birth to unnatural begetting, and eikon to portrait.[11]

In the story's first part, the moneylender appears only through his portrait. When Chartkov finds the gold coins in the portrait's frame, he surmises that the money in the frame might have been hidden there by "some grandfather [who] might have wished to leave his grandson a present," and he later "apostrophise[s] the portrait mentally, 'I don't know whose grandfather you are'" (113). The money Chartkov gets from the portrait, however, is not money passed on through natural begetting and succession; from its effects we know that it is the money of the usurer—who is neither a grandfather nor a father. Chartkov's error brings to the fore a difference between money grounded in natural begetting and succession and its opposite, money produced through usury.

With the money he finds in the portrait, Chartkov becomes a successful portrait painter. The demand for his portraits increases and this multiplication of orders and of portraits (127) resembles the miraculous growth, through interest, of the moneylender's wealth (more elaborated in the first version [1, 260]) and thus the growth of capital, its self-generation independent of a material base (goods, land). Chartkov's fame is self-generating and ungrounded, and eventually, rather than seeking fame, he starts amassing gold. As the narrator explains: "Fame cannot give pleasure to a man who has stolen it, to one who does not deserve it. . . . For this reason all his feelings and desires became obsessed with gold" (129). The relation between his portrait painting and the self-generation of money is highlighted in the scene of his agony and madness, where portraits are multiplied endlessly and they all have the eyes of the moneylender. This is probably the clearest instance in the text where "magic" growth or begetting links together portraits and usury: "He [Chartkov] began to be haunted by the long-forgotten, living eyes of the strange portrait. . . . The portrait was doubled and quadrupled before his eyes; all the walls seemed to be hung with portraits. . . . the room widened and lengthened endlessly to make room for more and more of those staring eyes" (136).[12]

Usury, however, can be understood not only as a diabolic multiplication and self-begetting of money out of money but also in terms of lack of adequation or equivalence. Usury is a deviation from what according to canonical law is the only authorized loan: one in which the amount lent and the amount paid back are the same. This even exchange means that there is neither excess nor lack; a loan with interest, on the other hand, produces "perverted" excess (and hence implies a corresponding lack).

Thus while portraits on/and money produce an extension of power in time and place, increase power through abstraction, portraits and usury are considered as unnatural breeding or reproduction and a disturbance of adequation through excess.

When Chartkov looks at the portrait, he feels that the portrait looks at him "with human eyes" (102) and that the eyes in/of the portrait are so "real" that "they seemed to have been cut out of a living man and put in there" (103). But the effect of this feat of realism is to "destroy the harmony of the portrait itself" (102–3); there seems to be an excess of realism here. At the same time, Chartkov's immediate association is with the story he heard from his professor about a portrait by Leonardo da Vinci that the artist thought of as unfinished (though others considered it a masterpiece): "The most finished thing about it was the eyes ... even the tiniest, hardly visible veins in them were not overlooked and were reproduced on the canvas" (102). The similarity between the portrait of the moneylender and Leonardo's painting is not only in the extreme accuracy of the depiction of the eyes but also in that they are both considered unfinished. We are not told exactly what it means that either one of them is unfinished: does it mean that part of the figure is not painted? That what is painted is not detailed enough? Or does it mean that it is very detailed but the details are not integrated into a whole? Be it as it may, in both cases a highly realistic depiction is judged unfinished by its painter: it clearly lacks something. At the same time, it also has something in it that exceeds certain limits and destroys "harmony."

That the hyperrealistic imitation of the eyes is "no longer art" (102) but life suggests that the portrait bears the trace of a transgressive desire to create life rather than merely imitate it (or by imitating it). This idea is further developed in the first version, when Chertkov continues his musings: "Does the highest art bring a man up to the line beyond which he captures what cannot be created by human effort, and snatches something living from the life animating his model? Why is the overstepping of the line, ordained as the limit for the imagination, so awful?" (I, 223). The second possibility he entertains is that "awful reality" intervenes as an "external shock" that throws the imagination off balance so that while the artist looks for "what is fine in man," he ends up discovering "what is revolting in man": the transcendent aspirations of the imagination are demolished by the eruption of the real. Finally he proposes the possibility that "too close an imitation of nature [is] as sickly as a dish that has too sweet a taste": the problem with the close imitation of reality may be that it is, paradoxically, excessive (I, 223).[13] In the second version, Chartkov's musings start where the first version left off—with the problem of hyperrealism, which is now seen as possibly "an offense that ... affect[s] you like a loud, discordant scream": rather than being adequate to the real, faithful imitation of nature, it creates a discord, lacks harmony. Next he thinks that the problem may be that painting reality "objectively and coolly" results in confronting "terrible reality" since it lacks "the light of some deep, hidden, unfathomable thought." This idea will have its equivalent, later in the passage, in the observation that "a landscape in nature, however beautiful it may be," seems to be missing something "if there is no sun in the sky" (103). The lack in realistic representation may be the lack of feeling or thought in the painter (deemed necessary for objective representation) or it may be a lack in the represented world itself—the lack of light, of spirit, knowledge, logos.

It would be a mistake to try to reconstruct a coherent reflection on representation from these two passages. What they register, to my mind, is a certain crisis in the understanding of representation as adequation. Whether he tries to transcend the real through the imagination or faithfully reproduces the real, the painter fails to produce an image that is "adequate"—neither excessive nor lacking. The harmony that, in the story of the old painter, marked religious images—which were neither transgressive nor mimetic and represented a world that did not lack spirit or light—is broken.

The operations of the moneylender show the "diabolic" ability of money to multiply itself, which we associate with capital as abstract money: the increase is not a matter of a growing pile of coins but rather is the result of a form of accounting, of mathematical, abstract operations. But besides increasing his capital through the abstract instrument of compound interest, the moneylender is also a pawnbroker, hoarding material objects of all sorts: "It was rumoured that his iron chests were filled to the very top with gold, jewellery, diamonds and all sorts of pledged articles of great value" (142). And the money Chartkov finds in the frame of the portrait is not paper money (insubstantial) but gold coins—that is, money as a material commodity rather than simply a token of exchange; the coins materiality—weight, sound, color—is emphasized in the text (they make a "heavy thud on the floor" [111]; they are "new and red hot" [112]). Thus if money is the root of evil, it is both because of its abstraction and because of its sheer materiality.[14]

The first part of the story starts in a shop where popular, mass-produced "art" ("lubki")[15] and miscellaneous engravings that Chartkov considers "grotesque" (94) are displayed. The shop also contains oil paintings—that is, "originals"—that are described as being all the same, as if mechanically reproduced, by an automaton (95).[16] The shopkeeper says they are fresh from the warehouse (95, 96), suggesting both mass production and the constant need for new articles of consumption that drives it. The description of the objects in the store suggests the disappearance of memory, of tradition, of the family, and growing anonymity: among the paintings "there were . . . old family portraits of people whose descendants could most probably no longer be traced anywhere; pictures of quite unknown people or torn canvases and frames that had lost their gilding" (96). As the last part of this quote suggests, the decay of art objects (which stands for the decline of art) is expressed by bringing to the fore their material aspect (canvas, frame, gilding). Indeed, the description of the objects in the shop shows works of arts that have become sheer matter since what is inscribed, or drawn, on that matter has been effaced, or is so covered with other matter—varnish, dust, and dirt—that they appear as no different from other, uninscribed objects: they are all sheer meaningless matter. In the description of the oil paintings what is emphasized is the thick paint that is smeared over everything and seems to obscure any lines or drawing that would have given this paint, this matter, any form or meaning. This is especially striking in the description of the picture of the holy city of Jerusalem, "with houses and churches unceremoniously bedaubed with red paint, which also covered part of the street and two praying Russian peasants in mittens" (93–94).[17] Chartkov's own paintings may be no different since according to his old professor they have an excess of color (matter) and lack line (inscription). He tells him: "Your colours seem to be getting out of hand. Much too slick those colours of yours are. . . . Your drawing, too, lacks strength. Sometimes it is very weak. No lines" (100).

The excess of color and of the material in general brings us back to the question of adequation or balance: between line and color, between form and matter, between art "as an 'ideal' object and [art as] a 'real' commodity,"[18] between gold as money, a token of exchange, whose value is guaranteed by the inscription on it and gold as a material commodity. What the story shows to be in excess in all these cases is the material; what is lacking is the nonmaterial (hence the story's lack of interest in paper money).

Thus money, and its relation to portraiture, appears in the story in three different guises: that of money's power of extension, of money's ability to breed unnaturally, and of money as material commodity. All these aspects have a correlative in the portrait as a representation. But the portrait's evil effect can be attributed not only to the various ways in which it is the analogue of money; it also has to do with the idea that portrait painting is a degraded and degrading art. And here we see a marked difference between the story's two parts. In the first part, dealing with the painter Chartkov, the portrait painter is seen as selling out, as betraying true art for money; money here is presented, rather conventionally, as what destroys true art. This idea is absent from the story's second part: the old painter is never paid for his portrait of the moneylender, who returns the half-finished portrait to him; no exchange of art for money takes place between them. The two parts of the story, then, represent differently the "evil" involved in the act of portraying. In order to understand this difference we need to take a closer look at the similarities and differences between the two painters, in the story's two parts.

The Two Painters

The idea that portraiture is a degrading art since the painter, rather than following his noble, artistic aspirations, paints to gain money and thus "sells" himself, is expressed explicitly in the story's first part, when Chartkov's professor warns him against becoming a portrait painter: "Start painting fashionable pictures, become a fashionable portrait painter, and all your money worries are at an end: you'll get lots of money. But remember, my dear fellow, that is the way to ruin your talent, not to develop it" (100). It is also stated, in the first version, in Chertkov's dream, where, significantly, it is the image of the evil old moneylender in the portrait that urges him to "Make haste and paint portraits of all the town! Accept every commission, but do not be in love with your work" (I, 229).

As his professor's admonitions also make clear, Chartkov has the potential to become a great artist but also has failings that could cause him to lose his talent: "you have talent," the professor tells him; "the trouble with you is that you are so confoundingly impatient.... You seem to be mainly working for effect" (100). Chartkov's negative qualities are realized when he becomes a portrait painter: his desire to work and succeed quickly (his impatience) is fulfilled with a vengeance when the high-class clientele he acquires wants its portraits painted in a hurry. Not only does he lose his freedom and has now to paint to please, but he has also turned himself into a commodity: at the very beginning of his career he advertises himself in the newspaper; he is "for sale." His wish to be recognized becomes his slavish subordination to the whims of his sitters.

Chartkov's "selling of his soul to the money devil" occurs when he allows his image of "Psyche" (the soul) to "pass" as the portrait of the society girl, Lise (Annette in the first version).[19] Both the portrait he paints of the girl and the sketch of Psyche which he has started earlier on, as one of his "studies," are described as conventional and idealized (122). But when he picks up the sketch, after the girl and her mother go away,

> [t]he features, shades and tones caught by him appeared on [the paper] in a refined form in which they occasionally appear on the paintings of an artist who, having made a close study from nature, moves away from it and creates a work of art which is like it and yet independent of it. Psyche began to come to life and the as yet faintly dawning idea began gradually to be clothed into a visible body. The type of the face of the young society girl was unconsciously transferred to Psyche's face and through this it received a unique individuality which entitles a work of art to be considered as truly original. (122–23)

It is this original work, in which a face appears in its "unique individuality" and which realizes the painter's "idea" and talent, that he agrees to sell as the portrait of the society girl. This is the beginning of his success as a portrait painter and of his degradation as an artist.[20]

Chartkov's behavior once he finds the money hidden in the frame of the portrait is characterized by conspicuous consumption (consumption that is not governed by need or use but by display).[21] The new apartment he rents has many mirrors in which he can look approvingly at himself in his new fashionable clothes. He also buys a lorgnette: self-display is complemented by seeing others in their self-display. His relation to time changes: he is now in a hurry all the time. This is because his clients are always in a hurry: the need to save time in the process of production (of the painter) is in service of the need to have leisure devoted to conspicuous consumption and display (of the sitters and the painter). In other words, in finding the money in the portrait's frame and becoming a portrait painter, Chartkov becomes like the fashionable sitters whose portraits he paints; he is their copy.[22]

Under the pressure of his sitters (and their money), Chartkov's portraits become more and more conventional, that is, both standardized and reproducible. The uniqueness of the sitter as well as the originality of the painter's way of seeing and skill with his brush disappear when "conventional colouring . . . daubed on mechanically" causes the "resemblance to the original" to disappear; it is replaced by "coldly ideal faces," "cold conventional features which did not seem to belong to any living body" (122). The insistence on the features and faces being "cold" suggests that the portraits are dead images of dead bodies. The "diversity and multiplicity" of his sitters disappear both because, always in a hurry, the painter can "capture merely the general expression as a whole" (124) and because his sitters do not want to be painted as they are: "What they wanted, in fact, was that their faces should be generally admired" (125). Chartkov himself, "beautifying his appearance in every possible way so as to make the best and most pleasing impression" (126), is like his portraits; he, too, wants to be "generally admired." As "his works and orders multipl[y]" (127), this process is accelerated; he more and more produces by rote "the same kind of portraits and faces, whose profiles and poses he now knew by heart" (127). As his paintings become "cold and lifeless" (128), he himself becomes a living dead, "one of those strange human beings who . . . seem to be walking coffins with a corpse where their hearts should be" (129); he is a dead body, an animated object.[23] The end of this process is that he loses interest not only in painting but also in fame; all he cares about is money. And he uses money to purchase works of art and destroy them. When he dies, none of his riches remain: he was his money.[24]

Thus in Chartkov's story art degenerates: rather than being pursued for its own sake, it becomes a way of making money. The painter who has sold himself destroys himself (loses his talent) and having become nothing but his purchasing power, destroys art. The death of art is manifested as the loss of originals (the portraits are all the same as if they were copies of each other) and of originality (the painter lost his genius; he is like everybody else). And it is caused by the commercialization of art, by art becoming a commodity. This idea is expressed also in the scene in the auction house, in the frame narrative of the second part. Like the shop where the first part of the story begins, the auction house shows the commercialization of art, considered as the death of art. The auction is compared to a funeral procession with "the funereal voice of the auctioneer . . . chanting a requiem for the poor arts" (138).

In the story of the old painter, as in that of Chartkov, painting a portrait or portraits has evil effects. But unlike Chartkov, the old painter represents an ideal of the painter that no other painter in the story will match.[25] That it is this ideal, archaic painter, with his striking portrait of the moneylender (rather than a vain, worldly painter with indifferent, conventional portraits)[26] who is at the root of all the evil is somewhat occluded by the story's structure: the reversal of temporal order (what comes first, chronologically, is told last) creates a sense of discontinuity, and thus presents the past as radically different from the present (in which Chartkov's part of the story takes place) rather than as its cause; conversely, the many parallels between the two parts may lead one to think that they both tell the same story—Chartkov's story.[27] This, in turn, obscures the fact that the old painter's story presents the "evil" of painting a portrait quite differently from Chartkov's story.

The old painter is presented as the painter of legends.[28] He is self-taught, which means that everything in his art comes from within him; he was not taught even the rules and laws of painting he follows but rather has found them in his soul, in his spirit. He does not imitate other artists, and though he is familiar with the work of Raphael, Leonardo, Titian, and Correggio, he does not follow any painter as his model or ideal. He is not affected by the reactions of others to his art; he does not try to please a public, has no worldly ambition, does not compete with others but, rather, helps fellow artists (147–48). He paints religious paintings: he works to please God (or his representatives on earth who are all presented as holy men) and to please himself, not in the sense of glorifying himself but rather in the sense of being true to his art. His inner integrity is seen in his paintings—in the exalted expression of the figures (148). It is important to emphasize that though he paints an inner vision, he is not a Romantic painter since he effaces his own personality, subordinates it to God, rather than being a Promethean rebel who competes with God. At the same time, his art is not mimetic (though it is representational); he does not imitate or reproduce nature, does not use models (as becomes obvious at the end of his story when he is a hermit).

In agreeing to paint the portrait of the moneylender, the old painter departs from his long practice of painting religious images for churches. Once he encounters the moneylender, he forgets the "inner inclination and personal conviction [that] guided his brush to religious subjects" (148). He is so "impressed by an exceptional subject for his brush" (I, 264), overcome by the "amazing features" (150) of the face, that, forgetting his religious commitments, he, astonishingly, says to himself: "If I am successful in getting him [the moneylender] even half as well as he is now, he'll kill all my saints and angels; they'll all pale into insignificance before him!" (150).

The old painter can be seen as an anachronistic representation of the artist in the mythic past before painting became separated from its religious, ritual, or magic function, that is, to use Hans Belting's term, "before the era of art"; in the first version he is specifically described as "one of those modest devout painters such as were only common in the religious middle ages" (I, 262).[29] Unlike Chartkov, he is not named since naming appears only as painting becomes independent of its cultic role—enters the "era of art" whose history, again as Belting puts it, is that of artists.[30]

Hence, "before the era of art" we cannot speak of images being "original" in the sense of "authentically reflect[ing] the artist's idea."[31] Eikons were essentially conventional images using repeated modes of representation and formal configurations since their production was governed by the religious authorities.[32] They were not signed, and their painting was often attributed to figures other than the actual painter.[33] Whereas "before the era of art" painting is subordinated to certain purposes, conventions, and practices as well as contained in certain spaces (church, monastery) and is evaluated according to its efficacy for these practices, its fitting for these purposes, when art "emerges" out of religious cult it "frees" itself from cultic practices and purposes while it also goes wider and wider into the world, becoming more and more exposable.[34] We can say that the painting of the moneylender's portrait is a reenactment of the mythical moment in which painting, still grounded in cult, is separated from cult and becomes "art." Situated at the threshold between cult and art, the portrait partakes of both: with its power to affect all those who come in contact with it, the portrait retains an "aura," in the religious sense of "an image exercising power over believers by its actual presence" (though in the case of the portrait the power is negative) while it also has the "aura" of a genuine work of art, "an 'original' . . . that authentically reflects the artist's idea."[35]

The circulation of the portrait in Gogol's story, which allows people in different places to see it and be affected by it (as described, for example, on page 158) can stand for the emergence of art, when, according to Walter Benjamin's argument in "The Work of Art in the Age of Its Mechanical Reproducibility," "cult value" is replaced by "exhibition value," or by what Benjamin called "Ausstellbarkeit," that is, the capacity or ability of being exhibited, being on view.[36] The story describes this shift and the emergence of art negatively, as a fall: the old painter can redeem himself and others only by regressing to the world of cult and becoming a hermit who paints eikons.

The moneylender's portrait appears to be the first instance in which the old painter engages in a mimetic representation. As a mimetic representation the portrait differs from religious images, where the represented figures are not "likenesses" of their subjects (the identity of specific figures is not indicated by their resemblance to their real referents but through emblems; the representation of face and body is highly conventional). The painter's need for a model arises when he wishes to represent evil—"all that weighs down and oppresses man" (149). Thus imitation and evil become associated with each other. In presenting evil in the form of a particular individual, the painter also anchors the existential-indexical aspect of the portrait in an individual whereas eikons were considered to derive their power from their indexical relation to the prototype. The evil the portrait represents is (also) the evil of its mode of representation, which relies on imitation, substitutes the individual for the prototype, produces a false prototype in the form of an allegorized individual.

The old painter's story is not concerned with the loss of the original and of originality. And though the moneylender's portrait is marked by its "Ausstellbarkeit" (what I called before, when discussing the portrait's relation to money, extension), its power over those who behold it or come in contact with it (its status as an image that belongs to cult rather than to art) is not lost or reduced because of its "extension."[37] The "evil" of the portrait, then, does not lie where we might have expected it—in reproducibility or exposibility. Rather, in this part of the story, "evil" is presented in terms of loss of "adequation": as we have seen, what is wrong with the portrait (in spite of the power of the image and the excellence of the artistic representation) is that it produces a sense of both excess and lack. If the portrait is judged in terms of adequation, it is because it is understood in the context of religious images (eikons) where, as in the case of money, it is adequation, rather than the relation between original and copy, that is the important factor. A perfect coin is not an authentic original to which all other coins of the same denomination and impression stand as inferior copies (hence mechanical reproduction of coins does not in itself reduce their value).[38] Rather, it is a coin in which the weight and purity of the inscribed metal are the exact equivalent of the value given by the inscription; in other words, it is a matter of perfect adequation between inscribed and inscription, res and intellectus (the terms used by Marc Shell), matter and spirit. An eikon is the equivalent of a perfect coin: it is "like a coin when its inscription's claim about the material qualities of the inscribed thing (weight and purity of substance) are 'true' or 'equal to' its actual qualities."[39] The eikon's power resides neither in its originality, nor in its likeness to its subject, nor yet in the indexical presence of the painter but in its "participation" in the prototype: the representation partakes of the prototype.[40] This "participation" was understood as an analogue to the incarnation; the eikon is thus matter infused with spirit.[41] The portrait as a figure for "art" fails to achieve such adequation; rather, it is defined by excess/lack.

Chartkov's portraits are contrasted with the masterpieces he could have created had he withstood the allure of money; his conventional, standardized, "mass-produced" copies are implicitly opposed to unique originals, painted by unique talents. That reproducibility inheres in the work of art (as Benjamin argues) is occluded in Chartkov's story by the opposition between, on the one hand, art for art's sake, which is outside the money nexus (Chartkov before the encounter with the portrait/money), and, on the other hand, art for sale, the entanglement of art in the market (Chartkov after the encounter). Thus, the first part of the story provides the familiar argument that money kills art. By contrast, the second part of the story places the root of the decline of art in its separation from cult—that is, at its moment of birth;[42] it locates the problem in the impossibility not of an original but of an adequate representation, treats not the danger posed to art by money but the impossibility for the work of art to be like the eikon, a perfect coin.[43]

There are, then, two different stories told in "The Portrait." The first is the story of Chartkov, and it tells of the destruction of art by money; it is centered around the opposition between original and copy. The second is the story of the portrait painted by the old painter, and it shows art as analogous to money; it centers around the notion of representation as adequation (or lack thereof). We should note that whereas the portrait was commonly seen as a lesser art or no art all (as we have seen in the introduction), in both parts of Gogol's story the portrait stands for art in general, though for two different reasons.

Critics tend to focus on Chartkov's story and on the loss of the original and of originality due to "mechanical reproduction"; they thus see the historical process of the decline of art (and through it of the "evils" of modernity) as that of growing commodification. But since the story of the old painter both precedes chronologically that of Chartkov and constitutes its cause, the process of decline has its starting point at an earlier moment: the moment when the power of the image is substituted for the originality of the painter and the authenticity of the work of art as an original—in other words, the moment when religious aura is substituted for the "aura" of the work of art. In the diagnosis offered by the story, then, the root problem would be not the *loss* of originality but the *introduction* of originality as a criterion for the production and evaluation of images. What would characterize the "decline" of art (and of the portrait), then, what has been lost, would be the power of the image or the valorization of and attention to this power.

Critics' tendency to focus on Chartkov's story and subsume in it that of the old painter is due, in part, to the perception that the issues raised by the former are relevant to our modern or postmodern life whereas the latter's preoccupation with eikons and diabolic moneylenders is not. This, however, is not quite the case, as we can see by briefly discussing the photographic portrait, a discussion that hopefully will resonate with issues raised earlier apropos of coins and/or eikons. Just as it does not make sense to ask for an "authentic" coin, so it does not make sense "to ask for the 'authentic' print" of photographic negative (Benjamin, "Work of Art" 224). In Benjamin's argument, therefore, photography stands for the loss of aura, of the original and authentic. But the lack of an original and the multiplicity of copies do not compromise the power of the photographic portrait to affect a viewer. This power does not reside (as it is sometimes argued) in the high degree of resemblance of the photographic portrait (its iconic aspect) but rather in its strong indexical relation to its subject.[44] Not since Butades's daughter traced on the wall the shadow of her sleeping lover and created the first portrait has there been such a strong causal (indexical) relation between a subject and his/her portrait as the one produced by a photograph. And it is the strong indexical presence of the photograph's subject that gives the photographic portrait is specificity. As Roger Scruton puts it, "the determining factor in the production of a photograph is the causal [i.e., indexical] relation between the referent and the image, rather than the intentional one between the photographer and the image" (587). Scruton adds that "the history of the art of photography is the history of successive attempts to break the causal chain by which the photographer is imprisoned, to impose a human intention between subject and appearance so that the subject can be both defined by that intention and seen in terms of it" (594). In other words, the attempts to transform photography into an "art," that is, a representation that reveals the photographer's "originality"—"style," "vision," or "intention"—are attempts to loosen up or minimize the importance of the indexical relation of the photographic portrait to its subject, the latter being perceived as restricting the freedom of the photographer. Thus the history of photography, like Gogol's story, reenacts the passage from the power of the image, grounded in its strong indexical relation to its subject, to the originality of the artist and the authenticity of the work of art.

As we have seen, however, in portrait *stories* the artist's "intention" or "vision" cannot be reduced to a matter of originality of artistic style or ideal; artistic styles and ideals, in turn, do not stand outside ideology but participate in it. The photographer's desire to "impose a human intention," to break free of the "causal chain," is, like that of the portrait painter, a desire to impose an interested vision—a vision that justifies and perpetuates the artist's power to represent. While the portrait is an index of the subject's existence, it is the painter's "intention" and power that shapes the way subjects are perceived (by themselves and by others). Gogol's valorization of the image "before the era of art"—that is, before the intention and vision of the painter became a determining factor—thus betrays nostalgia for a mythical world where subjectivities are independent of representation.

AFTERWORD

Reading Portrait Stories

In the preceding chapters, I have analyzed the way portraits function in the fictive world created by the literary texts in which they feature. I have argued that in one way or another portrait stories raise the question of the relation between representation and subjectivity (and therefore the question of how the power to represent is gained, kept, or lost); I have also showed how the portrait serves as a site for intersubjective relations among painter, sitter, and viewer(s). In all this, I was concerned with the fictive characters' experience and with the portrait as a particular kind of visual image. But though in the texts analyzed the portrait is a real image as well as a material object the characters can see, for us, the readers, the portrait is never visible. Just like everything else in the text, the portrait is made of black marks on a white page, marks that we read and interpret. No matter how much or how little we identify with the characters in the stories, our reading cannot be collapsed with their viewing or seeing experience. Portrait stories, therefore, do not raise the question of the relation between image and text in the way, say, a novel with illustrations does. In what follows I revisit some of the stories I have analyzed, this time with a focus on the way they represent the relation between portrait and story and what they tell us about reading.

"Long—long I read—and devoutly, devotedly I gazed," states the frame narrator in Poe's "Oval Portrait" (481). As we have seen, Poe's tale insists on the difference between portrait and story, between reading and gazing. The balance between reading and gazing suggests that, though different, they are of equal merit or importance. There is no question of establishing a hierarchy, a superiority of one form of expression over the other. At the same time, as we have also seen, they are not symmetrical opposites of each other: if they were, then a synthesis, an overcoming of their opposition would be, in principle, possible. Poe's neologism of sorts, "life-likeliness," evokes both portrait and story while keeping their heterogeneity and incompatibility intact. It is this heterogeneity and incompatibility *within* the portrait (and not only the difference *between* the story of the portrait's painter and that of its viewer, the frame narrator) that Poe's story asks us to read; misreading it means eliding what is different within the word, within the portrait, substituting for it what is common and known in advance.

Other texts also invite us to read portrait and story as neither the same nor opposites by introducing a third term between them or by doubling one or both of the terms. Thus in Balzac's *La Maison du-chat-qui-pelote*, the divergence I have discussed between the narrator's and the painter Sommervieux's view of representation can be seen as an opposition between writing (trace) and painting (plenitude), between the text of *La Maison du chat-qui-pelote* and the painting of "La Maison du chat-qui-pelote" (from which Augustine's figure is later on extracted and turned into her portrait). But this binary opposition is disrupted by the shop's signboard, which represents neither the shop's outside nor its inside (and thus differs from both the narrator's and the painter's representation of the shop). As the narrator explains, the signboard, on which one can see the image of a cat holding a racket, is a representation of an ancient practice, now extinct, whereby merchants attracted customers by displaying patiently trained animals to the amazement of the passersby. At the same time, the image of a "chat qui pelote" has to be read as the text "chaque y pelote" (here everybody feathers his nest). The picture on the signboard is both a trace of a mythical past (see chap. 4, n. 9) and a pictorial representation of a text, a visual play on words.

In Wilde's text, as we have seen, one result of Dorian's wish to trade places with the portrait is that the portrait becomes "a diary"—a picture becomes a story, a narrative of decay and degradation. But, as we have also noted, this does not eliminate the portrait since Dorian has taken its place; the two continue to coexist but each is divided within by the other. Man and portrait, subject and representation, unchanging portrait and a diary of change oppose each other but are also divided within and inextricably linked to the other. This otherness within both Dorian and the portrait (within both portrait and story) is reinforced by the doubling of each: the portrait is doubled by a mirror, and the story of Dorian's life is doubled by the infamous book Lord Henry gives him. Both mirror and book are doubles that are not quite the same as what they double. Just as the portrait is and is not a mirror (as we have seen), the portrait as a diary of Dorian's soul, registering his actions and their effects as they take place, is both similar to and different from the book, which "contains the story of his life written before he had lived it" (123).

Storm's story also presents us with a third term, situated between the portraits the painter Johannes paints and the manuscript he writes; this term is inscription. There are two inscriptions in the story. The first is the inscription C.P.A.S. on the dead child's portrait. As we have seen, the child narrator does not see it at first; his attention is fixed on the image of the child, with whom he identifies, and this blocks his attention from what seems extraneous to the image (but in retrospect is what the portrait is all about). Once he sees the inscription, he does not fully understand it. It is not until he reads the manuscript that his intuition about the inscription's meaning is confirmed. The portrait is supplemented (rather than doubled) by an inscription that is supplemented (rather than doubled) by the story told in the manuscript.

The second inscription is the one carved above the door of the house in town. This inscription, announcing the passing of all human life, is also noticed belatedly by the frame narrator: though he used to visit the baker's house in his school days, it is only now, as an adult, thinking back about his childhood, that he notices it for the first time. The inscription appears also in Johannes's manuscript. Unlike the narrator, Johannes has noticed the inscription from the very first; when the house on which it was carved was demolished, he bought the stone with the inscription and attached it to the house where he lived with his brother. Thus the inscription, perceived belatedly and transplanted from one site to another, is marked by temporal and spatial differences. This, however, does not oppose the inscription (language) to the portrait since, as we have seen, the portraits of the child and of Herr Gerhardus are similarly marked.

The inscription on the door of the house in Storm's story is also marked by the difference produced by reading. Though in the English translation the inscription mentioned by Johannes and the one mentioned by the narrator appear exactly the same, in the German original there is a difference. The inscription mentioned in Johannes's manuscript appears in "plattdeutsch" (431; 152). By contrast, the inscription in the frame narrative appears to us, the readers, in modern German while the narrator "reads" it in the original dialect. The narrator calls our attention to this difference: "an inscription in dialect caught my eye, which, translated would sound something like this [eine plattdeutsche Inschrift in die Augen fiel, die verhochdeutscht etwa lauten würde] . . . (384; 114). Though the text attempts to reproduce the appearance of the inscription (it is set in the center of the page, in two lines, just like the "real" inscription on the door), there is a difference between the inscription the narrator reads and the one the reader reads as well as between the inscription the reader reads in the frame narrative and the one he/she reads in the main narrative. In the story as a whole, the difference in language between the frame and main narrative is justified by the convention Storm establishes, according to which the seventeenth-century manuscript uses some archaic vocabulary and grammatical forms. But in the case of the inscription this means that a wedge of difference is inserted within what is supposed to be self-same. Between what is written and what is read there needs to be a translation; we are not reading the same thing the frame narrator reads (nor does he read the same thing as Johannes since the frame narrator reads the inscription in, or translates it into, modern German).

In both Storm's and Poe's stories, we have a frame narrator who finds a manuscript that he, in some sense, "reproduces" for us. This reproduction is presented not as a copying but rather as a reading. It suggests therefore that the difference that exists in any reproduction or copying also exists in reading: as we have seen already in the case of the inscription in Storm's story, the text we read is not exactly the same as the text written. Or, put otherwise: the written text is both discovered and produced (is re-produced with a difference) by its reader.

In Poe's story, the question of reading is raised through the difference between portrait and story. While we, the readers, cannot see the portrait the frame narrator sees, we do know his reaction to it: it is a strong affective reaction that he both savors and tries to neutralize. Conversely, though we read the same story he does, read it together with him—over his shoulder, so to speak, we do not know what his reaction to it is. If the frame narrator is the "implied reader" of the painter's story, we don't know what his reading implies to us. Though the story is "the same" for both narrator and reader, our reading of it is not predicted, remains unpredictable.

In Storm's story, too, we read the same manuscript the narrator reads, as he reads it. That the narrator reads the manuscript in the same room where Johannes wrote it contributes to the resemblance, carefully established also elsewhere in the text, between the frame and main narrative, here more specifically between the scene of reading (by the frame narrator) and that of writing (by Johannes). As we have seen, this resemblance, whereby frame narrative and main narrative each corroborate the other, is disrupted by a difference in one of the elements that was supposed to anchor it: the portrait the narrator and Johannes have at their side while reading/writing. No matter how much the reader within the text (the frame narrator) puts himself in the place of the writer, with whom he identifies in various ways, his reading exceeds what is "in" the text. What makes this excess legible (though, like Poe's "life-likeliness," it often remains unread) is the difference between two pictures that are supposed to be the same but are not, indeed cannot be. These pictures are already inhabited by difference: both of them are copies and grafts or transplants.

The sameness between the narrator's story and that of the main character Johannes—both end with the same words, the words that also give the story its title—is belied by the temporal distance that separates them and that divides also the *narrator-reader* himself. The short conclusion to the story starts with the phrase, "Here ended the manuscript"—that is, it starts at the moment when both we and the narrator finish reading Johannes's manuscript. But the sentences that follow register the passage of time—both in the past (Johannes's hope to become a famous painter proved illusory, what he "had once presumed to hope . . . were to be words spoken into empty air" [455; 170]) and in the narrator's presumed present: nothing is left of Johannes's artwork, the last work to be still mentioned in documents—the Lazarus picture—is lost, too, and so presumably is the picture the narrator had at his side while reading, lost between two paragraphs. This lapse of time within the narrator's present of narration anticipates the time of the reader who, no matter how much he identifies with the narrator, is separated from him by time and space. Storm's story thus insists on difference and spacing as constitutive of reading, writing, viewing, and painting.

Whereas in Poe and Storm we read the same text as the character, occupying the same place as the character, who holds the book for us, too, Wilde stages this situation *for Dorian* (while we, the readers, are told about Dorian's reading, rather than participate in it). What is at stake in the discussion of the book Lord Henry gave Dorian (chapter 11) is the difference between identification and influence and the relation of both to reading.[1] After telling us that "there were times when it appeared to Dorian that the whole of history was merely the record of his own life," the narrator states: "the hero of the wonderful novel that had so influenced his life had himself known this curious fancy" (138). On the one hand, there is a similarity between Dorian and the novel's hero—they both know "this curious fancy"—but it is far from clear that this similarity is the result of influence. On the other hand, the book has influenced Dorian, but it is not clear—nor is it logically necessary—that through its influence he became like the hero. Indeed, as we have seen (chap. 5, n. 40), this is not the case: while the hero is marked by his fear of mirrors, of growing old, Dorian is not and part of Dorian's pleasure—his "cruel joy" (123)—in reading the book lies precisely in this difference between him and the book's hero.

In the scene that follows, Dorian is reading the novel that has influenced him (its seventh chapter, to be precise), but we are not told what he felt or thought as he was reading, how the novel affected him, influenced him; nor do we read the novel together with Dorian, "as" Dorian. Rather, we read how the novel's hero, who is apparently also its narrator, "tells how . . ." he read. The passage describes the experience, common to Dorian and the novel's hero, of seeing their own story as already written. And this story is one of reading since it is by reading, by the mediation of a book, that they experience this commonness and this commonness is that of a particular way of reading (reading "as").[2] Hence the passage begins with Dorian reading a book where the hero tells how he sat reading, "as" Tiberius, "crowned with laurel," sat in his garden in Capri "reading the shameful books of Elephantis" (138). At this point, however, the passage changes direction since the "mise en abyme" is not sustained: Tiberius is not reading his own story in the "shameful books of Elephantis"—a Greek poetess who wrote about different modes of coition; rather, the implication is that Tiberius, as well as Caligula and Domitian, mentioned further on, were influenced (corrupted) by Elephantis's books. To collapse these two strands amounts to arguing that a book influences someone because it tells that person's story—but if this is what a book does, there is no room for influence. The influence the book exercises on Dorian and the similarity Dorian sees between himself and the hero (this similarity being that of seeing similarity with characters in a text) are not the same thing.

That reading one's own story in that of someone else and being influenced can get confused is already thematized at the very beginning of the novel when Dorian mistakenly thinks that in Lord Henry's words he can "recognize" a preexisting self whereas the words he hears, just like the book he reads, influence him, shape him, produce him.³ But again the difference between a portrait, where one can recognize oneself, and words or book that influence, is undermined. The portrait does not reflect a preexisting Dorian as he "truly is" while the book shapes, influences him, since Dorian's portrait is not his "likeness" in any simple way: produced by all three men, it represents their intersubjective relations and their influence on each other.

The actual reader can read "as" Dorian (see him/herself in Dorian, as Dorian and the book's hero do, see resemblance and sameness); this kind of reading can be staged in the text itself—as when Dorian and the book's hero read "as" a character in another text does. But reading a book can also influence the reader, who, at the same time, changes the text in the act of reading. What influence the book will have on the reader, how the reader will transform the text, are not things the book can foresee, let alone represent—and *The Picture of Dorian Gray* is a case in point—though the work of influence and transformation can be registered—as it is in the description of the production of the portrait.

As we have seen, portrait stories deal with the intersubjective relations among characters as mediated by a particular kind of image. The specific attributes of the portrait as an image are crucial for the way it functions in these stories. But while portrait stories are about portraits, "about" does not indicate duplication as sameness but rather introduces difference: difference between "real" portraits and portraits in stories, between portraits and stories as well as within them.

Portraits are supposed to fix forever the image of a person at a particular point in time, placing its subject beyond change and death, immortalizing it. This is the most basic way in which every portrait idealizes its subject. In portrait stories, however, time and difference are registered *within* the portrait in various ways: the temporal layering of the portrait in James's "The Tone of Time"; the decay of the portrait in Wilde's *The Picture of Dorian Gray*; the gradual coming into being of the portrait as Nicolo assumes its identity in Kleist's "Der Findling"; the portrait as representing a woman buried alive in Poe's "The Oval Portrait." Portraits in portrait stories are also transplanted and grafted onto a new context (as in Storm) or have a fictive context (as in "The Tone of Time") so that the very existence of the portrait's subject (of which the portrait is an index) is put into question. The reversal of the hierarchical relation between subject and representation we find in many stories further destabilizes the status of the portrait as a copy (in the sense of secondary in relation to a preexisting original). It is thus as an ungrounded image, marked by difference, by time, by loss and death as well as by dislocation and fictionality, that the portrait in many portrait stories provides the shifting and uncertain ground for the construction of identity and intersubjective relations.

Readers of these stories can "idealize" the text by seeing it as self-same, eternal, universal; and they can "recognize" themselves in the idealized text. But readers can also see the text as different and differing, registering the difference in time and place that always affects a reader's relation to it, creating/discovering the text in the process of reading while also being affected by it. Such a reading foregrounds the difference that interpretation produces and its ability to have an effect on other readers while at the same time accepting that all interpretations are inflected by particular interests, determined by power relations. Which is what portrait stories, in my reading, tell us.

NOTES

INTRODUCTION

1. For other nineteenth-century views of the portrait, see Heather McPherson's discussion of the modern portrait in France, where she quotes, for example, a critic's observation concerning portraits displayed in the salon of 1861: "The truth is that none of these portraits exist as a *work of art*" (qtd. 8).

2. Note that this "usefulness" already marks the portrait as having a practical purpose which, according to Jean-Luc Nancy, would account for its lowly status: the portrait "peut apparaître comme le seul genre de la peinture qui ait eu une finalité pratique bien déterminée: c'est d'ailleurs autour de cette finalité que s'est partagé longtemps le jugement sur sa dignité artistique" (38). Recently, Susan Gaylard has argued that the decline of "exemplarity" occurred already in the Renaissance. On the other hand, Hans Belting, in *An Anthropology of Images*, argues that one cannot speak "of the early portrait as presenting a resemblance to an individual, for that concept likewise could not have the meaning that it bears today—if indeed there was any such concept at all" (62). Édouard Pommier, who provides a nuanced history of theories of the portrait from the Renaissance to the eighteenth century, notes that the negative view of portraiture increases with its democratization (see, for example, 132–33).

3. Qtd. in Betzer 686. Betzer points out that the "servitude" of the portrait painter to his sitters was felt to be an issue particularly in the case of women subjects.

4. As Max J. Friedländer puts it, "aesthetic purists have wanted to exclude [portraiture] from the domain of artistic activity" (124). The origin of the valorization of the general over the particular is Aristotle's distinction, in *Poetics* IX 3–4, between poetry and history; the condemnation of the portrait for having a practical goal and being immersed in worldly interests and economic transactions derives from Kant's definition of the aesthetic in terms of purposelessness and disinterestedness, elaborated in the "Analytic of the Beautiful" in the *Critique of Judgement*. Critics often cite Hegel's comments on portraits (in his *Lectures on Fine Art* III.iii.1.2c) as the most important exception to the prevailing negative views of the portrait.

The tension between the general and the particular exists not only between genres (history painting vs. portrait, for example) but also within portraiture itself, and, as we shall see, several portrait stories deal with this tension (often expressed as that between the real and the ideal).

5. James Breckenridge argues that the earliest portraits are skulls, dated from 5000 BC and found in Jericho; they were modeled over with clay and fitted with eyes of shell to simulate the appearance of a particular person (15–18). For a history of the portrait from ancient civilizations on, see Francastel and Francastel. For portrait stories in classical antiquity, see Bettini; for portrait stories in the Renaissance and the Enlightenment, see Pommier; and Kris and Kurtz.

6. Other pre-nineteenth-century texts featuring portrait (or portraits) include Claude Henry de Fusée, abbé de Voisenon, *Tant mieux pour elle* (1760); Laurence Sterne, *Journal to Eliza* (1767); Sophia Lee, *The Recess* (1783–85); Johann Wolfgang von Goethe, *Wilhelm Meisters Lehrjahre* (1791–96); and Ann Radcliffe, *Mysteries of Udolpho* (1794), among others.

7. For nineteenth-century stories featuring a "haunted" portrait, see Ziolkowski; Kerry Powell's essay on *The Picture of Dorian Gray* studies what he calls "a curious efflorescence of novels and stories dealing with 'magic pictures'" in the late Victorian era (148).

8. See Maurice Beebe's discussion of this topic. For representations of the painter in fiction, see also Bowie; and Jeffares.

9. The tradition of the literary portrait goes back to classical antiquity; see Pommier 65–74. The question why the term "portrait" seemed particularly appropriate for James and Joyce to describe what they intended to do in their respective works is an interesting and important one but does not fall within the scope of my project, which deals with stories that feature an actual portrait.

10. For other differences, see Beebe 4.

11. Though it is in general true that the problematization of the portrait and of the act of seeing is characteristic of portrait stories featuring the portrait's painter, it can also be found in some nineteenth-century stories in which the painter either plays a minor role or is altogether absent. I will discuss two such stories—by Heinrich von Kleist and by Thomas Hardy—in chapter 5.

12. Peirce's theory of signs contains much more than the tripartite classification of signs into icon, symbol, and index; my presentation of this classification simplifies it considerably. For a concise discussion of Peirce's use of the terms "icon," "index," and "symbol," see Burks; Bal and Bryson 188–91; and Silverman, *The Subject of Semiotics* 14–25. The relation between icon and index is sometimes presented as homologous to that between

metaphor and metonymy. It is important to note, however, that index and metonymy are different in one crucial respect: whereas the metonymical relation is that of mere contiguity, for Peirce the indexical relation is grounded in causality and not in contiguity (as Bal and Bryson sometimes argue); the relation of the index to its object is therefore a necessary rather than a contingent one.

13. Resemblance in portraits, therefore, cannot be thought of naively as a copy of the real. As Richard Brilliant puts it, "Portraiture is not the transcription of people 'as they are'; 'as they are' is neither subject to replication nor can it be understood except in terms of 'as they are like.' Artists, therefore, represent people in portraits by means of established or invented schema whose recognizable content shapes the identity of the subject and convey it to the beholder" (38). However, the inflection of resemblance by convention per se does not play a role in portrait stories where the conflicts are always among persons.

14. Though portraits are rarely likenesses of their painters, there are cases of such iconic relation (see Gombrich, "The Mask and the Face" 42–43; I thank Moshe Ron for this observation). We find also a more general statement, not restricted to portraits, in the ancient saying that "ogni pintore dipinge se," to which Leonardo gave a particularly "mimetic" formulation: "Le peintre, qui aura les mains mal faites en donnera des semblables à ses figures, et fera de même pour tous les autres membres" (qtd. in Pommier 135).

15. Peirce himself saw the portrait together with its caption (or legend) as primarily an index of its subject: the portrait signifies the existence of this subject. He saw the iconic aspect of the portrait as a vehicle of such indexicality (see Steiner 112).

16. See Schneider 15.

17. Ernest Kris and Otto Kurtz suggest that once "the identity of picture and depicted," associated with magic and ritual use of images, "is in decline, a new bond makes its appearance to link the two—namely, similarity or likeness. . . . [T]he closer the symbol (picture) stands to what is symbolized (depicted), the less is the outward resemblance; the further apart, the greater is the resemblance" (77–78). For a critique of Kris and Kurtz's argument, see Freedberg 201–10. Freedberg's argument, however, is vitiated by his lack of interest in (or awareness of) the indexical relation between a portrait and its subject (due probably to his definition of his project as the power of images in general) so that even in the extreme case of Veronica's Veil he concludes that it is "accuracy" that generates the "efficacy" of the portrait, rather than the indexical relation (210).

18. See, for example, Francastel and Francastel, who argue that for

primitive people, "L'image possède . . . un caractère de réalité: elle ne *représente* pas, elle existe par elle-même et elle est capable d'agir, aussi bien que de subir une action venant d'autrui. Elle peut aussi servir d'intermédiaire et transmettre à distance le maléfice ou le bénéfice" (47).

19. For a discussion of this story, see Bettini 7–9.

20. In tracing the lover's shadow, Butades's daughter draws the contours of his body rather than the details of his face, a feature we will find in stories about male portraits, discussed in chapter 5.

21. We should note that as a perfect replica the portrait does not contain any trace of the painter's presence. In other words, the painter here merely copies the real—which, as we shall see, is a common way of presenting the woman painter.

22. Or, more precisely, convention (the portrait as symbol, in Peirce's sense of the term) determines here only the viewer's acceptance of a silhouette as a likeness.

23. The association of portrait stories with the fantastic also explains why critics sometimes find the presence of portraits in realist texts (especially those dealing with social conflicts) incongruous; see for example Anne-Marie Meininger's remarks about the portrait in Balzac's *La Maison du chat-qui-pelote*, discussed in chapter 4. It also led some critics interested in portrait stories to judge those that do not involve the fantastic and the supernatural as somehow falling short of what they should be (see Powell, e.g., 152) or to ignore such stories altogether (thus neither Ziolkowski nor Perosa include in their survey "realist" texts dealing with portraits, such as Balzac's novella or Storm's "Aquis submersus," though Perosa's discussion is more wide-ranging than Ziolkowski's).

24. Jacques Voisine, in an essay that deals with four nineteenth-century portrait stories, also considers the portrait a motif, though he does not trace a historical development. A. S. Byatt's *Portraits in Fiction* discusses actual portraits in relation to both literary portraits (character description) and actual portraits that appear in fiction; she mentions many of them without tracing a historical development or providing detailed reading.

25. Thus, for example, V. V. Gippius, in his study of Nikolai Gogol's story "The Portrait," argues that the lifelike portrait was "a favorite of the Romantics . . . [that] goes back to the hagiographic theme of icons coming to life; it even has a pre-Christian past . . . and ultimately it has its root in myth"; he therefore concludes that "the task of picking out Western parallels to 'The Portrait' is . . . of little value in the case of a motif which already has such a long tradition behind it" (51). As we shall see in chapter 7, Gogol's story cannot be reduced to the "motif" of the lifelike portrait, and the issues it raises are vastly different from those of the predecessors

Gippius assigns him (Charles Maturin, E. T. A. Hoffmann, Washington Irving, and others).

26. Ziolkowski, for example, emphasizes the continuity between the eighteenth and nineteenth centuries, arguing that the portrait of Manfred's grandfather in *The Castle of Otranto* "stalks directly into the literature of the nineteenth century, where in a variety of guises the haunted portrait plays a significant role" (79). The perception of continuity rather than a break is in part the result of limiting the portrait story to "haunted portraits," which, as I have mentioned above, most often do not feature a painter; or conversely, the investment in continuity may be one of the reasons why portrait stories that do not feature "haunted portraits" are not considered.

27. The focus on description is at the root of the tendency of literary critics to associate "portrait" first and foremost with the "literary portrait"—that is, character description. Thus, for example, for Michael Tilby, "portrait" in a literary work has only a metaphorical sense, and he compares Ingres's portraits to Balzac's character descriptions. As should be clear by now, in the fictive world of the literary texts I will be discussing, the portrait is a real object and not a metaphor for character description, and the stories they tell concern the characters' relation to the portrait and their relations to each other as mediated by it.

28. For examples of studies of James's portrait stories as concerned with art in general or with the relation between literature and the visual arts, see chapter 2.

1. POE'S "OVAL PORTRAIT"

1. By "gothic novel," I mean a genre that, according to most literary historians, begins with the publication of Horace Walpole's *The Castle of Otranto* in 1764 and ends around 1820 with the publication of Charles Maturin's *Melmoth the Wanderer*.

2. Thus Elisabeth Bronfen, for example, claims that both the painter and the frame narrator "repress death" by "localizing it away from the self, at the body of a beautiful woman" (*Over Her Dead Body* vi). Paula Kot, reiterating Bronfen's argument, claims that "the drama of the tale"—both parts of it—centers around "the male aesthetic gaze and its attempt to define woman as subordinate" (1); according to her, both the narrator and the painter have the same desire to "objectify" woman, and Poe, while criticizing the painter's and narrator's gesture, also repeats it. William Freedman speaks repeatedly about "the tale," suggesting that he does not see a difference between the frame narrative and the main narrative; so does Gerald Kennedy when he claims, for example, that "the tale . . . provides a condensed

allegory of death, life, and art" (60–61). Monique Dubanton goes further and argues that "Le peintre et le voyageur égaré ne sont sans doute qu'un seul et même homme" (108).

3. Bronfen discusses the story in terms of a woman's relation to a corpse and to a portrait. She then argues, using Peirce's terminology, that while the "reduplication" of the body by a corpse is iconic, "the replacement of the body by its portrait forms a symbolic relation," that is, a conventional and hence arbitrary one. She then links conventional signs with "paternal/patriarchal ideology" and indexical signs with the maternal (110–11). It is true that, as I have argued in the introduction, since no portrait resembles its subject absolutely (and indeed, absolute resemblance is no longer resemblance but identity), what counts as resemblance in portraits (as well as in other visual representations and, arguably, in life) depends to some extent on cultural conventions that vary across time and place. But this does not mean that the portrait no longer functions as an icon. Nor does the symbolic aspect of the portrait eliminate its indexical aspect (its being a trace of the subject's past presence). The opposition Bronfen establishes between the portrait, on the one hand, and the body (the corpse, the maternal), on the other, and the conclusions she draws from it seem to me highly questionable.

4. It is therefore wrong, in my mind, to refer to the story as "the prototypical treatment of the Pygmalion myth in American fiction" (Person 41).

5. Bersani, *The Culture of Redemption*. I thus disagree with Dubanton, who claims that there is a difference in the frame narrative between narrator and "hero," a difference that allows the narrator "sa lucidité" (104).

6. See, for example, Cixous 29; Dubanton 103; and Mollinger 150.

7. Critics, on the other hand, often slide from book to portrait as if they were the same object and the activities of gazing and reading were the same. While Poe makes a clear distinction, saying: "Long—long I read—and devoutly, devotedly I gazed" (481), Kot, for example, speaks about "gazing at the text" (1).

8. I therefore disagree with critics such as Bronfen and Kot who see the narrator as an example of an "aesthetic gaze" whose function is to allow "the male viewer to distance himself from his own weakness and serves to protect the self from the fear of dissolution and disintegration (Kot 4) or who claim that the narrator "re-aestheticizes" the woman by refusing to see her as a living person and insisting on her being "framed" in order to "circumscribe and devitalize" her once again (Person 43). The narrator indeed insists that what he is looking at is a painting, but his gaze is anything but distanced or re-aestheticizing.

9. There are no textual grounds for speaking, as does Kot, about "the narrator's pleasure in reading the critical account of the portrait" (3) or for claiming, as does Freedman, that "the volume's text provides the answer to the narrator's inquiry into the source of the power of the portrait" (12).

10. For example: Kot, pointing out that Poe "coins and highlights this word," goes on to misquote it as *"lifelikeness"* (4); Freedman quotes correctly, but in his frequent use of the term routinely changes it to "lifelikeness"; William Scheick misquotes *"life-likeness* of expression" (6), and Mollinger misquotes "absolute *life-likeness"* (151); Susan Williams quotes correctly but then speaks of the portrait "lifelikeness" (73, 77); Perosa misquotes "an absolute *lifelikeness of expression"* (88); Marie-Hélène Huet both misquotes and refers to the portrait as "life-likeness" (175, 176), as does Sylvie Richards (308, 309, 310).

11. See Burton R. Pollin, *Poe Creator of Words* 54. According to Pollin, Poe, in revising "The Premature Burial," changed "life-likeliness" to "life-likeness," though the American Library edition of Poe has "life-likeliness" (671). Poe did not change the word when he revised "Life in Death" into "The Oval Portrait."

12. See *The Complete Works of Edgar Allan Poe* 4: 318.

13. Kot points out that the use of the present participle, "ripening," suggests that "the woman in the portrait is both dead and undead" and concludes that "the woman in the portrait refuses to stay dead" (2). However, since the description is through the eyes of the narrator, and since we have no other account but his, it seems to me unwarranted to attribute "refusal" to the woman.

14. On the theme of premature burial, see Kennedy, chapter 2; and Arnold Goldman, "Poe's Stories of Premature Burial: 'That Ere Kind of Style,'" in *Edgar Allan Poe: The Design of Order*, ed. A. Robert Lee.

15. In a different context, and using a different conceptual framework, Georg Simmel argues that there is a clear and intimate relation between the understanding of death as "inhabit[ing] life from the outset" (an understanding that can be expressed, for example, by the figure of being buried alive) and the portrait as a representation of an irreducibly singular, that is, irreplaceable, individual (rather than a representation of a type or a representation of "the timeless qualitative essence of an individual" (71, 9). Comparing Rembrandt's portraits with those of the Renaissance, he writes: "If one grasps death not as a violent creature waiting outside—as a fate coming upon us at a certain moment—if one moreover comprehends its insoluble, deep immanence in life itself, then the death secretly casting its shadow out of so many Rembrandt portraits is only a symptom of how unconditionally, in his art, precisely the principle of life connects itself with that of individuality" (79).

16. For example, Cixous 28; Dubanton 103; and Kennedy, 60–61. When talking about the painter's tale as an "allegory," I use the word in its more conventional sense ("The representation of abstract ideas or principles by characters, figures or events in narrative, dramatic or pictorial form" [*American Heritage Dictionary*]) and not in the sense of the term as used by Walter Benjamin or Paul de Man.

17. The tension between the allegory of the painter and the story of the narrator's affective response to the portrait can be mapped onto the one described by Roland Barthes in his discussion of photography, between "the voice of banality (to say what everyone sees and knows) and the voice of singularity (to replenish such banality with the élan of an emotion that belongs only to myself)" (76). My argument is that critics have tended to hear only the voice of banality and that listening to and producing the voice of singularity is essential since only it can "replenish" a particular text and keep it "alive."

18. See, for example, Jean-Jacques Rousseau's "dialogue-préface" to *La Nouvelle Héloïse*, where N, the reader, tells R, the author: "Un portrait a toujours son prix, pourvu qu'il ressemble, quelque étrange que soit l'original. Mais, dans un tableau d'imagination, toute figure humaine doit avoir les traits communs à l'homme, ou le tableau ne vaut rien. Tous deux supposés bons, il reste encore cette différence, que le portrait intéresse peu de gens; le tableau seul peut plaire au public" (571).

19. I have discussed this "economy" of reading in my book *Economies of Change*, especially chapter 1.

20. For a discussion of art, power, and gender difference, see Linda Nochlin's essay "Women, Art, and Power" in *Women, Art, and Power and Other Essays*.

21. Solomon-Godeau, *Male Trouble: A Crisis of Representation* 9.

2. THE PORTRAIT'S TWO FACES: JAMES'S "THE SPECIAL TYPE" AND "THE TONE OF TIME"

1. James is partially responsible for this critical neglect since he included in the New York edition only a small number of the hundred or so stories he wrote. While "The Liar" was included, "The Special Type," "The Tone of Time," "Glasses," "The Story of a Masterpiece," and "The Sweetheart of M. Briseux" were not.

2. Thus, for example, Viola Winner mentions the short stories only in passing and repeatedly refers to "artists" in general; Marianna Torgovnick does not deal with the short fiction, and while she admits, in a note, that "a great many of James's tales deal with visual artists," she justifies her omission by claiming that "their uses of the visual arts would be quite likely different from the extended, developed uses possible in the novels"

(235n); Adeline Tintner's interest, in her chapter "The Portrait Gallery," in *The Museum World of Henry James*, is almost exclusively in James's references to actual works of art; thus, though she has a whole section entitled "The Vindication of the Portrait in *The Tragic Muse*," she does not even mention the passage where Nash provides this vindication. Similarly, she mentions James's essay on Sargent—another text where James discusses the merits of the portrait—but only in order to document James's relation to Sargent and references by James to Sargent's works. Both Frederick Wegener and Barbara Martineau discuss several portrait stories in some detail, but both end up presenting the "problem" of the portrait as that of "art" in general. Wegener's analysis is primarily concerned with proving the importance of Browning's "My Last Duchess" to James's understanding of portraits and portraiture; he concludes his analysis by stating that the "disquieting truth about the making of a portrait, or of any artistic image [is] that it reifies, by aestheticizing, its model" (567); Martineau concludes her discussion of "The Story of a Masterpiece" by saying that it shows "the surrender of artistic integrity to personal motive" (19). Of course, there are critics who paid attention to portrait stories but not necessarily because they deal with portraits; thus Donatella Izzo, for example, discusses various texts by James, including portrait stories, in terms of the representation of women; Tamar Yacobi analyzes "The Beldonald Holbein" to discuss the use of an artist as a center of consciousness. The one critic who paid systematic attention to the specificity of the portrait in James's work is Moshe Ron. My reflections on the subject are indebted to his work, especially to his essay on "The Liar," "The Art of the Portrait According to James."

3. One notable exception is the protagonist of "The Landscape Painter."

4. The phrase "last adumbration" may suggest a particular Hawthorne story, "The Prophetic Pictures," since the various meanings of the verb to "adumbrate" would apply to it. According to the *American Heritage Dictionary*, to adumbrate means: "to give a sketchy outline"; "to prefigure indistinctly, to foreshadow"; "to disclose partially or guardedly"; "to overshadow, shadow or obscure." The portraits in Hawthorne's story are doubled by a sketch; they foreshadow what will happen, disclose the future partially, but can also be said to overshadow their subjects.

5. To my knowledge, the only studies of these two stories are by David Wagenknecht (on "The Special Type") and John Vacca (on "The Tone of Time").

6. The "germ" for "The Special Type" is "what was told me the other day of the circumstances of W. K. Vanderbilt divorce: his engaging the *demi-mondaine*, in Paris, to *s'afficher* with him in order to force his virago of a

wife to divorce him." James further elaborates the plot: "the husband does not care a straw for the cocotte and makes a bargain with her that is wholly independent of real intimacy. He makes her understand the facts of his situation—which is that he is in love with another woman. *Toward* that woman his wife's character and proceedings drive him; but he loves her too much to compromise her" (Henry James, *Notebooks* 232; see also 288). A portrait does not make part of his original idea for the plot of this story. The "germ" for "The Tone of Time" is "the woman who wants a portrait of some non-existent (never-existent) person. . . . A woman who wants to 'have been' a *widow*—she wants to have in her house the portrait of her husband" (283); James further elaborates the details of the plot, including the coincidence by which "the lady-artist has really evoked and represented a (dead) reality—the man they both had loved" (284; see also 265–67, where the germ for this story is seen in relation to what will become the unfinished story "Hugh Merrow").

7. Edward Wagenknecht 204.

8. It is not entirely clear if the "date of the work" refers to the real date or the faked date. I take it to be the latter so that there are four layers of time: now (the painter as an old man looking at the portrait); the time of the painting; the pretended time of painting; and the period to which the clothes belong.

9. It is worth noting that the narrator's references to the portrait are always accompanied by references to time differences, sounding, as it were, the tone of time. The story is told in the past tense but with no references to the presence of narration that would mark the story as past—except in the case of references to the portrait: "The picture is before me now, so that I could describe it if description availed" (201); the face "has a charm that even, after all these years, still stirs my imagination" (201); "the subject of [the portrait] looks at me now across more years and more knowledge" (202); "This is an old man's tale. I have inherited the picture in the deep beauty of which, however, darkness still lurks" (215). The portrait is also related to anachronism, not being of one's own time (the man's clothes) and ghosts (dead men surviving death).

10. As we shall see in chapter 4, the language of this passage echoes the description of Flora at the end of "Glasses," where Flora appears as her own portrait: "The expression of the eyes was a bit of pastel put in by a master's thumb; . . . Yes, Flora was settled for life—nothing could hurt her further. . . . [S]he was fixed for ever, rescued from all change and ransomed from all doubt" (*Complete Tales* 9: 368).

11. See Barthes 96. Barthes rightly insists on the difference between portrait and photograph: while the photographic portrait is determined by

an indexical relation to its subject, the painted portrait also registers the intention or vision of the painter. This, however, does not mean that the indexical relation to the subject is missing entirely from the painted portrait; hence the painted portrait, too, says both "*This will be* and *this has been*" (96).

12. In order to determine whether or not this view can also be attributed to James himself, one will need to analyze the use of irony in this text and its relation to a first-person narration.

13. Belting, *An Anthropology of Images* 78.

3. THE PORTRAIT PAINTER AND HIS DOUBLES: HOFFMANN'S "DIE DOPPELTGÄNGER," GAUTIER'S "LA CAFETIÈRE," AND NERVAL'S "PORTRAIT DU DIABLE"

1. Huet 20. See also Bettini 189–203.

2. Huet 7.

3. For a discussion of another text that stages the encounter between the reproductive (female) imagination and the creative or transcending (male) imagination, see my essay "Imagination, Poetic Creation, and Gender: Hardy's 'Imaginative Woman.'"

4. See Bettini's discussion of the mother's invisibility as a sign of her faithfulness to her husand (191–92).

5. It is worth noting, however, that the woman's creation is linked to passive receptivity, usually associated with matter, so that in spite of her transgression of paternal authority and her power to subvert nature, the mother is still understood within the dominant paradigm according to which woman is passive matter whereas man is active spirit.

6. The gothic novel, originating in England, was popular in France, where translations of Horace Walpole's *Castle of Otranto*, Ann Radcliffe's *Mysteries of Udolpho*, and Matthew Gregory Lewis's *The Monk* were readily available. Charles Nodier played an important role in mediating between the gothic novel and the French tradition of the fantastic: his *Bertram ou le Château de Saint-Aldobrand* is closely modeled after Charles Maturin's *Melmoth the Wanderer*, and his essay on the fantastic, "Du fantastique en littérature," is the first theorization of this mode.

7. For the relation between the ideal and diabolic woman in Nerval, see Susan Dunn.

8. My reading of the painter Haberland's relation to the figure of the mother and to the question of procreation is indebted to Sarah Kofman's reading of Hoffmann's "Der Sandman" in "Le Double e(s)t le diable," in *Quatre romans analytiques*.

9. See *Discourses on Art*, Fourth Discourse 70.

4. ON PORTRAITS, PAINTERS, AND WOMEN: BALZAC'S *LA MAISON DU CHAT-QUI-PELOTE* AND JAMES'S "GLASSES"

1. Balzac's "La Vendetta," Sand's "Le Château de Pictordu," and James's "The Tone of Time" are among the very few portrait stories that feature a woman painter.
2. Wettlaufer, *Pen vs. Brush* 154.
3. In her introduction to *La Maison du chat-qui-pelote* in the Pléiade edition, Anne-Marie Meininger presents the final scene, in which the painter destroys Augustine's portrait, as forced and irrelevant to what she considers the "real" drama (35). Max Andréoli's short discussion of the portrait (73–74) is minimal and consists primarily of a paraphrase of the story; Paul Perron mentions the portrait only in the last paragraph of his analysis (40).
4. Bonard 22.
5. Wettlaufer, *Pen vs. Brush* 169.
6. See Wettlaufer, *Pen vs. Brush* 137–73; and Schuerewegen.
7. Although the narrator mentions the "unknown man" as if he were a vicarious observer, he usually differentiates himself from Sommervieux. Thus, after the narrator attributes to Sommervieux the enthusiasm of an archeologist (33; 16), he remarks that "the young man seemed very scornful of this essential part of the house" (34; 17)— that is, the part of the house the narrator has just described. As Wettlaufer has pointed out (*Pen vs. Brush* 156–57), the "representative" of the narrator in this scene is a hypothetical "flâneur" (33; 16) who is not the painter.
8. I thus disagree with Schuerewegen, who sees Sommervieux's paintings as continuing and extending the narrator's description (20–21).
9. It is hard to take literally the narrator's claim that, in the past, living animals actually performed the acts now merely represented on the signboards. The narrator's claim may be taken as an expression of his nostalgia for a time already thoroughly commercial but in which prosperity resulted from patient labor (the patience of the artisans who trained the animals whose accomplishments helped enrich the merchant [34; 18]). Alternatively, it can be taken as a sign of nostalgia for a mythically ideal time when representations were not necessary (since one had "the real thing") and linguistic signs were not arbitrary.
10. The narrator also sees Augustine as a masterpiece, characterizing the "calm of her eyes" as "immortalized long since [par avance] in the sublime works of Raphael." However, he also compares her to "day-blowing flowers [fleurs de jour]"—that is, subject to time (37; 20–21).
11. Surprisingly, Andréoli does not include this dichotomy in the long list of oppositions that in his view structure the novella (for that list, see

Andréoli 50). It seems clear that the Guillaumes' valorization of the interior is, according to Balzac, doomed to disappear since their worldview is anachronistic and resistant to change: at the height of Empire they hark back to the sixteenth century and oppose such current social trends as using riches to purchase class status through marriage. To the extent that Augustine is determined by her class origins, her failure and death announce the demise of that way of life. On the other hand, the association of the aristocracy (Sommervieux and the Duchess) with the valorization of the outside cannot be understood in a parallel fashion as presaging the triumph of that class, whose loss of power Balzac both witnessed and represented (for example, in the fall of Mme. de Beauséant at the end of *Père Goriot*). Rather, Balzac is using the aristocracy's historical investment in spectacle and exteriority to describe an emerging social world that is also predicated on the primacy of spectacle, but in which representations are no longer grounded in, say, "blood" or land.

12. Wettlaufer, *Pen vs. Brush* 154.

13. One should note that, unlike a bedroom, the boudoir is not a fully private space, nor is the affair between the Duchess and her lover a "private" one in the sense of hidden from the public eye. As Balzac makes clear in other texts (for example, *Père Goriot*), extramarital love affairs such as the one between the young d'Aiglement and the older Duchess were thoroughly institutionalized and publicly recognized and had a particular social function (the "sentimental education" of a young male).

14. In his essay "Homo Palpitans," Franco Moretti has argued that Balzac's originality resides precisely in creating plots that do not depend on such "unheard of" occurrences: "Balzac's extraordinary invention was to show that a young man's life could be exciting without his having to get shipwrecked on a desert island, sign a pact with the devil, or create homicidal life-size dolls. It is sufficient to write a theatrical review, lose one's heart to a light-headed actress, and lack an iron will. A touch of quite banal speculation transacted by not terribly trustworthy friends, the bank regulations on promissory notes, and the court will take care of the rest. Indeed, with Balzac the 'prose of the world' ceases to be boring" (*Signs Taken for Wonders* 115). My argument is that, if Balzac's novels show a world from which a certain kind of irrationality —associated with the belief in the supernatural, divine, or monstrous—has been banished, that world includes another kind of irrationality—this time associated primarily with the market and with simulacra.

15. Once they are no longer the inhabitants of the Maison du chat-qui-pelote, the Guillaumes console themselves by looking at the picture of the shop, which before they condemned as useless.

16. See Ron, "Portrait of the Artist without Glasses" 45–46, 61; and Izzo 111. The assumption that the relation between male and female involves a symmetrical opposition between seeing/not seeing, dominating/being dominated characterizes not only readings of the gender relations within the story but also comparisons between "Glasses" and Poe's "The Spectacles" (see, for example, Tintner "Poe's 'The Spectacles' and James' 'Glasses'"). Izzo argues that the gender change James introduced in rewriting Poe's story turns a comically improbable story of a myopic young man who refuses to wear glasses out of vanity into a tragic and "culturally representative, socially grounded, perfectly verisimilar" story of woman's willing objectification. But this is only because she considers the desire of Poe's hero to hide the weakness of his eyes (his "castration") as a "mere personal eccentricity" (Izzo 124). One could argue that Poe's story is "culturally representative" precisely insofar as it shows a man's weakness of sight (his narcissistic wound) to be the source of his compensatory idealization of woman. Moreover, once he wears glasses, Poe's Simpson does not see the "real woman" as opposed to an idealized one; rather, he sees an old hag—that is, woman as an image of death. The comic fairy tale ending that rescues Simpson from this "horror" does not erase the story's diagnosis of man's "vision."

17. Izzo 121, 106.

18. One can argue that the male gaze in this story (including that of the painter-narrator) fetishizes the face. As Kaja Silverman argues in another context, however, neither the identification of the male subject with vision (as opposed to the blindness of specularity associated with woman) nor the construction of woman as fetish assure the male subject a dominant position; indeed, the latter "carries with it certain dangers for male subjectivity" (*Subject of Semiotics* 229).

19. Following Freud's definition, Izzo describes Flora as "an extreme case of narcissism," a woman who "reveling in her own beauty, acquires 'a certain self-contentment,' which establishes her as her own love object" (99–100). But Flora has none of the self-sufficiency of Freud's narcissistic woman, who loves only herself. (For a feminist reading of the narcissistic woman in Freud, see Kofman, *Enigma of Woman*.) Later in her argument (following Simone de Beauvoir's definition of feminine subjectivity), Izzo redefines female narcissism as "Femininity = beauty = being looked at" (109), in effect identifying every woman in patriarchal society as narcissistic. In doing so, she robs the term of its specificity and so of its usefulness.

20. Izzo 102–3.

21. It is worth noting that the causal link between not wearing glasses and going blind is rather implausible, if not downright impossible. Adrian

Poole has argued that in the late 1880s spectacles became a consumer good that was advertised and promoted vigorously; the oculist's decree, then, may have more to do with marketing his goods than with supreme scientific knowledge. Poole also quotes from a popular book by John Browning entitled *How to Use Our Eyes: And How to Preserve Them from Infancy to Old Age with Special Information about Spectacles*, in which the author, sounding very much like the narrator and Mrs. Meldrum, argues that short-sighted girls should be encouraged to wear glasses because otherwise they will end up making a foolish marriage (9–10). The implausibility of the chain of cause and effect James has chosen casts doubt on those who promote it as undisputed knowledge and gives support to Flora's resistance to their decrees.

22. Poole 2, 14.

23. Significantly, the narrator, who, as Ron puts it, is a typical Jamesian voyeur, consumed by his curiosity about the affairs of others ("Portrait of the Artist without Glasses" 55), leaves the shop before the confrontation between Flora and Iffield takes place. By declining to watch—and represent—Iffield's behavior, the narrator thus contributes to Iffield's appearance as a figure of pure domination.

24. Ron, "Portrait of the Artist without Glasses" 47.

25. In other words, though the painter is a mediator he is not what Girard called an "external mediator," like God or an absolute king (as Ron claims in "Portrait of the Artist without Glasses" [59]) but rather an internal mediator, a position that can be occupied by anybody and is, hence, far from secure.

26. Ron, "Portrait of the Artist without Glasses" 51–52; Izzo 109–10.

27. The duality of Mrs. Meldrum can be read in her name which, combining "melody" and "drum," unites the semantic markers of beautiful voice and military appearance.

28. In this respect, Mrs. Meldrum plays the same role of "bad double" as Hawley, the narrator's fellow painter in James's "The Real Thing," whose comments about the Monarchs openly express the narrator's suppressed aggression toward them. Whereas Izzo takes Mrs. Meldrum's kindness at face value (109), Poole comments that "Mrs. Meldrum is supposed to have kind eyes but they do not rest with simple kindness on Flora. A strange violence enters her language" when she talks about her (3).

29. See also Izzo 115. The story as a whole, however, undermines a rigid position that equates beauty with femininity: Mrs. Meldrum is considered a woman and a possible object of desire despite her ugliness, and it is the "feminized" male —Dawling—who is ugly and not Lord Iffield.

30. Quoted in Tintner, "Why James Quoted Gibbon in 'Glasses'" 287.

31. Izzo notes that, "as Lynda Neal reminds us, 'the practice of applying paint to canvass has been charged with sexual connotations': the artist—a male, active, productive subject —is 'a man whose sexuality is channeled through his brush'" (120). The narrator's disparaging description of Flora as an artist who lays on colors too heavily thus also conveys envy of her power. Elsewhere, the narrator speaks hyperbolically about Flora's power: she will marry "Any one she likes. She is so abnormally pretty she can do anything" (323).

32. The interpretation that Flora appears to the narrator in the last scene as a successful painter-turned-picture is strengthened by the similarity of the language used in this scene to the description of the painter Mary in "The Tone of Time," discussed in chapter 2, pp. 39–40 and footnote 10. In both stories, the narrator sees in the woman turned picture the accomplishment of his own (frustrated) desire for immortality, though as we have seen, in "The Tone of Time" this immortality may also mean the loss of life; for "Glasses," see Ron, "Portrait of the Artist without Glasses" 64.

33. James's own motivation for writing "Glasses" the way he did may or may not parallel the narrator's. Poole has suggested that in the final scene of "Glasses" (which "displays an image not of mere success but of triumph"), "James is drawing, at some level, on his own bitter sense of humiliation regarding the opening night of Guy Domville" (8). George Bishop links the metaphors of thread and string of pearls to a notebook entry from August 11, 1895, in which James expresses his need (and ability, after his failure in the theater) to control the narrative line (36–39). A more explicit (and probably more relevant) reference to a string of pearls is discussed by Susan Winnett, who quotes a letter James wrote in 1900 to Mrs. Everard Cotes: "I think your drama lacks a little line —bony structure and palpable, as it were, tense cord—on which to string the pearls of detail. It's the frequent fault of women's work— and I like a rope (the rope of the direction and march of the subject, the action) pulled, like a taut cable between a steamer and tug, from beginning to end. [Your plot] lapses on a trifle too liquidly" (qtd. in Winnett 516).

5. PORTRAITS OF THE MALE BODY: KLEIST'S "DER FINDLING," HARDY'S "BARBARA OF THE HOUSE OF GREBE," AND WILDE'S *THE PICTURE OF DORIAN GRAY*

1. Denys Dyer is the only critic, to my knowledge, to point out, in his study of Kleist, the resemblance between "Der Findling" and Hardy's "Barbara of the House of Grebe" (see Dyer 55n11).

2. Needless to say, a portrait of the body by necessity includes the face, but the reverse is not true. Moreover, as Louis Marin puts it, while "in the 'real,' the body is as individual as the face," this is not the case in

representation, where "the body individuates together with the face but not without it, while the face individuates without the body" (227; translation modified). My interest is in the necessity, in these three stories, for representing the body.

3. As Peter Brooks, among others, puts it in his discussion of "the body in the field of vision," "while the bodies viewed [in realist fiction] are both male and female, vision is typically a male prerogative, and its object of fascination the woman's body, in a cultural model so persuasive that many women novelists don't reverse its vectors" (88).

4. Brooks 97. Since this act is often represented as unveiling or denuding, it is important to note that in all three texts the represented male figure is fully clothed.

5. Cave 391.

6. George Reinhardt recognizes the problematic nature of this experience but ultimately does not answer his own questions: "What, for example, are we to make of Nicolo's inability to recognize his own *Doppelgänger* as he confronts Colino's portrait? And how can Elvire remain unaware of the similarity of the two men to each other?" (268).

7. One could describe the first type of relations as grounded in contracts or legal transactions whereas the resemblance between Nicolo and Colino (and hence Nicolo's relation to Elvire), which is central to the second strand of the narrative, points to a relation grounded in blood and the body; one could then argue that the story opposes document to body. But the point is that most of the contractual relations are violated and the biological relation is never affirmed in the text; resemblance, as I will argue, is shown to be a construction rather than a "fact." On body and document in Kleist, see Weineck.

8. See, for example, Ellis's discussion of the story, esp. 4–5; Niekerk 109–10; and Wagner, 283–84. These substitutions can be described as metonymical; this is clearest in the case of the "original" substitution between Piachi's son, Paolo, and Nicolo, due to the accident of "contagion"—a metonymical process. These metonymical substitutions produce the impression of "sameness" or "likeness"; likewise, as we shall see, the resemblance or likeness between Nicolo and the image of Colino is produced by metonymies (for example, clothes standing for the person). Thus in both strands of the story we find metonymies being taken for metaphors, relations of contiguity, for resemblances. I would like to thank Claudia Brodsky Lacour for suggesting this interpretation.

9. Another relation of substitution that resembles Nicolo's taking the place of the image in the portrait is Piachi's forging Xaviera's handwriting.

10. Other critics read the story in terms of the question of identity and

subjectivity but along different lines than mine (see Newman; Ryder; and Webber, "Kleist's Doppelgänger"). Gelus discusses critically (rather than taking at face value) the topic of resemblance (545–47) but with the goal of showing "fallibility and limitations of consciousness" on the part of both narrator and characters (541).

11. For a discussion of point of view, see Parkes.

12. I therefore cannot agree with Webber, who states that in this scene Nicolo "is lured into seeing himself narcissistically in the picture, rather than recognizing its alterity" (110). Newman's account is more precise: she rightly states that Nicolo "suddenly confronts his self in the face of the image, a self who is paradoxically at the same time completely unknown to him" (though the focus on the face here and also on page 293 is misleading: it is always a question of body and clothes and never of face). But it is inaccurate to characterize the scene as one in which "the proto-subject is captivated by its image as whole and powerful" and that it produces in him a "burning passion to recognize the face in the picture" (292–93) since, as Newman herself points out, recognition and desire appear only retrospectively and through the mediation of others.

13. That neither Elvire nor Piachi see a resemblance between Nicolo and Colino (or Colino's portrait) in the course of their habitual, daily relations with him also suggests that "recognition" in this story does not belong to the sphere of normal daily life. Recognition in the story always happens in a flash and always disrupts what is habitual, continuous, normal. Nor does it ever occur under conditions that promote clear visibility: in the open, in a well-lit space, from the proper distance, and so on. All this suggests the exceptional, disruptive, and problematic nature of seeing resemblance.

14. Klara's exclamation may not be as clear as it first appears since it can also be read as claiming that Nicolo is her father.

15. Gelus 544.

16. It is therefore imprecise to say, as does Newman, that in that last scene "Nicolo dons 'exactly' the same Genovese costume he had worn in the accidental encounter with Elvire after the carnival, rendering himself 'exactly' like the portrait" (295). The text suggests, rather, that the *portrait* becomes like Nicolo—in other words, that it is through Nicolo's imitation that the portrait becomes full and concrete.

17. On this, see also Gelus 545.

18. The portrait in this case resembles the "transitional object" theorized by the psychoanalytic theory of object relations. Like the transitional object, the portrait "stands midway between what is created by the inner world and that which exists in the environment": it is not completely created by the subject, but it is the subject who gives it life (Modell 35).

19. I do not agree with Marroni's claim that Edmond's beauty is "negated" (36); rather, the narrator's comment calls attention to Edmond's other, inner qualities, such as bravery and the ability to forgive, which Barbara's investment in his external appearance ignored.

20. As Naomi Schor puts it, sculpture "functions as the degree zero of the detail" (*Reading in Detail* 27).

21. Ebbatson's discussion of the story minimizes the role of the body in the story, claiming, somewhat self-contradictorily, that "Willowes's bodily grace is concentrated in his facial beauty" (102). By contrast, I argue that the function of the statue depends on its being of a full body and that the damage to the face, voice, and hand has to do with the destruction of a fantasmatic image of the body as impenetrable.

22. Gross 17, 30.

23. See "The Ego and the Id," where Freud argues that the ego is "first and foremost, a bodily ego; it is not merely a surface entity, but is itself the projection of a surface" (*Standard Edition of the Complete Psychological Works* 19: 27).

24. As Kristin Brady puts it, Barbara's only choice is "between two statues: Willowes's dead image of beautiful warmth and Uplandtowers's living embodiment of cold 'sculptural repose'" (61).

25. As Barbara's mother says maliciously after the accident, "his wonderful good looks" were "the one little gift he had to justify [Barbara's] choice of him" (257). As a "gift" of nature, a distinction that is not earned or worked at, beauty is often seen as an analogue to aristocratic status; thus Lord Henry, in *The Picture of Dorian Gray*, will call Dorian a "prince" because of this beauty.

26. Whereas Uplandtowers's name suggests solidity (land, tower), Edmond's family name, Willowes, suggests the grace and flexibility of the willow tree, thus both calling attention to his body and signaling that if Edmond has beauty, it is Uplandtowers who has the fixity, immobility, and solidity of a statue.

27. See Ron, "The Uncanny Harbingers of Death" 318.

28. Voice is another individuating trait and also connects inside to outside: thus, when Barbara cannot decide whether the figure that came back is or is not Edmund, she notes that "the tones were not unlike the old tones" but "the enunciation was so altered as to seem that of a stranger" (261).

29. At the end of the story the narrator mentions that many years later, "while digging in the grounds [of the Hall] . . . the broken fragments of a marble statue were unearthed. They were submitted to various antiquaries, who said that, so far as the damaged pieces would allow them to form an opinion, the statue seemed to be that of a mutilated Roman satyr; or, if not,

an allegorical figure of death." Though the comment can be read as ironic (both the reader and "one or two old inhabitants" know "whose statue those fragments had composed"), these interpretations suggest that the mutilation of the statue, like that of the body, destroys its status both as a representation of the human (it is a satyr) and as defying death (an allegory of death).

30. My discussion here is indebted to Michael Taussig's theorization of defacement as "mimetic repetition" (44) that "draws out" of the statue what is already there, hidden because tabooed or repressed (52).

31. Shumaker rightly notes that "Edmond's burns disrupt the border between the inside and the outside of his body"— violating the integrity of the body; but I don't think there is any textual support for her claim that the burns therefore show the skeleton or the eruption of bodily fluids (4).

32. In this respect, Barbara's relation to the statue is similar to the fetishist's divided belief—"Je sais bien mais quand même . . ."—as Octave Mannoni formulated it in an essay by this name.

33. See Taussig's discussion of the exposure of what he calls "the public secret" (211–17).

34. As the word "diary" clearly indicates, one result of this inversion/literalization is that the portrait becomes like a narrative: "the picture of Dorian Gray" becomes *The Picture of Dorian Gray*. I will discuss this topic and the question of reading in the afterword.

35. Though the shift is produced by the inversion cum literalization of the two clichés about portraits, the tension between the two versions of the wish persists in the novel: thus for Lord Henry change is only a question of being in time whereas Basil sees change in moral terms, as affecting the soul. For a different reading of the shift, see Audrey Jaffe.

36. Here as elsewhere in the text, "personality" means "personhood." For the concept of "personality" in the novel, see Hovey, p. 30.

37. For a somewhat different reading of the dynamics of seeing in this novel, centered more on questions of spectatorship, performance, theatricality, as well as the relation of identity to social groups, see Hovey 17–44; see also Craft; and Gomel.

38. In his comments on the novel, Lee Edelman presents Basil's pronouncement that the sitter "is merely the accident, the occasion" for the portrait as one of the moments in the text where a totalizing notion of identity expressed through the "metaphoric privileging of the image, misrecognizes the contingency, the 'accident' that produced it" (16). In asserting that Dorian's presence in the portrait as "style" contradicts Basil's assertion about Dorian's "accidental" relation to the portrait, I do not intend to recover the "metaphoric" notion of identity as essence; rather, the indexical and iconic presence of the sitter in the portrait indicates precisely

that the portrait is the site of both metaphorical and metonymical definitions of identity (an index being a particular form of metonymy).

39. Edelman 16–17.

40. Dorian's relation to the hero of the "poisonous book" Lord Henry gave him is similar to his relation to the picture: he sees the hero of the book as "a kind of prefiguring type for himself" (123) but with the important difference that the book's hero does change with age and loses "what in others, and in the world, he had most dearly valued": his remarkable beauty. Hence the hero's "grotesque dread of mirrors," which Dorian does not share. Both similar to and different from the book's hero, Dorian feels a "cruel joy" (narcissistic and masochistic) in reading the end of the novel, where the hero's loss is described (123), similar to the pleasure he experiences in watching the picture.

41. As Jeff Nunokawa put it, "the abuse suffered by the picture of Dorian Gray is a form of corporal punishment meted out" for homosexual love (165).

42. I borrow this term, as well as the notion of "knowing what not to know" from Michael Taussig, who associates both terms with what he calls "the public secret" (225; 2). My own analysis, however, differentiates between what I call, following D. A. Miller, the "open secret" ("Secret Subjects, Open Secrets," in *The Novel and the Police*) and what Taussig calls "knowing what not to know." For a reading that challenges this notion of the open secret and elaborates, instead, a reading of the novel in terms of the tension between appearance and essence, see Glick.

43. Basil thus has internalized the dominant view of homosexuality as a vice that is written over the body, of the homosexual as a man with "lust written in his face" (John Addington Symonds, qtd. in Edelman 5).

44. Nunokawa also draws attention to the generality of the terms Lord Henry uses: "Lord Henry endorses *every* feeling, thought, dream, and impulse, rather than any in particular." He sees this generality as a strategy for "sheltering" his own desires (158).

45. In a passage toward the end of the novel, Lord Henry asks Dorian to play for him on the piano, saying: "It seems to me that you are the young Apollo, and that I am Marsyas listening to you" (206). The sentence can be read as referring to Dorian's unchanging beauty in comparison with which the wrinkled, worn, and yellow Lord Henry (205) appears as a satyr. But as John Hamilton convincingly argued in his analysis of the Marsyas myth, Marsyas can be read as "question[ing] the voice's reduction to linguistic meaning" (39), that is, as standing for music and voice as purely material sound.

46. For a different reading of these repetitions/reversals, see Otten 299–301.

47. They invite us especially to complicate the Lacanian thesis that "the

mirror image would seem to be the threshold of the visible world" (Lacan, "The Mirror Stage"). For a discussion of this claim, see Kaja Silverman, *The Threshold of the Visible World*.

6. PORTRAITS, PARENTS, AND CHILDREN: STORM'S "AQUIS SUBMERSUS" AND SAND'S "LE CHÂTEAU DE PICTORDU"

1. Schor, *George Sand and Idealism* 44; emphasis in the original.

2. On the understanding of the relation between parents, children, and portraits in classical antiquity, see Bettini 187–212. In the gothic novel, from Walpole to Maturin, portraits of ancestors abound since, as I have noted in the introduction, the emphasis there is on past, unresolved conflicts. Nathaniel Hawthorne's *House of the Seven Gables* and the short story "Edward Randolph's Portrait" both deal with portraits of ancestors. Only one of Henry James's many portrait stories deal with the relation between parents and children: the unfinished "Hugh Merrow." Theodor Storm's interest in the relation between parents and children produced several portrait stories: "Viola Tricolor," "Eekenhof," "Im Schloss," and "Im Nachbarhaus links."

3. Goux 226, 213, 222.

4. *The Standard Edition of the Complete Psychological Works of Sigmund Freud* 10: 235–42.

5. For a summary of criticism dealing with the subject of "guilt," see W. N. B Mullan; see also John Pizer. Gerhard Kaiser reads the father's guilt in terms of Storm's own biography as well as in terms of the institution of the family. My own analysis is closest to that of Mark Ward, who sees "guilt" as "neither a metaphysical nor a personal category. It is socially engendered and socially attributed" (464). But whereas Ward's interest is in showing how Johannes's guilt is socially produced, my own interest is in showing how the story reveals the "fault" within the social world order.

6. In *The Truth in Painting*, Jacques Derrida argues that what constitutes the *parergon* "is not simply [its] exteriority as a surplus, it is the internal structural link which rivets [it] to the lack in the interior of the *ergon*. And this lack would be constitutive of the very unity of the *ergon*. Without this lack, the *ergon* would have no need of a *parergon*. The *ergon*'s lack is the lack of the *parergon*" (59–60). On the supplement in Derrida see also ". . . That Dangerous Supplement . . ." in *Of Grammatology* 141–64.

7. Schneider 10, 15.

8. Woodall 4.

9. An explicit expression of this "complaint" can be found in the twice-repeated anguished address to the missing "guardian [Hüter]": "Oh, guardian, guardian, was your call so far from me?" (419; 143); "O guardian, guardian, was your call so distant?" (450; 167).

10. For a discussion of the relation between portraits and father-son relation and of St. Augustine's definition of both as resemblances *in deterioribus*, see Bettini 187–98.

11. In the second part of the main narrative, the discussion between Johannes and the pastor about the painting of the Virgin Mary implicitly draws the same analogy between biological transmission of traits and portraits, but again not in the context of father and son: the pastor says that he has removed the image of Mary from the church since "the features [die Züge] of our Savior's mother . . . have not been transmitted [handed down, sind nicht überliefert worden]" (438; 157). It is not clear whether the pastor means that they were not transmitted biologically—to her son—or by means of a portrait made during her lifetime.

12. For the controversy about the "Urahne" (the evil ancestress), see Pizer 1002–3.

13. Johannes also comments to Katharina that the face of her own mother does not resemble that of the evil ancestress (407; 133); this is a curious remark since there is no reason why two wives of a Gerhardus should resemble each other. It suggests that resemblance, or lack thereof, is thought of in a nongenealogical context. This strengthens the argument that attributing a resemblance that is not grounded in heredity in the case of Wulf and the evil ancestress is not simply "a slip on Storm's part" as some critics (e.g., Mullan 234) have argued.

14. Leonard Duroche noted some of the obvious similarities between the frame narrative and the main narrative (3). See also the discussion of the frame in E. Allen McCormick 99–107; on the frame structure in Storm, see David Dysart 53–56.

15. Holub 128–29.

16. Though it is true that in both cases the portraits are made soon after death, before the onset of rigor (not to mention decomposition or decay), they are still representations of death (what Phillipe Ariès called "beautiful death").

17. In his brief comments on the novella, Andrew Webber states that "The enterprise of artistic revival serves only to resuscitate ghosts, with the return of the uncanny to the family home. The 'Lazarusbild' as allegory of a true revival is consigned paradigmatically to oblivion" ("The Uncanny Rides Again" 869). As we have seen, the "Lazarusbild" undermines "revival" even before it is forgotten.

18. For an exhaustive study of portraits of the dead, see A. Pigler. His long essay demonstrates that portraying the dead was a recognized genre, markedly different from portraiture. He traces the history of this genre in several national traditions, from the fifteenth century to the end of the nineteenth.

19. Elisabeth Bronfen argues that the narrator recognizes the water lily as the painter's signature ("Inszenierung der Grenze" 329). This is true only to the extent that the water lily allows us to conclude that the two paintings were painted by the same painter. In this sense, her argument complements and supports my own: it is the presence of the gratuitous, supplemental object—the water lily—that allows one to recognize as the same not only the portraits' subject but also their painter.

20. Achim Nuber, for example, sees the lily as an allegorical sign of both death and purity (232); Arndt states that "the white flower together with the presumably white, laced pillow allegorically convey the innocence displayed in the picture" (596) and again, "allegorically the white lily represents innocence" (604); she adds that "the lily is also the allegorical flower of death" (612n32). If the water lily conveys "the innocence displayed in the picture" (meaning, presumably, in the representation of the child since the flower is in the picture too), then it is a superfluous detail, an excess; if it represents innocence "allegorically"—that is, as an objectified attribute—it means that the image of the child could not express his innocence (or could not do it satisfactorily). Thus the water lily is an excess that points out to a lack: a supplement. What is true about the water lily is also true about the portrait as a whole: in the description of the painting we read that it is "the innocent portrait of a child" (381; 112); the "innocence" is metonymically attributed to the portrait (rather than the subject) just as it was attributed to the water lily rather than to the image of the child.

21. The water lily does not fit within theories of the inessential detail such as Barthes's notion of the "effet de réel" or the "punctum": unlike the former, it is not a detail devoid of any thematic or symbolic meaning, which by its very emptiness declares, "I am the real," thus producing the effect of the real. As to the latter, though Barthes calls the punctum a "supplement" (*Camera Lucida* 47) that has the power to move the spectator, he also remarks that what is added by the viewer is "already in the image" (55); and since the image is a photograph, it is also already there, in the real, though the artist did not intend to represent it and may have not even noticed it. Johannes, by contrast, fully intends to represent what is not there in front of him, trying to fill in what he perceives/interprets as missing in the real. This difference suggests the variety of meanings attached to "realism."

22. Though critics often refer to the flower as a lily, what Johannes paints is a *water lily*. This is important to note since water in this story—whether that of the ditch where the child drowns or of the sea that floods the land—is a dangerous and destructive element. Thus the water lily that fills the empty hands of the child is also a reminder of the cause of his death.

23. The inscription on the door of the house in town complicates this relation: whereas in Johannes's narrative the inscription appears in dialect, in the frame narrative the narrator comments that it is written in dialect but translates it into standard German. This difference inserts a wedge within the self-sameness of the inscription that Johannes and the frame narrator see and read, within the "original" (the real) of which both narratives are "copies" (representations): it is and it is not the same inscription. It thus undermines "the impression of both authenticity and immediacy" that Holub argues realism and recollection produce (125). I will further discuss the inscription in the afterword.

24. Thomas Kamla misreads the passage in which Johannes describes how he made a copy of Lord Gerhardus's portrait in the gallery and later used this copy "for a larger portrait, which is still my most precious company here in my lonely chamber" (402; 129). He states that Johannes "reflects on the picture he had painted showing Gerhardus holding his drowned grandson," adding that it was Gerhardus's "youthful features as a young man on the genealogical wall he reproduced on canvas together with the drowned child" (41). As we shall see, Johannes never mentions a picture of Gerhardus holding his dead grandson, and the oil painting that represents him holding the dead child is not of a young man but of an elderly man. Holub states, erroneously, that "the anonymous narrator is able to authenticate Johannes' account by merely lifting his glance to the painting mentioned in the manuscript" (124; see also 136). Dysart quotes Holub's erroneous statement in support of his own argument about the structuring role of the paintings in the story (104). Nuber argues that the correlation between writing and reading is produced by the narrator reading the manuscript in the place where Johannes wrote it and also because the painting of Gerhardus is present in the same space during both the act of writing and the act of reading (239). McCormick makes the same mistake as Kamla, equating the portrait of Gerhardus with the painting of Herr Gerhardus with the dead child and failing to notice that one is of a young man, the other of an elderly one. But he does realize that the oil painting exceeds the limits of Johannes's story: "We may assume that a number of years pass before Johannes finally brings himself to paint Gerhard and to place the dead child in his arms. . . . Significantly, the portrait of Gerhard and the child is the only painting outside the story proper" (128–29). But since he omits to mention that Johannes tells us that the portrait of Herr Gerhardus (which he takes to be the painting of the grandfather holding the child) "is still my most precious company here in my lonely chamber" (402; 129), he does not explain how a painting that was by Johannes's side as he was writing the manuscript could be painted after the manuscript was

completed; in other words, he does not explain what it means that the frame both diverges from the story it frames and exceeds it.

25. The link between the breaking of the dikes that causes drowning and the fault/guilt of the father is the topic of the novella that many consider to be Storm's masterpiece, "Der Schimmelreiter" (*The Rider on the White Horse*), published in 1888. The dikemaster Hauke, who denies the omnipotence of God, sees his responsibility as protecting the entire community where he lives against "God's sea" (749; *The Rider on the White Horse* 272). He assures his feeble-minded daughter, who trusts in his power, that the dike he built will protect her but finally has to recognize that he failed in his responsibility; as a result, both his daughter and wife die by drowning when the dike breaks.

26. Gerhard Kaiser reads "culpa patris" as referring to God (see, for example, 411, 414); but for him the story is an accusation against an evil God who drives people into calamity against their will rather than an acknowledgment of the inability of God to protect.

27. Wettlaufer, "Representing Artistic Identity" 313. Wettlaufer reads the story as a "rejection of the oppressive law of the father and return to the Lacanian realm of the maternal imaginary" (312), a view that my reading seeks to problematize.

28. Schor, *George Sand and Idealism* 161, 165.

29. Flochardet's practice can be read as a caricature of Hegel's statement that even though the portrait painter is the least interested among painters in the ideal, he has to flatter, that is, has to leave out all external particularities of the sitter. In Hegel, however, the result of this "flattery" is that what *is* represented are the permanent spiritual properties of the sitter (see *Aesthetics: Lectures on Fine Art* I.iii.a1.155).

30. Ernst Bloch, "A Philosophical View of the Novel of the Artist," in *The Utopian Function of Art* 266.

31. See Schor, *George Sand* 130.

32. The similarity between Sand's tale and Gautier's "La Cafetière," which I discussed in chapter 3, is worth noting. In both stories, the main character "sees" during the night painted images come to life, bringing back a past considered aesthetically superior to the present; in both, we find an aspiring or young painter drawing a portrait without quite knowing what she/he is doing; in both cases, the drawing proves to be that of a dead woman whom neither painter knew either in life or through a representation. But in Gautier, the emphasis is on the male painter's idealization of the lost woman, which the story ironizes; in Sand, by contrast, the idealization of the real mother is presented as necessary for Diane's becoming a painter.

33. J. Hillis Miller 8.

34. See Schor, *George Sand* 53: Indiana's "dream of being freed from patriarchal bondage is inseparable from a dream of emancipating the victims of colonialism."

35. Thus Sand in this story imagines a possible scenario for women different from the one that Sandra Gilbert, in "Notes toward a Literary Daughteronomy," characterized as the inevitable lot of the daughter in patriarchal society. According to Gilbert, what the female predecessor transmits to a woman artist is the message that "You must bury your mother; you must give yourself to your father. Since the daughter has inherited an empty sack and cannot *be* a father, she has no choice but to be *for* the father—to be his treasure, his land, his voice" (265).

36. On the question of matter in its relation to the feminine and the maternal, see Judith Butler; and Vicky Kirby.

7. GOGOL, "THE PORTRAIT"

1. For the first version, I will be using Constance Garnett's translation in *The Overcoat and Other Stories*; for the second version, I will be using David Magarshack's translation in *The Overcoat and Other Tales of Good and Evil*. References to the first version will have a Roman numeral I before the page number. I will refer to the painter by the name Chartkov or Chertkov according to which version I am discussing.

2. T. E. Little observes apropos of *Dead Souls* the absence of "love interest" as well as "the non-existence in Gogol's works of genuine, mundane, cordial friendship and affection"; characters rarely "express simple affection or exchange friendly information" (109). Helen Muchnic points out that Gogol's works do not have "characters" in the usual sense of the term (7). Donald Fanger quotes S. A. Vengerov's claim that there are no heroes in Gogol since his characters are collective figures (115); Fanger also argues that besides the artist in "The Nevsky Prospect" and Chartkov in "The Portrait," "Gogol's characters all incline towards facelessness" (116). It is hard to think of the moneylender as being "faceless" since the text insists on his striking features, on his difference from the people who surround him; rather, as I will argue, the portrait turns the moneylender into an allegory in which his face signifies.

3. In the first version, the harm caused by the moneylender is often death or sickness. In the second version, the narrator of the second part questions the veracity of such occurrences, saying they may be only rumor or "absurd superstitious talk" (142). Instead, he presents two "case studies" that describe the evil effects of the moneylender as that of turning people envious. A well-known, admired, philanthropic statesman who supports the arts and a handsome, noble lover, "the ideal hero of novels and women" (145), each

needs money and as the result of borrowing it from the moneylender becomes excessively envious. Each needs money in order to perpetuate a certain image of himself as someone who is admirable and enviable because he has the power (of money) to get or do what he wants (continue support of the arts, marry the woman he loves). It is the desire to be admired by others, which, as we shall see, is shared by Chartkov's sitters and by Chartkov himself, that they want to sustain. By showing that they have become envious as a result of borrowing the money, what is revealed is that they borrowed it because what they wanted was to be envied. That the effect of the moneylender and his portrait is to generate envy is made also clear in the two parallel scenes in the first and second part where the old painter and Chartkov each becomes envious of another painter who has produced a great work of art.

4. On the money devil, see Shell, *Art and Money* 63–72.

5. My discussion of the relation between the portrait and money is indebted to the work of Marc Shell, who has devoted many books to studying the relation between money, art, and religion, especially to his *Art and Money*. On money and the portrait more particularly, see "Portia's Portrait."

6. See, for example, Henry James's "The Liar," where Sir David Ashmore is said to have "his pet superstition. He was sure that if [his portrait were painted] he would die directly afterwards" (*Complete Tales* 6: 388).

7. See Steiner 112–13.

8. See, for example, Gippius 101; and Peace 116.

9. When the son finishes the story and everybody realizes that the portrait is not there, one other explanation is proposed, besides the possibility that it was stolen: the possibility that the portrait never existed, that it was all an illusion, a trompe l'oeil. This could have led to an argument about art as make-believe, as illusion, which often, as Shell has argued, is related to paper money. This line of thought is not developed in the story.

10. For Aristotle's discussion of usury, see *Politics* I, chap. 10. Aristotle's argument against usury is that it substitutes means for ends. Money was intended to be used as a means for exchange, but usury tries to make it grow as though it were an end in itself. In begetting money out of money, usury works against nature because money is sterile and only natural organisms can breed an offspring.

11. I will be using this spelling for the religious eikon in order to distinguish it from the sign-function Peirce called "icon." This is necessary since, as we shall see, the religious eikon is not a Peircean icon.

12. This scene echoes (or anticipates) the one in the second part of the story where the envy the old painter feels at his pupil's success "stimulated

[his] brush" (153); in the picture he produced under the evil influence of the moneylender's portrait, the eyes multiply: all the figures have "the usurer's eyes" and gaze at the viewer with "demon-like intensity" (152).

13. Chartkov's meditation curiously seems to accord with Hegel's remark, in the introduction to the *Aesthetics*, that "There are portraits which, as has been wittily said, are 'disgustingly like'" (introduction 6.iii.43). Jean-Marie Pontévia argued that Hegel's comment that the successful portrait "is more like the individual than the actual individual himself" (III. iii.1.2c.867) means that the portrait is inherently marked by excess and implies, at the same time, that reality is lacking (23).

14. For a general discussion of the question of matter in Gogol, see Michal Oklot.

15. "The lubok was a form of primitive folk art: a broadsheet consisting of a crude print illustration, frequently accompanied by a text"; it originated in the Ukraine (Shapiro 58).

16. Maguire 144.

17. See Oklot's discussion of the scene in the shop and the question of matter (84–91); on the erasure of inscription as a variation on the abolition of difference between background and foreground, see 126.

18. Shell, *Art and Money* 135.

19. For another reading of this scene, see Oklot 94–101.

20. Oklot pointed out that the name of the girl in the first version—Annette—spelled in the Russian original "Anet," is a pun on "'a-no' [a-net]" (96n187). In painting her portrait as the image of Psyche, Chartkov, according to the mother, shows that he is a great painter, as good as the one who made the girl's portrait as a child and whose name is "Monsieur Nohl," meaning "zero [nol]" in Russian (Maguire 146). Thus the scene is coded as that of Chartkov's annihilation.

21. This term comes from Thorstein Veblen's *Theory of the Leisure Class*.

22. As Maguire argued, "The sitters are probably imitating portraits they have seen" (149), so the portraits Chartkov paints are copies of copies, and Chartkov, in painting them, is "Merely imitating the already imitative expectations of others . . . he really 'becomes' everything he imitates . . . merely another version of each of the poses he renders" (150; see also 151).

23. The image of a coffin with a corpse without a heart suggests an analogy between Chartkov and the moneylender. According to Anne Derbes, Saint Anthony is said to have invited his audience to open the coffin of the usurer to show that he had no heart (Derbes 40). I would like to thank Scott Hiley for referring me to this work and for discussing usury with me. That Chartkov is described as a body without spirit (corpse) rather than as a ghost correlates with the emphasis in the story on gold coins, "associated

with the substance of value" as opposed to insubstantial paper money, which was often associated with ghostliness. See Shell, *Money, Language, and Thought* 6.

24. Maguire notes that after Chartkov's death there is no trace of his wealth and concludes: "he has turned himself completely into money and in spending the money he spends himself. When it is gone, so is he" (154).

25. Maguire argues that "The Portrait" is very different from other texts by Gogol since it does include a positive ideal in the figure of the old painter; he neglects to point out that this positive figure is also the source of all subsequent evil. The two other painters, who form the foil for the lapsed old painter and for Chartkov, can be seen as positive ideals, but they are not the subject of the story.

26. I do not think there is textual support for Maguire's claim that the portrait of the moneylender is "a prime example of bad art and is recognized as such by Chartkov" and that Chartkov himself "is fated to create art very much like it" (145). Chartkov's reaction to the portrait (see 96–97), as that of all those who see it and would like to own it, is that it is a striking, arresting picture, showing superb technique.

27. Thus Peace, for example, claims that "Chartkov is the hero of the story" (120). The reason Peace gives for this judgment—that Chartkov alone is named—is factually true; but as we shall see, the anonymity of the old painter has nothing to do with his importance, or lack thereof, in the story.

28. On the hallmarks of the painter of old legends, see Kris and Kurz.

29. *Likeness and Presence: A History of the Image before the Era of Art.* According to Belting, "After the Middle Ages . . . art took on a different meaning and became acknowledged for its own sake—art as invented by a famous artist and defined by a proper theory" (xxi).

30. "Art becomes the sphere of the artist, who assumes control of the image as proof of his or her art" (Belting, *Likeness and Presence* 16).

31. Belting, *Likeness and Presence* 484.

32. The eikon is thus not an "icon" in the sense Peirce gives to this term. It is partially what Peirce has called a "symbol" (determined by convention) and, as we shall see, a special kind of index (participates in the prototype).

33. For example, to Saint Luke (see Freeland 53–54; Belting, *Likeness and Presence* 4).

34. Chartkov's story can be read as arguing against Benjamin's claim that "mechanical reproduction emancipates the work of art from its parasitical dependence on ritual" (224). According to the story, this "freedom" is illusory: instead of being constrained by religious authorities, the painter is

enslaved to the foolish whims of his clients; the manifestation of this enslavement is "mechanical" reproduction in response to demand.

35. Both quotes are from Belting, *Likeness and Presence* 484.

36. "With the emancipation of the various art practices from ritual go increasing opportunities for the exhibition of their products. The ability to exhibit [die Ausstellbarkeit] of a portrait bust that can be sent here and there is greater than that of a statue of a divinity that has its fixed place in the interior of a temple. The ability to exhibit [die Ausstellbarkeit] of a painting is greater than that of the mosaic or frescoes that preceded it" (Benjamin 225; translation modified). As Samuel Weber argues, Benjamin uses frequently the suffix -barkeit (as in "Ausstellbarkeit" and the better-known "Reproduzierbarkeit" or "reproducibility") to indicate "a virtual condition," "a structural possibility that is potentially 'at work' even there where it seems factually not to have occurred" (7, 6).

37. Thus the story suggests that the object of ritual is not determined, as Benjamin argues, by "the location of its original use value" (224).

38. The same is true for a photograph. I will come back to the question of photography at the end of the chapter.

39. Shell, *Art and Money* 10. And Shell continues: "The traditional definition of truth as adequatio res et intellectus—the unifying adequation of the thing with the intellectual conception of it—is, as Heidegger seems to suggest in 'On the Essence of Truth,' in this sense, numismatic."

40. As David Hawkes argues, defenders of eikons "draw inspiration from Plato's theory of the prototype, as expressed in such texts as the *Symposium* and the *Timaeus*. . . . For Plato the image actually participates 'in' the prototype and it cannot be conceived of separately from its original. . . . From here it was a short step to perceiving the *pneuma* of divinity inhabiting the *eikon*" (58–59).

41. The eikon "bears witness to the transfiguration of matter by light which is realized by incarnation in the person of the Son of God" (Goux 149).

42. See Philippe Lacoue-Labarthe's discussion of Benjamin's essay (57–61), where he argues, among other things, that art, defined by its "exposibility" destroys itself and that hence the "essence of art" "n'est pas l'art, mais le religieux" (60).

43. This explains why the lack of adequation is expressed primarily as excess of materiality (rather than the more common thesis of the loss of material support or ground): The materiality of eikons is infused with spirit; but to the "rational" gaze (as well as to the gaze of the iconoclast), the eikon is not the saint it "represents"; it is just a piece of wood with gold on it, sheer matter.

44. See Barthes *Camera Lucida*, passim.

AFTERWORD: READING PORTRAIT STORIES

1. My reading of the scene of reading in *The Picture of Dorian Gray* owes much to Garrett Stewart's discussion of it (346–52). Stewart, however, does not seem to make a distinction between being influenced and "reading as"—which is the main point of my own discussion.

2. It is worth noting that though "reading as" is a somewhat curious expression, painting someone "as" someone else is a very common practice (e.g., Sir Joshua Reynolds's *Mrs. Siddons as the Tragic Muse*, among many others). Indeed, the beginning of the passage on reading curiously echoes an earlier passage dealing with painting, where Basil tells Dorian how he painted him "as" a series of figures from antiquity: "I had drawn you as Paris in dainty armour, and as Adonis with huntsman's cloak and polished boar-spear. Crowned with heavy lotus-blossoms you had sat on the prow of Adrian's barge, gazing across the green turbid Nile. You had leant over the still pool of some Greek woodland, and seen in the water's silent silver the marvel of your own face" (110). Basil tells Dorian about the difference between the historical paintings in which he painted Dorian as someone else—in which Dorian is "prefigured"—and a portrait; but as we have seen the portrait cannot be understood as "painting Dorian as he truly is" since the portrayed Dorian is a product of Lord Henry's influence as well as of Dorian's own influence on Basil.

3. Stewart, indeed, reads this scene as a scene of silent reading, since Basil does not seem to hear anything Lord Henry has been telling Dorian (352).

WORKS CITED

Andréoli, Max. "Une nouvelle de Balzac: 'La Maison du chat-qui-pelote': Ébauche d'une lecture totale." *L'Année balzacienne* (1972): 43–80.
Ariès, Philippe. *Images of Man and Death*. Trans. Janet Lloyd. Cambridge: Harvard University Press, 1985.
Aristotle. *Poetics*. Trans. Anthony Kenny. Oxford: Oxford University Press, 2013.
———. *Politics*. Trans. Carnes Lord. Chicago: University of Chicago Press, 2013.
Arndt, Christiane. "On the Transgression of Frames in Theodor Storm's Novella *Aquis submersus*." *Monatshefte* 97 (2005): 595–614.
Bal, Mieke, and Norman Bryson. "Semiotics and Art History." *Art Bulletin* 73 (1991): 174–208.
Balzac, Honoré. *At the Sign of the Cat and Racket*. Trans. Clara Bell. London: Dent, 1910.
———. *La Maison du chat-qui-pelote*. Ed. Anne-Marie Baron. Paris: Garnier-Flammarion, 1985.
Barthes, Roland. *Camera Lucida: Reflections on Photography*. Trans. Richard Howard. New York: Hill and Wang, 1981.
———. "L'Effet du réel." *Communications* 11 (1968): 84–89.
Beebe, Maurice. *Ivory Towers and Sacred Founts: The Artist as Hero in Fiction from Goethe to Joyce*. New York: New York University Press, 1964.
Belting, Hans. *An Anthropology of Images: Picture, Medium, Body*. Trans. Thomas Dunlap. Princeton, N.J.: Princeton University Press, 2011.
———. *Likeness and Presence: A History of the Image before the Era of Art*. Trans. Edmund Jephcott. Chicago: University of Chicago Press, 1994.
Benjamin, Walter. *Illuminations*. Trans. Harry Zohn. Ed. Hannah Arendt. New York: Schocken, 1973.
Bersani, Leo. *The Culture of Redemption*. Cambridge: Harvard University Press, 1990.
Bettini, Maurizio. *The Portrait of the Lover*. Trans. Laura Gibbs. Berkeley: University of California Press, 1999.
Betzer, Sarah. "Ingres's Second *Madame Moitessier*: 'Le Brevet du Peintre d'Histoire.'" *Art History* 23 (2000): 681–705.

Bishop, George. *When the Master Relents: The Neglected Short Fictions of Henry James*. Ann Arbor, Mich.: UMI Research Press, 1988.
Bloch, Ernst. *The Utopian Function of Art and Literature: Selected Essays*. Trans. Jack Zipps and Frank Mechlenburg. Cambridge: MIT Press, 1988.
Bonard, Olivier. *La Peinture dans la création balzacienne: Invention et vision picutrales de* La Maison du chat-qui-pelote *au* Père Goriot. Geneva: Droz, 1969.
Bowie, Theodor. *The Painter in French Fiction*. Chapel Hill: University of North Carolina Press, 1950.
Brady, Kristin. *The Short Stories of Thomas Hardy*. New York: St. Martin Press, 1982.
Breckenridge, James. *Likeness: A Conceptual History of Ancient Portraiture*. Evanston, Ill.: Northwestern University Press, 1968.
Brilliant, Richard. *Portraiture*. London: Reaktion, 1997.
Bronfen, Elisabeth. "Inszenierung der Grenze realistischer Repräsentation." *Die Trauben des Zeuxis: Formen künstlerischer Wirklichkeitsaneignung*. Ed. Hans Körner. Hildesheim: G. Olms, 1990. 306–34.
———. *Over Her Dead Body*. New York: Routledge, 1992.
Brooks, Peter. *Body Work: Objects of Desire in Modern Narrative*. Cambridge: Harvard University Press, 1993.
Burks, Arthur W. "Icon, Index, and Symbol." *Philosophy and Phenomenological Research* 9 (1949): 673–89.
Butler, Judith. *Bodies That Matter: On the Discursive Limits of "Sex."* New York: Routledge, 1993.
Byatt, A. S. *Portraits in Fiction*. London: Chatto and Windus, 2001.
Cave, Terence. *Recognitions: A Study in Poetics*. Oxford: Oxford University Press, 1988.
Cixous, Hélène. *Three Steps on the Ladder of Writing*. Trans. Sarah Cornell and Susan Sellers. New York: Columbia University Press, 1993.
Craft, Christopher. "Come See about Me: Enchantment of the Double in *The Picture of Dorian Gray*." *Representations* 91 (2005): 109–36.
de Man, Paul. *The Rhetoric of Romanticism*. New York: Columbia University Press, 1984.
Dean, Sharon. "The Myopic Narrator in Henry James's 'Glasses.'" *Henry James Review* 4 (1983): 191–95.
Derbes, Anne. *The Usurer's Heart: Giotto, Enrico Scrovegni, and the Arena Chapel in Padua*. University Park: Pennsylvania State University Press, 2008.
Derrida, Jacques. *Of Grammatology*. Trans. Gayatri Chakravorty Spivak. Baltimore: Johns Hopkins University Press, 1974.
———. *The Truth in Painting*. Trans. Geoff Bennington. Chicago: University of Chicago Press, 1987.

Dowell, Richard W. "The Ironic History of Poe's 'Life in Death': A Literary Skeleton in the Closet." *American Literature* 42 (1971): 478–86.

Dubanton, Monique. "L'Ovale du portrait: La fonction de l'écriture chez Edgar Poe." *Poétique* 37 (1979): 102–10.

Dunn, Susan. "Nerval et les portraits." *Australian Journal of French Studies* 12 (1975): 286–94.

Duroche, Leonard L. "Like and Look Alike: Symmetry and Irony in Theodor Storm's *Aquis submersus*." *Seminar* 7 (1971): 1–13.

Dyer, Denys. *The Stories of Kleist: A Critical Study*. London: Duckworth, 1977.

Dysart, David L. *The Role of the Painting in the Works of Theodor Storm*. New York: Peter Lang, 1992.

Ebbatson, Roger. *Hardy: The Margin of the Unexpressed*. Sheffield: Sheffield Academic Press, 1993.

Edelman, Lee. *Homographesis: Essays in Gay Literary and Cultural Theory*. New York: Routledge, 1994.

Ellis, John M. *Heinrich von Kleist: Studies in the Character and Meaning of His Writings*. Chapel Hill: University of North Carolina Press, 1979.

Fanger, Donald. *Dostoevsky and Romantic Realism: A Study of Dostoevsky in Relation to Balzac, Dickens, and Gogol*. Evanston, Ill.: Northwestern University Press, 1998.

Francastel, Galienne, and Pierre Francastel. *Le Portrait: 50 siècles d'humanisme en peinture*. Paris: Hachette, 1969.

Freedberg, David. *The Power of Images: Studies in the History and Theory of Response*. Chicago: University of Chicago Press, 1989.

Freedman, William. "Poe's Oval Portrait of 'The Oval Portrait.'" *Poe Studies* 24 (2001): 7–12.

Freeland, Cynthia. *Portraits and Persons*. Oxford: Oxford University Press, 2010.

Freud, Sigmund. *The Standard Edition of the Complete Psychological Works of Sigmund Freud*. Trans. James Strachey. London: Hogarth Press, 1966.

Friedländer, Max J. *On Art and Connoisseurship*. London: Bruno Cassirer, 1942.

Gautier, Théophile. *My Fantoms*. Trans. Richard Homes. New York: New York Review of Books, 2008.

———. *Récits fantastiques*. Bournemouth: Parkstone Press, 1994.

———. *Spirite and the Coffee Pot*. Trans. Patrick Jenkins. New York: Dedalus, 1995.

Gaylard, Susan. *Hollow Men: Writing, Objects, and Public Image in Renaissance Italy*. New York: Fordham University Press, 2013.

Gelus, Marjorie. "Displacement of Meaning: Kleist's 'Der Findling.'" *German Quarterly* 55 (1982): 541–53.

Gilbert, Sandra. "Notes toward a Literary Daughteronomy." *Daughters and*

Fathers. Ed. Lynda E. Boose and Betty S. Flowers. Baltimore: Johns Hopkins University Press, 1989. 256–77.

Ginsburg, Michal Peled. *Economies of Change: Form and Transformation in the Nineteenth-Century Novel*. Stanford, Calif.: Stanford University Press, 1996.

———. "Imagination, Poetic Creation, and Gender: Hardy's 'Imaginative Woman.'" *Modern Philology* 110 (2012): 273–88.

Gippius, V. V. *Gogol*. Trans. Robert A. Maguire. Ann Arbor: Ardis, 1981.

Girard, René. *Deceit, Desire, and the Novel: Self and Other in Literary Structure*. Trans. Yvonne Freccero. Baltimore: Johns Hopkins University Press, 1965.

Glick, Elisa. "The Dialectics of Dandyism." *Cultural Critique* 48 (2001): 129–63.

Gogol, Nikolai. *The Overcoat and Other Stories*. Trans. Constance Garnett. London: Chatto and Windus, 1923.

———. *The Overcoat and Other Tales of Good and Evil*. Trans. David Magarshack. New York: Norton, 1965.

Gombrich, Ernest, et al. *Art, Perception, and Reality*. Baltimore: Johns Hopkins University Press, 1972.

Gomel, Elana. "Oscar Wilde, *The Picture of Dorian Gray*, and the (Un)Death of the Author." *Narrative* 12 (2004): 74–92.

Goux, Jean-Joseph. *Symbolic Economies after Marx and Freud*. Trans. Jennifer Gage. Ithaca, N.Y.: Cornell University Press, 1990.

Gross, Kenneth. *The Dream of the Moving Statue*. Ithaca, N.Y.: Cornell University Press, 1992.

Hamilton, John T. *Music, Madness, and the Unworking of Language*. New York: Columbia University Press, 2008.

Hardy, Thomas. *Wessex Tales and A Group of Noble Dames*. Ed. F. B. Pinion. London: Macmillan, 1977. The New Wessex Edition.

Hawkes, David. *Idols of the Marketplace: Idolatry and Commodity Fetishism in English Literature, 1580–1680*. New York: Palgrave, 2001.

Hegel, Georg Wilhelm Friedrich. *Aesthetics: Lectures on Fine Art*. Trans. T. M. Knox. Oxford: Oxford University Press, 1975.

Hoffmann, E. T. A. *Gesammelte Werke*. Vol. 4. Hamburg: Standard Verlag, 1964–65.

———. *Selected Writings of Hoffmann*. Vol. 1. Trans. Leonora J. Kent and Elizabeth C. Knight. Chicago: University of Chicago Press, 1969.

Holub, Robert C. "Realism and Recollection: The Commemoration of Art and the Aesthetics of Abnegation in *Aquis submersus*." *Colloquia Germanica* 18 (1985): 120–39.

Hovey, Jaime. *A Thousand Words: Portraiture, Style, and Queer Modernism*. Columbus: Ohio State University Press, 2006.

Huet, Marie Hélène. *Monstrous Imagination*. Cambridge: Harvard University Press, 1993.

Izzo, Donatella. *Portraying the Lady: Technologies of Gender in the Short Stories of Henry James*. Lincoln and London: University of Nebraska Press, 2001.
Jaffe, Audrey. "Embodying Culture: Dorian's Wish." *Aesthetic Subjects*. Ed. Pamela R. Matthews and David McWhirter. Minneapolis: Minnesota University Press, 2003. 295–312.
James, Henry. *The Complete Tales of Henry James*. Ed. Leon Edel. London: Rupert Hart-Davis, 1964.
———. *The Notebooks of Henry James*. Ed. F. O. Matthiessen and Kenneth B. Murdock. New York: Oxford University Press, 1947.
———. *The Tragic Muse. Novels 1886–1890*. Ed. Daniel Mark Fogel. New York: Library of America, 1989.
Jeffares, Bo. *The Artist in Nineteenth Century English Fiction*. Buckinghamshire: Colin Smythe, 1979.
Kaiser, Gerhard. "Aquis submersus—versunkene Kindheit." *Euphorion: Zeitschrift für Literaturgeschichte* 73 (1979): 410–34.
Kamla, Thomas A. "Transitoriness and Christian Transcendence in Storm's *Aquis submersus*." *Forum for Modern Language Studies* 39 (2003): 27–52.
Kant, Immanuel. *Critique of Judgement*. Trans. Creed Meredith. New York: Oxford University Press, 2007.
Kennedy, J. Gerald. *Poe, Death, and the Life of Writing*. New Haven, Conn.: Yale University Press, 1987.
Kirby, Vicky. *Telling Flesh: The Substance of the Corporeal*. New York: Routledge, 1997.
Kleist, Heinrich von. *The Marquise of O—And Other Stories*. Trans. Martin Greenberg. New York: Signet Classics, 1962.
———. *Sämtliche Erzählungen und Anekdoten*. Munich: Carl Hanser Verlag, 1977.
Kofman, Sarah. *The Enigma of Woman: Woman in Freud's Writing*. Trans. Catherine Porter. Ithaca, N.Y.: Cornell University Press, 1985.
———. *Quatre romans analytiques*. Paris: Galilée, 1973.
Kot, Paula. "Painful Erasures: Excising the Wild Eye from 'The Oval Portrait'." *Poe Studies* 28 (1995): 1–6.
Kris, Ernst, and Otto Kurz. *Legend, Myth and Magic in the Image of the Artist: A Historical Experiment*. New Haven, Conn.: Yale University Press, 1979.
La Fayette, Madame de. *Romans et nouvelles*. Ed. Emile Magne. Paris: Classiques Garnier, 1961.
Lacan, Jacques. "The Mirror Stage as Formative of the Function of the 'I' as Revealed in Psychoanalytic Experience." *Écrits: A Selection*. Trans. Alan Sheridan. New York: Norton, 1977.
Lacoue-Labarthe, Phillipe. *Portrait de l'artiste, en général*. Paris: Christian Bourgeois, 1979.
Lee, A. Robert, ed. *Edgar Allan Poe: The Design of Order*. London: Vision Press, 1987.

Lee, Vernon. *Euphorion: Studies of the Antique and the Medieval in the Renaissance*. London: Unwin, 1885.
Little, E. T. *The Fantasts*. Amersham, England: Avebury, 1984.
Maguire, Robert A. *Exploring Gogol*. Stanford, Calif.: Stanford University Press, 1994.
Mannoni, Octave. *Clefs pour l'imaginaire ou l'autre scène*. Paris: Éditions du Seuil, 1969.
Marin, Louis. *Portrait of the King*. Trans. Martha M. Houle. Minneapolis: University of Minnesota Press, 1988.
Marroni, Francesco. "The Negation of Eros in 'Barbara of the House of Grebe.'" *Thomas Hardy Journal* 10 (1994): 33–41.
Martineau, Barbara. "Portraits Are Murdered in the Short Fiction of Henry James." *Journal of Narrative Technique* 2 (1972): 16–25.
McCormick, E. Allen. *Theodor Storm's Novellen: Essays on Literary Technique*. Chapel Hill: University of North Carolina Press, 1964.
McPherson, Heather. *The Modern Portrait in Nineteenth-Century France*. Cambridge: Cambridge University Press, 2001.
Meininger, Anne-Marie. "Introduction." Balzac, Honoré. *La Maison du chat-qui-pelote*. In *La Comédie humaine*. Ed. Pierre-Georges Castex. Vol. 1. Paris: Gallimard, 1976. Pléiade edition. 25–38.
Meltzer, Françoise. *Salome and the Dance of Writing: Portraits of Mimesis in Literature*. Chicago: University of Chicago Press, 1987.
Miller, D. A. *The Novel and the Police*. Berkeley: University of California Press, 1988.
Miller, J. Hillis. *Versions of Pygmalion*. Cambridge: Harvard University Press, 1990.
[Miss Elliott]. *The Portrait*. London, 1783.
Modell, Arnold H. *Object Love and Reality: An Introduction to a Psychoanalytic Theory of Object Relations*. London: Hogarth Press, 1969.
Mollinger, Robert N. "Edgar Allan Poe's 'The Oval Portrait': Fusion of Multiple Identities." *American Imago* 36 (1979): 147–53.
Moretti, Franco. *Signs Taken for Wonders: Essays in the Sociology of Literary Forms*. Trans. Susan Fischer et al. London: Verso, 1983.
Muchnic, Helen. *The Unhappy Consciousness: Gogol, Poe, Baudelaire*. Baltimore: Barton-Gillet Co. [published by Smith College], 1967.
Mullan, W. N. B. "Tragic Guilt and the Motivation of the Catastrophe in Storm's 'Aquis submersus.'" *Forum for Modern Language Studies* 18 (1982): 225–46.
Nancy, Jean-Luc. *Le Regard du portrait*. Paris: Galilée, 2000.
Nerval, Gérard de. *Oeuvres complètes*, Vol. 3. Ed. Jules Marsan. Paris: Champion, 1928.
Newman, Gail. "Family Violence in Heinrich von Kleist's *Der Findling*." *Colloquia Germanica* 29 (1996): 287–302.

Niekerk, Carl. "Men in Pain: Disease and Displacement in 'Der Findling.'" In *Kleists Erzählungen und Dramen: Neue Studien*. Ed. Michael Lützeler and David Pan. Würzburg: Königshausen and Neumann, 2001. 107–19.

Nochlin, Linda. *Women, Art, and Power and Other Essays*. New York: Harper and Row, 1988.

Nodier, Charles. *Oeuvres de Charles Nodier: Rêveries*. Paris: Librairie d'Eugène Renduel, 1832.

Nuber, Achim. "Ein Bilderrätsel: Emblematische Struktur und Autorefererntialität in Theodor Storms Erzählung *Aquis Submersus*." *Colloquia Germanica* 26 (1993): 227–43.

Nunokawa, Jeff. "The Importance of Being Bored: The Dividends of Ennui in *The Picture of Dorian Gray*." *Novel Gazing: Queer Readings in Fiction*. Ed. Eve Kosofsky Sedgwick. Durham, N.C.: Duke University Press, 1997. 151–66.

Oklot, Michal. *Phantasms of Matter in Gogol and Gombrowicz*. Champaign and London: Dalkey Archive Press, 2009.

Otten, Thomas J. "Slashing Henry James (On Painting and Political Economy Circa 1900)." *Yale Journal of Criticism* 13 (2000): 293–320.

Parkes, Ford B. "Shifting Narrative Perspectives in Kleist's 'Findling.'" *Journal of English and Germanic Philology* 76 (1977): 165–76.

Peace, Richard. *The Enigma of Gogol*. Cambridge: Cambridge University Press, 1981.

Perosa, Sergio. *From Islands to Portraits: Four Literary Variations*. Amsterdam: IOS Press, 2000.

Perron, Paul. "Système du portrait et topologie actantielle dans *La Maison du chat-qui-pelote*." *Le Roman de Balzac: Recherches critiques, méthodes, lectures*. Ed. Roland Le Huenen and Paul Perron. Montréal: Didier, 1980. 29–40.

Person, Leland, Jr. *Aesthetic Headaches: Women and Masculine Poetics in Poe, Melville, and Hawthorne*. Athens: University of Georgia Press, 1988.

Pigler, A. "Portraying the Dead." *Acta Historiae Artium* 4 (1956): 1–75.

Pizer, John. "Guilt, Memory, and the Motif of the Double in Storm's *Aquis submersus* and *Ein Doppelgänger*." *German Quarterly* 65 (1992): 177–91.

Poe, Edgar Allan. *The Complete Works of Edgar Allan Poe*. Vol. 4. Ed. James A. Harrison. New York: AMS Press, 1965.

———. *Poetry and Tales*. Ed. Patrick F. Quinn. New York: Library of America, 1984.

Pollin, Burton R. *Poe, Creator of Words*. Baltimore: Enoch Pratt Free Library, 1974.

Pommier, Édouard. *Théories du portrait: De la Renaissance aux Lumières*. Paris: Gallimard, 1998.

Pontévia, Jean-Marie. *"Ogni dipintore dipinge sè": Écrits sur l'art et pensées détachées*. Bordeaux: William Blake, 1986.

Poole, Adrian. "Through 'Glasses' Darkly." *Henry James: The Shorter Fiction, Reassessments.* Ed. N. H. Reeve. New York: St. Martin's Press, 1997. 1–16.

Powell, Kerry. "Tom, Dick, and Dorian Gray: Magic-Picture Mania in Late Victorian Fiction." *Philological Quarterly* 62 (1983): 147–70.

Reinhardt, George W. "Turbulence and Enigma in Kleist's 'Der Findling.'" *Essays in Literature* 4 (1977): 265–74.

Reynolds, Sir Joshua. *Discourses on Art.* Ed. Robert R. Wark. New Haven, Conn.: Yale University Press, 1975.

Richards, Sylvie. "The Eye and the Portrait: The Fantastic in Poe, Hawthorne and Gogol." *Studies in Short Fiction* 20 (1983): 307–15.

Ron, Moshe. "The Art of the Portrait According to James." *Yale French Studies* 69 (1985): 222–37.

———. "Portrait of the Artist without Glasses." *Hebrew University Studies in Literature and the Arts* 14 (1986): 40–65.

———. "The Uncanny Harbingers of Death." In *Uncanny Portraits: An Anthology* (in Hebrew): 266–333. Ed. Moshe Ron. Tel Aviv: Ha-kibbutz ha-meuhad, 2001.

Rousseau, Jean-Jacques. "Préface dialoguée." *Julie ou La Nouvelle Héloïse.* Paris: Garnier-Flammarion, 1967.

Ryder, Frank G. "Kleist's Findling: Oedipus Manqué?" *MLN* 92 (1977): 509–24.

Sand, George. *Contes d'une Grand-mère.* Vol. 1. Ed. Philippe Berthier. Meylan: Les Editions de l'Aurore, 1982.

———. *Tales of Grandmother.* Trans. Margaret Bloom. Philadelphia: Lippincott, 1930.

Scheick, William. "The Geometric Structure of Poe's 'The Oval Portrait." *Poe Studies* 11 (1978): 6–8.

Schneider, Norbert. *The Art of the Portrait: Masterpieces of European Portrait-Painting, 1420–1670.* Trans. Iain Galbraith. Cologne: Benedikt Taschen, 1999.

Schor, Naomi. *George Sand and Idealism.* New York: Columbia University Press, 1993.

———. *Reading in Detail: Aesthetics and the Feminine.* New York: Routledge, 1989.

Schuerewegen, Franc. "La Toile déchirée: Texte, tableau et récit dans trois nouvelles de Balzac." *Poétique* 65 (1986): 19–27.

Scruton, Roger. "Photography and Representation." *Critical Inquiry* 7 (1981): 577–603.

Shapiro, Gavriel. *Nikolai Gogol and the Baroque Cultural Heritage.* University Park: Pennsylvania State University Press, 1993.

Shell, Marc. *Art and Money.* Chicago: University of Chicago Press, 1995.

———. *Money, Language, and Thought.* Berkeley: University of California Press, 1982.

———. "Portia's Portrait: Representation as Exchange." *Common Knowledge* 7 (1998): 94–144.
Shumaker, Jeanette Roberts. "Abjection and Degeneration in Thomas Hardy's 'Barbara of the House of Grebe.'" *College Literature* 26 (1999): 1–17.
Silverman, Kaja. *The Subject of Semiotics*. Oxford: Oxford University Press, 1983.
———. *The Threshold of the Visible World*. New York: Routledge, 1996.
Simmel, Georg. *Rembrandt: An Essay in the Philosophy of Art*. Trans. and ed. Alan Scott and Helmut Staubmann. London: Routledge, 2005.
Solomon-Godeau, Abigail. *Male Trouble: A Crisis in Representation*. London: Thames and Hudson, 1997.
Steiner, Wendy. "The Semiotics of a Genre: Portraiture in Literature and Painting." *Semiotica* 21 (1977): 111–20.
Stewart, Garrett. *Dear Reader: The Conscripted Audience in Nineteenth-Century British Fiction*. Baltimore: Johns Hopkins University Press, 1996.
Storm, Theodor. *"Aquis submersus."* Trans. Jeffrey Sammons. *German Novellas of Realism*. New York: Continuum, 1989.
———. *Novellen*. Frankfurt: Deutsche Klassiker Verlag, 1987.
———. *The Rider on the White Horse and Selected Stories*. Trans. James Wright. New York: Signet Classics, 1964.
Taussig, Michael. *Defacement*. Stanford, Calif.: Stanford University Press: 1999.
Tilby, Michael. "'Telle main veut tel pied': Balzac, Ingres and the Art of Portraiture." *Artistic Relations: Literature and the Visual Arts in Nineteenth-Century France*. Ed. Peter Collier and Robert Lethbridge. New Haven, Conn.: Yale University Press, 1994. 111–29.
Tintner, Adeline. *The Museum World of Henry James*. Ann Arbor, Mich.: UMI Research Press, 1986.
———. "Poe's 'The Spectacles' and James' 'Glasses.'" *Poe Studies* 9 (1976): 53–54.
———. "Why James Quoted Gibbon in 'Glasses.'" *Studies in Short Fiction* 14 (1977): 287–88.
Torgovnick, Marianna. *The Visual Arts, Pictorialism, and the Novel: James, Lawrence, and Woolf*. Princeton, N.J.: Princeton University Press, 1985.
Vacca, John. "The Art of Memory in James's 'The Tone of Time.'" *Studies in Short Fiction* 35 (1998): 259–65.
Veblen, Thorstein. *The Theory of the Leisure Class*. New York: Viking, 1967.
Voisine, Jacques. "La magie de la peinture: Variations sur le motif du portrait au XIXe siècle." *Rivista di letterature moderne e comparate* 49 (1996): 63–82.
Wagenknecht, David. "Getting the Picture: The Aesthetics of Hysteria in Henry James's 'The Special Type.'" *ELH* 66 (1999): 801–29.

Wagenknecht, Edward. *The Tales of Henry James*. New York: F. Ungar, 1984.
Wagner, Irmgard. "*Der Findling*: Erratic Signifier in Kleist and Geology." *German Quarterly* 64 (1991): 281–95.
Walpole, Horace. *The Castle of Otranto*. *Three Gothic Novels*. Ed. E. F. Bleiler. New York: Dover, 1966.
Ward, Mark G. "Narrative and Ideological Tension in the Works of Theodor Storm: A Comparative Study of *Aquis Submersus* and *Pole Poppenspäler*." *Deutsche Vierteljahrsschrift für Literaturwissenschaft und Geistgeschichte* 59 (1985): 445–73.
Webber, Andrew. "Kleist's Doppelgänger: An Open and Shut Case?" *Publications of the English Goethe Society* 63 (1994): 107–27.
———. "The Uncanny Rides Again: Theodor Storm's Double Vision." *Modern Language Review* 84 (1989): 860–73.
Weber, Samuel. *Benjamin's–abilities*. Cambridge: Harvard University Press, 2008.
Wegener, Frederick. "'Looking As If She Were Alive': The 'Duchess Effect,' the Representation of Women, and Henry James's Use of Portraits." *Centennial Review* 38 (1994): 539–77.
Weineck, Silke-Maria. "Kleist and the Resurrection of the Father." *Eighteenth-Century Studies* 37 (2003): 69–89.
Wettlaufer, Alexandra K. *Pen vs. Brush: Girodet, Balzac and the Myth of Pygmalion in Post Revolutionary France*. New York: Palgrave, 2001.
———. "Representing Artistic Identity: Sand's Femmes Peintres." *George Sand: Intertextualité et polyphonie*, Vol. 1. Ed. Nigel Harkness. New York: Peter Lang, 2011. 301–13.
Wilde, Oscar. *The Picture of Dorian Gray*. New York: Penguin Classics, 2000.
Williams, Susan S. *Confounding Images: Photography and Portraiture in Antebellum American Fiction*. Philadelphia: University of Pennsylvania Press, 1997.
Winner, Viola. *Henry James and the Visual Arts*. Charlottesville: University Press of Virginia, 1970.
Winnett, Susan. "Coming Unstrung: Women, Men, Narrative, and Principles of Pleasure." *PMLA* 105 (1990): 505–18.
Woodall, Joanna, ed. *Portraiture: Facing the Subject*. Manchester: Manchester University Press, 1997.
Yacobi, Tamar. "'The Beldonald Holbein': The Artist's Power and Its Dangers as Narrative Center." *Henry James Review* 27 (2006): 275–84.
Ziolkowski, Theodore. *Disenchanted Images*. Princeton, N.J.: Princeton University Press, 1977.

INDEX

Aesthetic, 2, 5, 47, 108, 128, 135, 136, 167n4, 171n2, 172n8
Aesthetics, 127, 129, 135, 139
Affect, 20, 23–25, 42, 96, 97, 161
Allegory, 11, 22, 23, 59, 137, 142, 172n2, 174n16, 186n29, 193n2
Aristotle, 167n4, 194n10
Art: as commodified, 69, 70, 73, 75, 147, 148, 151; and cult, 152–55; decline of, 148, 151, 155; and exhibition, 63, 66, 153; and life, 9, 17, 18, 28, 31, 33, 40, 64, 100, 119, 134, 146; as make-believe, 57, 194n9; and money, 12, 18, 149, 151, 155; photography as, 156; portraits relation to, 1–2, 24, 25, 30, 57, 58, 73, 79, 97, 141, 149, 154, 155; relation to the real, 22, 23, 43, 53, 122, 139, 152; as a separate sphere, 25; woman's access to, 126

Bal, Mieke, and Norman Bryson, 169n12
Balzac, Honoré de, 41, 179n14; *La Maison du chat-qui-pelote*, 11, 12, 53, 54, 58, 59–69, 78–80, 110, 138–39, 165; *Illusions perdues*, 69; *Père Goriot*, 179nn11,13
Barthes, Roland, 174n17, 176n11, 190n21
Belting, Hans, 152, 167n2
Benjamin, Walter, 153, 155, 156, 196n34, 197n37
Bettini, Maurizio, 9, 110
Body: degradation of, 102; vs. face, 70, 81, 90, 108, 170n20, 182n2, 184n12; as general form, 86, 90, 94; ground for identity formation, 89, 91, 108; integrity of, 94, 95; and labor, 139; and the material, 139–40; phantasmatic view of, 91, 94; male body, representation of, 12, 81, 91, 92, 94, 98–99, 108; woman's body, 82, 108, 140, 171n2, 172n3
Brilliant, Richard, 5, 6, 169n13
Bronfen, Elisabeth, 171n2, 172nn3,8, 190n19
Brooks, Peter, 183n3
Butades's daughter, 7–8, 156, 170n20

Cixous, Hélène, 24
Class, 60, 80, 92, 111, 112, 115, 127, 132, 140, 178n11; and the power to represent, 138–39
Coin, 143, 145, 147, 154–56, 195n23
Color, 76, 136, 182n31; vs. line, 137; relation to matter, 147, 148
Convention, 8, 48, 98, 153; determining resemblance, 5, 6, 169n13, 170n22
Copy: relation to original, 12, 30, 62, 78, 114, 123, 124, 154, 155, 165; perfect copy, 8; painter as, 45, 150; of the real, 22, 47, 56, 132, 169n13

de Man, Paul, 133–35
Dead, portraits of, 39, 41, 42, 119
Death: as immanent in life, 8, 23, 42, 173n15; portrait as overcoming, 8, 29, 31, 38, 41, 42, 68, 119, 141, 142, 143, 164, 165; as caused by the painting of a portrait, 14, 18, 23, 43, 55, 60, 194n6
Derrida, Jacques, 188n6
Desire: man as object of, 12, 81; mimetic, 12, 82, 87, 88, 89, 97, 109; mother's desire, 47–48; painter's desire, 12, 48, 74, 156, 182n32; shaped by representations, 37, 73, 77; to transcend the individual, 2, 11, 43
Devil: and illusion, 52, 58; as a double, 52; and money, 141, 142, 144, 145, 147; as a figure for the painter, 44, 46, 50, 54, 57, 58

209

Double: image as a double, 1, 30, 45, 48, 52, 58, 102, 160; of the painter, 52, 53, 55, 57; of the self, 46, 48, 51, 52, 56, 84, 89, 91, 92, 97, 122, 181n28

Edelman, Lee, 186n38
Eikon, 145, 153–56. *See also* Image, sacred.
Ekphrasis, 10
Elliott, Miss 4
Face: vs. body, 70, 81, 90, 98, 170n26, 182n2; of the mother, 126, 131, 132, 136, 140; relation to particularity, 94, 108, 150, 152; woman as, 12, 69, 70, 75, 76, 77. *See also* Prosopopeia
Fantastic, 2, 8, 49, 170n23
Father, 54, 57, 60, 85, 92, 112–26 passim, 127; and daughter, 128, 130, 132, 135–37; and son, 12, 47; power of, 47, 111. *See also* Idealization, of the father; de-idealization; Transmission, paternal
Freedberg, David, 169n17
Freud, Sigmund, 111, 127, 180n19

Gautier, Théophile: "La Cafetière," 11, 49–53, 56–58, 59, 114; "Onuphrius," 52
Gaze, 17, 18, 19, 20, 23; male, 25, 61, 82, 171n2, 172n8, 180n18; the painter's, 63; source of morality, 136; punishing, 102, 136
Gender: bias, 67; relation to beauty, 75; difference, 11, 25, 60, 72, 180n16; and the real/ideal distinction, 11; and power, 2, 12, 59, 80, 139; and transmission, 12
Ghost: portrait as, 11, 34, 38, 39; and paper money, 195n23
Gogol, Nikolai: "The Portrait," 12, 68, 141–57
Gothic fiction, 4, 13, 14, 15, 16, 49
Goux, Jean-Joseph, 111
Gross, Kenneth, 91

Hardy, Thomas: "Barbara of the House of Grebe," 11, 12, 81–82, 89–97, 107, 108–9, 138
Hegel, Georg Wilhelm Friedrich, 167n4, 192n29, 195n13
Hoffmann, E. T. A., 18; "Die Jesuiterkirche in G.," 43; "Die Doppletgänger," 11, 41, 43–48, 52–53, 56–58, 59, 110, 111
Huet, Marie Helene, 47

Icon, 7, 28, 106, 168n12, 172n3, 196n32
Iconic, 5–8, 98–100, 124, 156, 169n15, 186n38
Ideal: painter's search for, 48, 53, 56, 129; and the real, 11, 18, 43, 44, 52, 111, 136, 140, 148, 168n4; woman as figure for, 45, 46, 50, 51, 57, 58, 110–11, 132, 133
Idealization, 10; de-idealization, 12, 111, 132; of the father, 111, 127; of man, 12, 32, 81, 90, 108; of the mother, 127, 137, 192n32; of reality, 63; of woman, 50, 51, 53, 63, 126, 180n16, 192n32
Identification, 3, 10, 77, 97, 107, 109; and influence, 163; with an image, 12, 25, 56, 70, 86, 87, 108; of the portrait's subject, 5, 13; with the portrait's subject, 7; narcissistic, 12, 82, 88, 89, 109
Identity, 2, 7, 46, 84, 85, 153, 165, 169n13, 186n38; relation to body, 91, 104; painter's, 39, 67; viewers', 86, 87, 89, 108, 164; portrait as a token of, 3, 5, 39. *See also* Self; Subjectivity
Idol, 63, 87, 93, 94, 96
Idolatry, 87, 88, 89
Image, 3, 9, 10, 23, 24, 30, 45, 48–54 passim, 69–78 passim, 83, 92–100 passim, 118–123 passim, 133, 137, 149–64 passim; idealized, 63, 82, 91, 102, 106, 109; role in identity formation, 88–89, 90, 96, 108, 165; mirror, 38, 46, 84, 96, 101, 102; power of, 7, 47, 68, 103, 153, 155, 156; sacred, 125, 140, 147, 152. *See also* Identification, with an image.
Imagination, 19, 111, 122, 136, 139, 146, 147; the mother's, 47–48; reproductive, 56, 177n3
Imitation, 3, 37, 39, 46, 98, 109, 111, 122, 153–54; defacing as, 95; as destruction, 89, 97, 108; of the portrait, 86–87, 184n16; of the real, 122, 129, 146
Index: defined, 7–8, 169n12; of the painter, 28, 41; of the portrait's subject, 41, 157, 165, 169n15; treated as an icon, 106. *See also* Trace

Index

Indexical: defined 6–8; relation of portrait to painter, 48, 56, 57, 99, 124; relation of portrait to subject, 34, 41, 100, 143, 154, 156, 169n17, 186n38; in photography, 156
Individual, 23, 56, 58, 94, 108; portrait's relation to, 1, 2, 11, 25, 57, 142, 154, 167n2, 173n15; desire to transcend, 2, 8, 11, 18, 43, 57, 91, 94, 108
Influence, 7, 98, 100, 101, 103, 104, 105, 106, 107, 109, 163
Intersubjective relation(s), 3, 10, 30, 101, 109, 141, 158, 164, 165

James, Henry, 5, 27, 30, 137; "Glasses," 12, 25, 60, 69–78, 79, 80, 138; "The Special Type," 11, 31–42; "The Tone of Time," 11, 31–42, 44, 57, 110, 164; *The Tragic Muse*, 28–31
Joyce, James, 5

Kant, Immanuel, 167n4
Kleist, Heinrich von: "Der Findling," 12, 81–89, 90, 97, 107, 108, 109, 164
Kofman, Sarah, 177n8
Kris, Ernst and Otto Kurz, 169n17
Künstlerroman, 5, 131

Lacan, Jacques, 102, 187n47
Lacoue-Labarthe, Phillipe, 197n42
Lafayette, Madame de, 3
Likeness, 47, 54, 67, 79, 89, 118, 133, 153, 154, 164, 170n22; portrait as, 1, 5–11 passim, 21–40 passim, 47, 100, 114, 137; stealing of, 8, 46, 48, 56, 57, 63, 64, 68. See also Icon; Resemblance
Loss, 56, 62, 118, 125, 131, 132, 136, 165; as lack, 42; of the original, 151, 154, 155, 156; portrait's relation to, 31, 33, 35, 40, 41; of self, 57, 64, 68; of the ideal woman, 49, 53; of the real woman, 48

Magic, 7, 9, 30, 48, 68, 98, 137, 145, 152
Mannoni, Octave, 186n32
Marin, Louis, 108, 182n2
Materiality, 147, 197n43; and woman, 65, 140; and the mother, 132, 133; and lower class, 140
Matter, 138, 154, 177n5; color as, 137; and form 90, 111, 148; and idea, 111

Mediation, 38, 73, 84–86, 109, 132, 163
Mediator: painter as, 36, 37, 38, 48, 73, 74, 78, 83, 84, 85, 87, 109, 163
Meltzer, Françoise, 10
Miller, D. A., 187n42
Miller, J. Hillis, 135
Mirror, 45, 46, 48, 52, 56, 91, 150, 163; and portrait, 70, 101–2, 106, 109, 160. *See also* Image, mirror
Misrecognition, 3, 10, 63, 84, 88, 101, 109
Money, 32, 34, 36, 37, 40, 71, 113, 116, 142; and art, 33, 130, 149, 151, 155; and portraits, 12, 143–50, 154; power of, 35, 144
Moretti, Franco, 179n14
Mother, 72, 74, 115, 126–40; as an artist, 47, 48, 56, 58. *See also* Imagination, the mother's; Materiality, and the mother; Transmission, maternal

Nancy, Jean-Luc, 167n2
Narcissism, 70, 101, 102
Nerval, Gérard de: "Le Portrait du diable," 11, 42, 53–56, 57–58, 59

Original, 6, 23, 29, 74, 148, 153, 155; the portrait's, 87, 88, 137, 143. *See also* Copy, relation to original; Loss, of the original
Originality: the painter's 45, 129, 150, 151, 154, 155, 156

Painter: ambivalence towards portrait, 2; and class, 138–40; emergence in fiction, 4–5, 10, 13; freedom of, 1; interestedness of, 3, 12, 43, 58, 60; male, 12, 25, 48, 53, 57–60, 78; and money, 1, 33, 36, 37, 144, 149; presence in portrait, 5–7, 29, 39, 54–57, 68, 99–100, 124; relation to portrait's subject, 18, 22–25, 28, 30, 32, 33, 35, 43, 59, 74; painter's subjectivity, 2, 3, 5, 11, 44, 48, 53–57, 67; type of, 17–18, 23, 25, 37, 39, 43, 45, 46, 112–13, 122, 126, 129, 132, 145, 151–52; viewer's relation to, 7; woman as, 37, 41–42, 57, 110, 126–27, 132, 170n21. *See also* Devil, as a figure for the painter; Double, of the painter; Ideal, painter's search for; Identity, painter's;

Painter *(continued)*
  Mediator, painter as; Originality, the painter's; Power, of the painter; Vision
Parergon, 112, 121, 122. *See also* Supplement
Peirce, Charles Sanders, 5, 6, 7, 8, 168n12, 169n15, 170n22, 172n3
Performative, 98, 106, 119, 135
Perosa, Sergio, 8, 170n23
Phantom: portrait as, 30, 31
Photography, 156–57
Poe, Edgar Allan: "The Oval Portrait," 11, 13–26, 42, 43, 57, 59, 161–62, 164, 180n16; "Premature Burial," 21–22
Power, 1, 30, 108, 115, 165; of beauty, 72, 103; of the father, 12, 47, 111, 112, 122, 126, 130; and gender, 2, 25, 48, 58, 60, 67, 69, 79–80, 139, 182n31; of images, 7, 47, 68, 103, 125, 154–56, 169n17; of the imagination, 47, 56; of money, 35, 36, 148, 151, 194n3; of the painter, 3, 6, 11, 25, 35–36, 37, 45, 46, 58, 66–67, 73, 74, 77, 137; of the portrait, 2, 7, 12, 20, 24, 59, 68, 73, 79, 142, 143, 144, 146, 153, 154, 156; to represent, 12, 25, 35, 60, 73, 80, 112, 138, 157, 158; of representations, 45, 69; of the portrait's subject, 143; of words, 105–6
Prosopopeia, 133–35

Reader, 10, 12, 16, 17, 24, 84, 123, 138, 158, 161–62, 164, 165
Reading, 10, 12, 14–17, 19–20, 24, 25, 45, 80, 134, 158–59, 161–65, 172n7
Realism, 23, 37, 124, 146–47, 190n21, 191n23
Realist, 33, 45, 59, 60, 68, 82, 122, 129, 139, 143, 170n23
Recognition, 57, 91, 110, 139, 165; of the portrait's subject, 6, 22–23, 34, 38, 39, 41, 51, 54, 63, 82, 101, 108, 109, 120–21, 123, 124, 133, 164, 184n13; of the painter, 6, 39, 48, 56. *See also* Misrecognition
Representation (also re-presentation), 16, 30; as/and adequation, 12, 145, 146, 147, 148, 154, 155; as deception, 39, 44, 50, 52, 58; and/as exhibition, 66, 153; function of, 7, 35; relation to loss, 33, 41, 42; means of, 60, 73, 77; mimetic, 8, 52–53, 89, 100, 153; as preservation, 11, 62; primacy of, 78; relation to the real, 31, 45, 58, 93, 101; as a social practice, 2, 165; relation to the represented subject, 68, 87, 88, 89, 93, 95, 98, 107, 143; relation to subjectivity, 2, 30, 67, 91. *See also* Power, of representations; Realism; Realist
Resemblance, 4, 21, 50, 52, 54, 82–90, 98, 113, 164; as affinity, 115, 116, 189n13; and convention, 5; of copy to original, 48, 114; disagreement over, 6; between frame and main narrative, 162; between paintings, 120, 137; perfect, 46, 52; of portrait to its subject, 5, 7, 23, 38, 98, 150, 153, 156; of son to his father, 47, 114, 115. *See also* Icon; Iconic; Likeness; Seeing resemblance
Reynolds, Sir Joshua, 57
Rivalry, 10, 18, 76, 88, 142; between doubles, 46, 77; between men, 89, 91–92, 97, 107, 109; between women, 31, 32, 37, 38
Ron, Moshe, 181nn23,25
Rousseau, Jean-Jacques, 174n18

Sand, George: "Le Château de Pictordu," 5, 11, 12, 41, 47, 111–12, 126–40
Schor, Naomi, 126–27, 185n20, 193n34
Scrutton, Roger, 156
Seeing, 5, 17, 30, 33, 54, 55, 68, 96, 102, 150; relation to gender, 69, 73, 79; problematization of, 3, 5, 34, 38, 41, 50–51, 63, 82, 88, 119, 122, 135; and reading, 12, 17, 158; seeing resemblance, 83–87. *See also* Recognition; Viewer; Vision
Self, 3, 6, 56, 84, 95; ideal, 107; loss of, 52, 64, 68, 96; inner, 67, 78, 79, 85, 86, 88, 93, 101, 106, 164. *See also* Identity; Selfhood; Subjectivity
Selfhood, 45, 46, 48, 89. *See also* Self; Identity; Subjectivity
Shell, Marc, 154, 197n39
Silverman, Kaja, 180n18
Simmel, Georg, 173n15
Simulacrum, 11, 30, 31, 41, 58, 68
Sitter, 1, 2, 3, 6, 28, 29, 30, 34, 35, 39, 79, 151. *See also* Subject

Stewart, Garrett, 198nn1,3
Storm, Theodor: "Aquis submersus," 11, 12, 42, 111–26, 128, 130, 138–40, 160–61, 162, 164, 192n25; "Der Schimmelreiter," 192n25
Subject, of a portrait, 20, 31, 33, 39, 44, 46, 54, 82, 84, 102, 109, 112, 120, 121, 129, 142; and gender, 12; relation to painter, 1–11 passim, 25, 157; relation to portrait, 3–11 passim, 24, 28–30, 32, 35, 41, 58, 60, 81, 90, 96–97, 100, 114, 118–19, 124, 142–43, 156–57, 164–65; relation to representation, 5, 11, 42, 56, 58, 87, 89, 93, 98, 103, 107, 153; relation to viewer, 3, 7, 13, 22, 23, 28, 82; woman as, 15, 43. *See also* Painter, relation to portrait's subject; Sitter
Subjectivity, 83; formation/production of, 2, 3, 108, 109; relation to image, 88–89; of the painter, 11, 44; as an open secret, 104; relation to representation, 2, 3, 5, 7, 79–80, 103, 157, 158; of the viewer(s), 109. *See also* Identity; Self
Supernatural, 2, 8, 68, 98, 143, 144
Supplement, 60, 62–63, 112–14, 116, 118, 120, 121, 122, 125, 160, 190nn19, 20. *See also* Parergon
Symbol, 6

Taussig, Michael, 186n30, 187n42
Trace, 34, 54, 56, 62, 63, 100, 105, 107, 125, 133, 165. *See also* Index
Transmission, 15, 16, 115, 118, 189n11; and gender, 12; maternal, 47, 111, 126–27, 140; of the past, 128; paternal, 111, 114, 121; portraits as means of, 12

Uncanny, 8, 9, 30, 38, 48, 68, 86
Ut picture poesis, 10

Viewer, 6, 11–14, 23–25, 39, 99, 120, 158, 159, 172n8; relation to painter, 7; relation to portrait, 2, 3, 81, 84, 108–9, 156; relation to subject, 7, 23; subjectivity of, 5, 82, 108–9. *See also* Seeing
Violence, 16, 107, 139
Vision: "double vision," 28–31, 137; and gender, 12, 25, 79, 81, 180nn16,18; the painter's, 6, 11, 30, 38–40, 41, 43, 45, 48, 56, 57, 129, 133, 136–37, 139, 152, 156–57
Voice, 74, 100, 105, 126, 131–37, 140

Walpole, Horace, 4
Wilde, Oscar: *The Picture of Dorian Gray*, 11, 12, 81–82, 97–109, 114, 159–60, 162–64
Woman, 15, 54, 23, 24, 60, 69, 71, 74, 75, 89, 136, 137; woman's body, 82, 108; and death, 14, 15, 16, 18, 22, 42, 68, 140, 164; ideal/real, 43–44, 45, 48, 49, 50–51, 53, 57, 58, 110, 133; identification with, 25; as site of lack, 41–42; as object, 31, 59–60, 69, 70, 71, 73, 79, 171n2; as painter, 37, 41, 47, 57, 58, 110, 126, 170n21; relation to portrait, 17, 18, 43, 78; as portrait's subject, 11, 12, 44, 50, 54, 58, 59, 69, 78
Woodall, Joanna, 113

Ziolkowski, Theodore, 8, 9, 170n23, 171n26